D0449972

CALIFORNIA
CHARACTERS

CHARLES HILLINGER

CAPRA PRESS
SANTA BARBARA

MECHANICS' INSTITUTE LIBRARY
57 Post Street
San Francisco, CA 94104
(415) 393-0101

Copyright © 2000 by Charles Hillinger
All rights reserved.
Printed in the USA.

Cover and book design by Frank Goad, Santa Barbara.

All photos by author unless otherwise indicated.
Cover photo of Hillinger reading his article to Clint Wescott by R.L. Oliver.

LIBRARY OF CONGRESS CATALOGUING-IN-PUBLICATION DATA

Hillinger, Charles.
California characters : an array of amazing people
from Dr. Tinkerpaw to Spaceship Ruthie / Charles Hillinger.
p. cm.
ISBN 0-88496-443-4 (paper : alk. paper)
1. Eccentrics and eccentricities—California—Biography.
2. California—Biography. I. Title.

CT9990 .H55 2000
920.0794—dc21
[B]
00-028947

Capra Press
Post Office Box 2068
Santa Barbara, CA 93120

CALIFORNIA CHARACTERS

Dec. 5, 2005

To Patrons of
        Mechanics' Institute —

Hope you find this a good
read + enjoy meeting this
colorful cast of California
characters.

All my best!

Charly Hillinger
Rancho Palo Verdes

I have a story about Mechanics'
Institute in my book
Hillinger's California: Stories
from all 58 Counties

979.4
465cc

CONTENTS

FOREWORD: by OTIS CHANDLER   Page 11

CHAPTER ONE: FREE AS A BIRD IN A DOWNTOWN NEST   Page 13

CHAPTER TWO: ESOTERIC PRACTICES, CALIFORNIA STYLE   Page 22
Full Mooners: Chanting On A Mountain Top   Page 22
Do You Realize Dog Is God Spelled Backwards?   Page 24
One of The Most Exclusive Cults In America   Page 26

CHAPTER THREE: FOUR PEAS IN A POD   Page 30
Walkin' George   Page 30
Seldom Seen Slim   Page 33
Shopping Cart Dougherty   Page 34
Dr. Tinkerpaw Of Nitwit Ridge   Page 36

CHAPTER FOUR: A WRETCHED MESS   Page 38

CHAPTER FIVE: DESERT DWELLERS   Page 41
Hubcap Lucy   Page 41
Gasless Gas Station   Page 42

CHAPTER SIX: THE OUTER SPACE CONNECTION   Page 44
Spaceship Ruthie   Page 44
"Le Grand Papa" Of Flying Saucers   Page 46
Psychics Convention   Page 48

CHAPTER SEVEN: SMALL, BUT LIVELY   Page 50
A Store From Another Century   Page 50
Smallest Free Republic In The World   Page 52
The People Of Peanut   Page 54

CHAPTER EIGHT: A ZEST FOR Z'S   Page 56
Zzyzx And The Old-Time Medicine Man   Page 56
Last Name In The Phone Book   Page 61

CHAPTER NINE: A CRAZY RACE & PROPHET OF SOAP — Page 63
    People-Powered Sculptures — Page 63
    Peace Plan On Soap Label — Page 66

CHAPTER TEN: A COUPLE O' POETS — Page 68
    Every Poet Should Have A Few Acres — Page 68
    The Gravy Poet — Page 71

CHAPTER ELEVEN: LAST SPEAKER OF ANCIENT LANGUAGE — Page 74

CHAPTER TWELVE: HERMITS — Page 76
    An Odd Duck And A Scholarship Fund — Page 76
    Hermit Of Hardrock Gulch — Page 79
    "To Hell With Everybody" — Page 80
    Desert Fats — Page 83

CHAPTER THIRTEEN: MINERS — Page 85
    Sweetwater Clyde — Page 85
    Down The Road Dugan — Page 87
    Alleghany Lu — Page 89
    "Gonna Strike It Rich Before We Die" — Page 90
    Salmon River Steve — Page 92
    Anti-American, Pro-Russian Shrine — Page 95

CHAPTER FOURTEEN: SCIENTISTS — Page 98
    Bat Lady — Page 98
    Ants In His Pants — Page 100
    World's Oldest Oologist Is Rare Bird — Page 101
    Flat-Footed Fly Expert — Page 102
    Oldest Living Thing On Earth — Page 104

CHAPTER FIFTEEN: ODD JOBS — Page 106
    Outhouse Nate — Page 106
    Cleaning Up America — Page 107
    Riding The Rails In A Bright Yellow Bug — Page 108
    Carver Of Wooden Indians — Page 110
    King Of Queen Bees — Page 111
    Chimney Sweeps' Convention — Page 112

CHAPTER SIXTEEN: MORE ODD JOBS — Page 114

   Stagecoach Ginny — Page 114

   Paid To Watch TV, All She Sees Is Fish — Page 115

   Drawbridge Blues — Page 117

   Backyard Geyser — Page 118

   The Cactus King — Page 119

CHAPTER SEVENTEEN: SOUP & TORTILLAS — Page 121

   500 Gallons Of Soup Every Sunday — Page 121

   Queen Of Tortillas — Page 122

CHAPTER EIGHTEEN:
OF WINDMILLS, GOATS, A SKINFLINT, & A "MOLE" — Page 124

   King Of The Windmills — Page 124

   Goat Lady in the Valley of Giant Redwood Stumps — Page 125

   Monument To An Old Skinflint — Page 127

   Human Mole Has Subterranean Estate — Page 128

CHAPTER NINETEEN: TOWN CHARACTERS — Page 131

   The Greeter — Page 131

   Volunteer Street Sweeper — Page 133

   The Town Communist — Page 135

CHAPTER TWENTY: FIVE HAMLETS — Page 137

   Turn-Back-The-Clock Town — Page 137

   Backward Village — Page 139

   Haunted Hamlet — Page 140

   Hallelujah! — Page 141

   Callahan's Emporium — Page 143

CHAPTER TWENTY-ONE: OBSESSIONS — Page 145

   Charlie Spurlock's Perpetual Motion Wheel — Page 145

   George Haynes' Perpetual Motion Machine — Page 146

   They Never Miss A Train — Page 148

   Isky Cannot Pass Up A Bargain — Page 150

   Antiques To Him, Junk To the BLM — Page 151

CHAPTER TWENTY-TWO: A COUPLE OF WEIRD ARTISTS — Page 154
The Great Razooly — Page 154
5,000 Teeth Standing On End In The Desert — Page 156

CHAPTER TWENTY-THREE: FOUR SPECIAL WOMEN — Page 159
Martha's Café — Page 159
Millionaire Fry Cook — Page 161
Squirrel Gulch Elly — Page 162
Trained Steers: "Too Much Like Family" — Page 163

CHAPTER TWENTY-FOUR: FIVE FASCINATING WOMEN — Page 165
Soaring Jenkins — Page 165
"Help Yourself Baby" — Page 168
Guardian Of A Strange Tunnel — Page 169
$35-A-Month Librarian — Page 171
Mad Rose, Nun Who Knows The Odds — Page 172

CHAPTER TWENTY-FIVE: THE OLDEST PROFESSION — Page 174
Plaque For Scarlet Women — Page 174
Sally Stanford, Madame-Turned-Politician — Page 175

CHAPTER TWENTY-SIX:
MR. LIGHTHOUSE, MOON LEE, REDHEADS & RUBELIANS — Page 178
Mr. Lighthouse — Page 178
Moon Lee And The Taoist Temple — Page 181
Twelve Million Redheads — Page 182
What Is A Rubelian? — Page 183

CHAPTER TWENTY-SEVEN: MORE FROM THE LIGHT SIDE — Page 186
Warmly Ormly — Page 186
Laughing In The Library — Page 188
Joke Professor — Page 189

CHAPTER TWENTY-EIGHT: BIRDS OF A FEATHER — Page 192
Town Under Attack By Woodpeckers — Page 192
Bird Dialect Expert — Page 194
"The Owl" Is His Legal Name — Page 195
Pelican Man — Page 196

CHAPTER TWENTY-NINE:
OF SCALES, SNAILS, CHIRPS & WRIGGLES . . . . Page 198
   Mystery Monster Tuna . . . . Page 198
   California Snail Problem . . . . Page 200
   Crickets Galore . . . . Page 202
   The Bloodworm Business Is Booming . . . . Page 204

CHAPTER THIRTY: CAMPUS CAPERS . . . . Page 206
   Students Take Cows To College . . . . Page 206
   Billy Goat Davis . . . . Page 208
   Campus Brewery . . . . Page 209
   Prevention Of Progress . . . . Page 210
   Vampire Professor . . . . Page 211

CHAPTER THIRTY-ONE: UNUSUAL BARBERS . . . . Page 213
   State's Oldest Barber Shop . . . . Page 213
   Hymns And Prayers Come With Haircuts . . . . Page 214
   Wild Willie Slade . . . . Page 215
   Cuts Hair, Traps Raccoons . . . . Page 217

CHAPTER THIRTY-TWO: THAT'S SHOW BIZ . . . . Page 219
   Life And Times Of Old Abe . . . . Page 219
   The Wild Bunch . . . . Page 221

CHAPTER THIRTY-THREE: JFK LYING IN STATE . . . . Page 223

CHAPTER THIRTY-FOUR:
HIKERS, A DUST DEVIL & THE PRINCE . . . . Page 225
   Hundred Peakers Club . . . . Page 225
   Dust Devil Dan . . . . Page 227
   The Prince Of Pisgah . . . . Page 229

CHAPTER THIRTY-FIVE: WRITERS OF THE WEST . . . . Page 231
   Nettie Brown And The Blue Angels . . . . Page 231
   The Widow's Tears . . . . Page 233
   Of Mac And Maggie . . . . Page 234
   Chronicling The West Since The 1930s . . . . Page 235

CHAPTER THIRTY-SIX: HIGH FLYERS — Page 237
   Half Man, Half Bird — Page 237
   Human Fly — Page 239
   One-Winged Eagle — Page 240
   Flying Saucer Pilot — Page 243

CHAPTER THIRTY-SEVEN: TALES FROM THE SLAMMER — Page 245
   Convicts Build Airplane — Page 245
   Country Club Of Prisons — Page 246
   "Now We're Going To The Gas Chamber" — Page 248

CHAPTER THIRTY-EIGHT: KITES & PUMPERNICKEL — Page 251
   Kite Flyer — Page 251
   Kings of Pumpernickel — Page 252

CHAPTER THIRTY-NINE: OF POTBELLIES, GUM & GARLIC — Page 254
   Potbellies — Page 254
   Gum — Page 256
   Garlic — Page 257

CHAPTER FORTY: POTPOURRI — Page 259
   Ed And Junior's Half Acre — Page 259
   A 19th Century Man — Page 261
   Grandma Prisbrey — Page 262
   Root Beer Foam — Page 263

CHAPTER FORTY-ONE: MELL'S MOMMA — Page 265

CHAPTER FORTY-TWO:
A Big Finish With The GALLOPING GHORMLEYS — Page 268

ABOUT THE AUTHOR — Page 270

FOREWORD

by

OTIS CHANDLER

former publisher *Los Angeles Times*

CHUCK HILLINGER AND I ARE THE SAME AGE. We worked together during the last half of the 20th Century at the *Los Angeles Times*. I was publisher. He was the paper's roving reporter. His bylines came from all over California, from every state, from exotic places all over the world during his 46 years at the *Times*. And I paid all his expenses, but it was worth every penny! Chuck's words, his character and his insights brought a unique dimension to the paper. I always looked forward to his pieces. So did our readers. I told him next to being publisher of the *Los Angeles Times* he had the best job in journalism. Charles Kuralt called him his hero. Hillinger went everywhere. No other newspaper had a reporter with his range. The world was his oyster. He interviewed people from all walks of life, from presidents and kings to people like Clint Wescott, the man in the weeds under the 4th street bridge who appears on the cover and is the subject of the first story in *California Characters*.

Chuck's columns, about 6,000 in all, not only appeared in the *Times* but also were syndicated to 600 other newspapers. The stories that had a particular fascination for millions of readers were his profiles of colorful California characters told with warmth and compassion. California, perhaps more than any other state, is home to a variety of amazing eccentrics who follow their own unbelievable paths. And Chuck traveled throughout every remote corner of the state, seeking, finding and writing about them. In the pages that follow you will meet, be entertained, amused and enlightened by the likes of Seldom Seen Slim, Shopping Cart Dougherty, Salmon River Steve, Hubcap Lucy, Spaceship Ruthie, Allegheny Lu, Dr. Tinkerpaw of Nitwit Ridge, Desert Fats, Down the Road Dugan, and Zachary Zzzzra, just to name a few.

Charles Hillinger's columns about real people of a different bent were a lively and refreshing contrast to the hard news stories of the day. So, climb aboard and join Chuck on his incredible 46-year odyssey throughout the Golden State as he revisits this wonderful cast of colorful California characters. Take my word, you will be enchanted with every story that follows.

DEDICATED TO

Clint Wescott, Spaceship Ruthie, Seldom Seen Slim, Walkin' George,
Shopping Cart Dougherty, Down the Road Dugan, Soaring Jenkins,
and all the other incredible California characters I have
been privileged to know and write about
during the last half-century,

and to the greatest California character of all:

ARLIENE
my wife of 52 years.

CHAPTER ONE

Clint Wescott refusing letter from Charles Hillinger informing him that he has money in a New York bank. (Photo by R.L. Oliver)

FREE AS A BIRD IN A DOWNTOWN NEST

CLINT WESCOTT lived in the heart of Los Angeles, ten years at the same place, when we first met him and during that period had not once received any mail, not one letter. "Ain't got no address, that's why," the bearded, flop-hatted, 51-year-old explained. No address, but his "estate" was two blocks from the County Courthouse in the hub of the nation's second largest city. Wescott's home had no walls, no floors, no ceiling, no roof.

"It's just the way I like it. I couldn't stand starin' at four walls every day. I require fresh air, space. Can't stand being hemmed in. That's why I live here," he said. Every day thousands passed by Wescott's place— but few ever saw it. "We're out of sight here. I don't bother nobody. Nobody bothers me or the boys who drop in to stay awhile," said

Wescott. His home was a broken down couch with outcroppings of stuffing, a discarded office chair, an old mattress, a campfire and a dozen large rocks for guests to sit on.

The "Old Man" as Wescott was affectionately called by his friends, lived at the base of a Bunker Hill cliff on the east side of Flower Street, under the 4th Street Bridge. He was like scores of Skid Row habitués in 1968 who slept on slopes of undeveloped weed-covered hills in downtown Los Angeles, under bridges, in bushes. Except he had established somewhat of a record for occupancy—ten years in that spot. Wescott was well known to other Skid Row transients. He never left his "estate." He was always at home. He had visitors every day.

"It's a great life," he related. "The boys are in and out. Now and then someone throws out a $5 bill and says, 'Let's go!' A run is made for a couple big jugs. And we go on a grand one for a day or two." The "Old Man" had admittedly been a bum for 13 years, "the last time I paid income tax," he said. "Ever since I've been as free as a bird. No worries. I stay out of people's way." Wescott didn't mind talking about himself, his friends, his shortcomings, his failures, his hopes. "Ain't never been married," he said with a chuckle. "I was in love once, but the girl wasn't. I grew up normal like. Graduated from high school in Burnt Hills, N.Y. I thought I was going to make it like every other kid. Make a success in business or something."

Clint blamed his last job for his taking off and "living a different way of life than most—just laying in the weeds, letting the rest of the world go by. I was working under so much strain over there in Reno—running a rock crusher. I set on the crusher pushin' buttons. I'd watch those buttons all day. Someone would holler up, 'Don't forget to push the right button.' I'd push a button and there'd be a spill on No. 4. I should have hit No. 1. It was just too damn much strain. I just had to stop and take a drink for a few years."

Wescott figured he was having a good life "for the present. I'm going to get on the ball someday, I'm pretty sure. I'd like to have a home, a family. Still the same idea." He hadn't used a telephone in 13 years. He slept on and under newspapers, leaving his old mattress for his guests. He never washed himself or bathed. "I don't go much for that any more. Just keep laying here in the weeds. What's the use," he reasoned. He said he "gets in jail a couple times a year for being drunk. It does me good. I get a chance to dry out and clean up, to eat regular for three,

CHARLES HILLINGER

four weeks."

His friends brought him food they shared over his campfire. They'd get their money panhandling, he noted. Wescott said he never had been seriously sick although he was an asthmatic and was 4-F during World War II because of it. "Every time I go to jail I get enough asthma pills to see me through till next time I'm tossed in the clink." But he did admit to unhappy days around his camp in the heart of the city. "Two fellows died here. Got down in a rut and couldn't get out. Didn't want to. Wouldn't eat. Died of starvation pneumonia."

He found his shirts and trousers in trash barrels. "You can always find old shoes behind shoe shops at night," he said. He never wore underwear or socks because they made him nervous. Now and then during rainy weather friends put him up in a cheap hotel. But he never stayed. "I just can't stand sleeping indoors under blankets. I feel penned in like an animal. I got to get out to sleep under newspapers in the weeds."

He read discarded newspapers. He knew what was going on. "We talk about everything that's happening in the city, in America, in the world when we sit around our campfire. You'd be surprised how much we know. Several years ago one of my brothers found me living under the bridge and tried to talk me into going back home with him. I told him to sit down and have a drink," recalled Wescott. "He said I was the filthiest man he'd ever seen. He handed me a $5 bill and took off. What a character." Is he ever bothered with rats or mice living and sleeping where he does? "Rats eat out of my hand," he replied. "Sometimes I lay a sack with food down next to me and go to sleep. I wake up in the night. What the hell's rattlin' the bag, I ask myself. It's a rat. 'You son of a gun. I hope you leave some for my breakfast,' I tell the rat."

Asked if he thought the story I was doing for the newspaper about his lifestyle and his "estate" might create a problem for him with the police, Wescott answered: "The cops all knowed I'm living under the bridge. I knowed every cop that goes by. I've got to move on soon anyway. I knowed that for sure. High-rise is comin' in here. It won't be long 'for I'll have to move down the line a little ways and find a new place..."

The story about Clint Wescott, the man living in the weeds under the 4th Street Bridge was a Sunday feature I did for the *Los Angeles Times*. It was syndicated and carried in newspapers across America, around the world. Attorney John P. Brown in Burnt Hills saw the story in the Schenectady Gazette. Wescott had been quoted about growing up in Burnt Hills. Brown called the *Los Angeles Times* and told me he had been searching for Wescott for seven years.

"Finding Clinton is a great relief. I have $19,219.68 of his money in two bank accounts, I want to hand over to him," related the attorney. "It's money due him on a gas station he built in Burnt Hills and abandoned when he hit the high road and headed West. There was a foreclosure. The gas station was sold with $15,124.38 banked to Clinton Wescott's credit by the New York Superior Court when efforts to locate him proved fruitless. Interest had been accumulating to the point where Clinton's fortune was nearing $20,000." Attorney Brown's law firm was appointed by the state of New York to handle the matter.

"You know Clinton was a popular, industrious person—a lifelong resident of Burnt Hills. He built his gas station with his own hands," noted Brown. "Then suddenly 15 years ago he said to hell with it and took off never to be seen again."

Brown sent a letter to me to deliver to Clint Wescott. Enclosed was a copy of the order showing the man in the weeds had the sum of $19,219.68 credited to his accounts in two banks in Saratoga County. "I have set forth in my letter to Clinton that he could discuss with you what course of action to take in this matter," Brown wrote.

Armed with the documents, photographer Dick Oliver and I set out to find Wescott. We spent two hours early in the morning hiking through steep weed, brush and tree-covered slopes next to and then under the 4th Street Bridge, awakening more than a dozen down-and-outers, asking if they had seen Clint. We talked to "One-Eyed Jack," "Big Swede," "Missing Man," (so called because his pals said he was always missing when he had a bottle he didn't want to share), "Lacey," Herman Honeycutt, and other cronies of Wescott,—"around somewhere," they told us.

He was finally found asleep in a pile of newspapers under the bridge. Told of his fortune worth nearly $20,000, Wescott, dressed in rags and with 44 cents in his pockets, chose to ignore what his dirt-encrusted ears were hearing. He turned his back on the money. "I'd rather stay at the bottom of the barrel," said the 51-year-old bum. "I'm not ready to go over to the other side. Not yet. Hand me a dollar. I'll take it and buy a little drink, a little smoke. But I don't want a huge wad of money like that.

"Sure someday I want to get out of the weeds. But I have no thought of moving out now. I want this life," he insisted. "Being a wino agrees with me. It's not a bad life. No cares. A man lives in the weeds with $30, $40 in his pockets, it's a different story. A few dimes, pennies. There's no danger of anything. Hah!" he laughed, showing his few misshapen, broken teeth. "Lookit here." He dug into his pockets and counted out the 44 cents. "I'm rich. This is all the richer I want to be. Enough to buy a short jug. That's all I want out of life now. One of these days I'll go straight. I'll climb out of the bottom of the barrel. But I'm not ready. Not now, anyway. Don't mention the gas station or any of that out of the past. I don't want to hear about it. I like it the way it is. I don't have any worries. This disrupts everything. It's a shame you had to wake me up and tell me. Going back is a blind alley at this time in my life. I'm not ready. I've got to stay here in the weeds, take more rest. I'm not ready for the responsibility you're talking about."

"But Clint," I interrupted, "you've been resting for 15 years. Why not make the break now? You said someday you want to get on the ball, to have a home, a family. Here's your chance. My God, Clint, you've got a bigger savings in those New York banks than most people have ever had in a lifetime." "I know...I know," Clint mused, nervously moving back and forth in a chair, rapidly inhaling and blowing smoke into the air. "God, I need a drink," he said. He pulled a fifth of tokay out of a beat-up overcoat given to him by a stranger during a downpour.

"Here, Clint. Here's the letter from your attorney. Open it. Read his suggestions on what you should do," I urged. "No. I don't want to think about it. I don't want to touch it," he replied excitedly. He refused to allow it to be opened. "No. I don't want to have any part of it. No. I can't," he insisted.

Then he began reminiscing: "What a time us winos have had the past 10 years I've been living here. What a time. No worries, except where the next bottle's coming from. Free as a bird. No taxes. No rush to work. Rush home from work. Nothin'. Oh, we've had good times, especially when a fellow comes in with $5 or $10 and we make a run for wine. You know all I want out of life is a loaf of bread, a pound of baloney, a hunk of cheese, good health. I got all that here. I'm at peace with the world.

"Sure I'd like to get a little place, maybe in upstate New York where I lived. A little place where I could hunt and fish and not bother nobody. Do a little work. I ain't scared of work. I remember when I bought a new car right off the floor. It was pretty hard to make car payments with the money I made. That's it right there. I'm not ready for all that—not yet. I can't take the money. I can't skip out of here now.

"You know I never smoked or drank none before I went on the bum. Not a drop. Not a cigarette. But smoking and drinking been a comfort to me. It soothes my nerves. It's nice to lay in the weeds, think and reflect without letting your stomach get boiled up with problems. I can't leave I'm enjoying life here..." Wescott promised if he had a change of mind, he'd stop by the newspaper and read his attorney's letter. But it was obvious he was afraid of the world outside the weeds under the 4th Street Bridge. His security was there.

In a way it was a shame he had to be told he had a fortune waiting. "It disrupts everything," as he said. The world of Clint Wescott had been shattered and would never be the same. He avoided people for 15 years, now they would be chasing him—and the $19,219.68 he suddenly found waiting for him in Burnt Hills. And although Wescott didn't want any part of his fortune, there were plenty of others who did. And the day the story appeared about his windfall they began appearing under the 4th Street Bridge, showing up with ideas on how the bearded drifter should spend his money.

A parking-lot owner driving a new Lincoln Continental drove up, parked, walked over to Wescott and shouted with a big grin: "Hey, Clint baby. Remember me? Your pal. Your old buddy. I've known you for years, haven't I baby? You've always been my boy. You need a manager for all that money, Clint—for that 19 thou. You've always been my boy, Clint. OK, Clint baby?"

A man who said he represented a Christian group in Pasadena was out looking for Clint in the weeds and when he found him said: "Give us the money, Clint, and we'll put it to good use. It's for a good cause. We have a boys' club. It will give kids a life, give boys a chance. Remember when you were a boy, Clint? You can live in the back of our place. We'll put you up."

Wescott used the telephone for the first time in 13 years and talked to attorney John P. Brown. "I can't take the money, not now. I'm not ready to leave this life," Clint told him. "I'd rather not talk about it, not at this time, thank you." The attorney responded: "It's your money, Clint, all of it, and yours alone. You can have it now or leave it sit drawing interest as it has the past seven years." Brown also informed him he was actually worth more than $24,000 as his father had died and left him $4,000. "I'm sorry to hear about my father. I had no idea he died," sighed Wescott. "Did you say he left me $4,000? Oh no, not more money. No. No. No," he mumbled, shaking his head. Then the letters started pouring in from all over the world

Clint Wescott, the Bunker Hill bum, who hadn't received a letter in 10 years, hit the jackpot. Within a few days thousands of letters were sent to Clint, nearly all asking for the fortune he wasn't interested in accepting. He had marriage proposals, appeals from brides-to-be, from college students, ministers, inventors, from cons in prison who wanted the money to prove their innocence, from a host of people in dire straits.

If he were able to carry out the wishes of those writing him he would be one of the great philanthropists of all times. Wescott read some of his letters to wino friends under the downtown Los Angeles bridge where they lived. He chuckled as he scanned the huge pile of mail, exclaiming: "They're all the same. They all want the money." He fumbled through his mail. "Look at this. Someone wants to name a baby after me."

"I'm soon to be married," read the letter from a woman living in Lawrence, Kansas. "This money would come in handy. If you mail it to me, I'll do you the favor of naming a child after you." A man from Ft. Washington, Pennsylvania, wrote: "Send the money in the enclosed envelope. I'll send you a carton of smokes every month. What's your brand?" A woman from Louisiana said she had three brothers and a sister who have cancer. "I have prayed for God to get enough money to bury them when they die. Will you help? I rote to John Wain, Bob Hope, Dean Marten, Loretta Young, Dorothy LaMoore. No luck. They never even answered my letters."

A man obviously awaiting a plane at the San Francisco International Airport, addressed a letter to Wescott on TWA Ambassadors Club stationery: "No requests, just admiration for your sticking to your beliefs. I'm making $20,000 a year working three jobs, keeping a family of four children, a wife and also a 'friend.' I envy you. I may join you someday." A Pennsylvania man who sent along photographs of himself and his family, said he, too, was a Wescott, and "the name goes back to Stukely Wescott on the Mayflower. I'm sure we're related. I could pay all my debts."

A young woman in Attalla, Alabama, enclosed a snapshot of her 2-year-old daughter. "I love my child very much and I want a little home for me and her. Could you help?" One letter invited him to be a guest of honor at a wine-tasting party. A little girl in Kalamazoo, Michigan, wrote: "Please send me enough to buy a horse and enough money to feed him." From Berlin came an urgent plea in German from a "poor sailor" who wrote of losing $6,000 in a recent fire. "If you send me the $6,000 I will do you a favor and visit you someday."

Some of the letters were sent special delivery. Some were addressed simply: "To Clint Wescott. The Man in the Weeds. Los Angeles, California." For many, Wescott obviously represented a last hope. Some asked for a loan, but most were outright demands for the $19,219. "I'll just get to the point," wrote a Detroiter. "I'm asking you for your money. Just send it to me."

"Consider this one of the repulsive letters," began another from Vancouver, B.C. "If you still have an odd thousand left, send it along." "Say Clint," began still another. "I built an exercise machine. The big problem—hell, just like always—I need the money to get it off the ground. Call me collect."

Some of the troubled included the following: "Sick daughter with four children. Four thousand would help."—Monroe, Louisiana. "Three house payments behind. Two light bills. Three months' phone bills. Bills...bills...bills."—Alexandria, Virginia. "We are about to lose our home, our car, our furniture. We got into too much debt, too fast. Could you lend us $3,950? Honestly you are our only hope. This is no hoax. I will send you the bills."—Houston. A Californian wrote: "I have a son facing a prison term. I can get him out on bail for $1,000." An 80-year-old Omaha man suggested Clint "build a bathhouse where your friends can have a bath for a nickel. That will help them with their health."

A handful were not interested in Wescott's money. "You should take it and start a new life," wrote a Portland, Oregon, woman. "Two years ago my husband and I gave you clothes. Oh, Mr. Wescott, please don't sell out. How marvelous life must be without everyday cares or worries," a Los Angeles woman wrote. "Please use the enclosed $1 for your few needs and God bless you for sticking to your convictions," a Tustin woman wrote. "You remind me of my dad. Don't let anyone tell you what to do."

A Florida man wrote: "Accept the money in paper currency. Buy a

CHARLES HILLINGER

gallon of gas. Soak the currency in the gas and burn it." By the end of two weeks more than 5,000 letters were sent to Clint from throughout America, from the far corners of the Earth, a total request in excess of $100 million dollars from people seeking the wino's money. But Clint Wescott never did take the money.

His sister, Minnie Gateby, 79 in 1999, wrote to tells us: "We hadn't heard one word from Clint for 15 years, from the time he abandoned his gas station and went out West until we read about him living under the 4th Street Bridge in the weeds in downtown LA. When your stories about Clint came out members of the family thought we would hear from him, but we never did, not one phone call, not one letter," she explained.

Clint never changed his life style. He never stepped forward to claim his money. As he expected, he had to move out from under the 4th Street Bridge when "high rise" came in. He lived and slept in near-by parks, and despite his continuing bouts with asthma he lived a remarkably long life, considering the way he lived. He died at the age of 76 in 1992. But what happened to the money?

The state of New York held it, waiting for Clint to claim it until the day he died. Eight years after his death, Clint Wescott's heirs, his three sisters and other surviving relatives—he was a lifelong bachelor—were involved in a complicated still-unresolved lawsuit trying to get the state to release the money to them.

The problem is, Clint didn't want anybody to get his money. He didn't want it. He didn't want his relatives to have it. He didn't want the government to get it. He wanted everybody to simply forget it. But you don't forget about a bunch of money just sitting there drawing interest. Sooner or later something has to happen to it. Right?

CHAPTER TWO

Meditation Mount, where Full Mooners gather to chant and celebrate the full moon.

ESOTERIC PRACTICES, CALIFORNIA STYLE

FULL MOONERS: CHANTING ON A MOUNTAIN TOP

A SMALL KNOT OF PEOPLE stood on the summit of Meditation Mount under the brilliant full moon on the crisp, clear night, chanting: "Love to all human beings, north, south, east, west, above, below. Love to all human beings. Light, harmony and peace to all human beings." A calico cat named Gemini pranced nervously back and forth where the Full Mooners had gathered. A coyote howled mournfully in the distance. The "blessing to the world" chant culminated the monthly 90-minute celebration of the full moon by the Meditation Group at its world headquarters on the mountaintop overlooking Ojai Valley.

It was dusk and 35 men and women from throughout Southern California, from many walks of life, assembled on the summit of

Meditation Mount. As the moon loomed large and bright over nearby Topa Topa peak, Montford Smith, a physicist who worked on the atomic bomb project at Los Alamos, N.M., welcomed the group to the Tibetan-style auditorium, a glass-walled, carpetless room with a painting of the full moon and starlit sky on the wall. "Welcome to Meditation Mount and to the full moon of the Capricorn," Smith said. "Let us begin."

The Meditation Group, which claims 8,000 followers in this country and several thousands overseas, was founded in 1956 by New Yorker Florence Garrigue, a metaphysicist, and six others prominent in the field of psychic phenomena. Garrigue, 95 at the time of our visit, lived on Meditation Mount, a $1 million complex of Tibetan structures including Meditation House, a barren room with a round carpet with crystals, the focal point of meditation, in the center.

In the auditorium, Frances Moore, 73, the associate director of Meditation Group, gave the full-moon message: "As we all know, meditation is far more effective at the time of full moon. A band of golden light energy streams forth between the sun and the moon. Let it stream forth into the hearts and minds of men and women everywhere. The force of energy radiating from the full moon is not a myth. It is a living reality, ongoing, never-ending, always happening at this time of month. Let us have a recognition of the revelations from the countless realms of the soul, from the unwalled world whose center is everywhere, whose circumference is nowhere."

Moore asked those assembled to close their eyes, to lay their hands on their laps: "Let the mind become tranquil, centering the consciousness at the top of the head. Silence the thought machine, let us meditate..." For the next 13 minutes she stood at the podium, her eyes closed, her body rigid, with no sign of movement. Everyone in the room sat in deep meditation. There were no coughs, no creaking chairs, no rustling of clothes.

The light of the full moon streamed down into the auditorium. It was so quiet one could hear the blood rushing through one's ears. Finally Frances Moore softly spoke: "Let us come back from silence, slowly and gently." Organist Lorraine Babbitt played "Go Tell It on the Mountain." Phyllis War, a former TRW secretary who is an official of the group, noted that "the Bible is full of full moon. Druids and other groups such as ours have gathered down through the centuries to meditate under the light of the full moon." Later, after the 90-minute celebration, those on the mountain talked among themselves about the energies received from the full moon. "For me the full moon sends out an electromagnetic field of feminine energy," said Chery Fenley, 29, an artist with a red rose on each side of her head pinning her hair back. "The full moon is like a religion to me."

"DO YOU REALIZE DOG IS GOD SPELLED BACKWARDS?"

THE REV. J. CALVIN HARBERTS was minister of a one-church denomination, the Bubbling Well Church of Universal Love in Napa. "Do you realize dog is God spelled backwards?" Harberts asked as he held a plaque that read: "If Christ had a little dog, it would have followed him to the cross." The church doubled as a pet cemetery that Harberts insisted is the largest and most beautifully landscaped of the approximately 500 such cemeteries in the United States.

In 1977, Harberts incorporated the cemetery as a church. That same year he was ordained as a mail-order minister through Universal Life Church. He filed and received a tax-exempt status as a church in California. In 1980 a U.S. Tax Court in Washington D.C. denied the Bubbling Well Church of Universal Love a federal tax-exempt status. Harberts appealed the denial to the 9th Court of Appeals because the minister-pet undertaker insisted Bubbling Well Church of Universal Love is, indeed, a bona fide church.

"We have regular services in our chapel at the pet cemetery. The chapel has an altar, stained-glass windows, an organ, pews, a bell in the church tower. We also have an outside altar in the cemetery where people come to meditate, pray and remember their departed pets. The church has 300 members. To be a member, one must have a pet buried in the cemetery."

On the chapel altar, instead of a cross or other religious symbol, there is a large metal sculpture of a German shepherd custom made for Harberts in Guadalajara, Mexico. Harberts said his services are similar to those of other denominations. "We believe any Supreme Being who puts the breath of life in you and me and these little four-legged creatures is not going to forget man's cherished pets in the hereafter.

"At our church services, the congregation and I say prayers for our departed pets and for sick pets. I read from the Scriptures, recite poetry about pets, talk about the roles pets play in our lives. We sing hymns about pets," explained Harberts.

Funeral services for pets were occurring in the chapel almost daily. At times, there were weddings—for humans—in the pet cemetery chapel, where couples took their vows while holding living pets. "Members of my church believe in the hereafter not only for humans but for pets as well," he continued. "The Bible is not explicit that pets do not have a soul, do not go to heaven. To many pet owners, the loss of a pet takes on the same importance as a loss of any other member of the family. We talk life and death with every one of the pet owners who come here to inter their beloved four-legged creatures.

"I spend a good part of my time consoling people, telling them they will see their pets again in heaven. Organized religion doesn't help them. They have to turn to someone. That is where the religious aspect of the Bubbling Well Pet Memorial Park and the Bubbling Well Church of Universal Love come together."

However, the federal Tax Court ruled that Harberts failed to show his earnings were not being used for purely personal purposes, or that his expenditures were used exclusively for religious and charitable purposes as the law requires. In one of his tax returns, Harberts listed $61,170 in "donations and free will offerings." His $61,543 in expenditures included a European trip he took with his wife, Catherine, and son, Dan.

His wife was secretary-treasurer of the church and his son, vice president. He believed his church was the beginning of a religious movement that would spread worldwide. He planned to establish other pet cemetery-churches, ordain other ministers. "Millions of people all over the world feel this way about pets," he maintained.

Harberts expected that in time he would "become a bishop, maybe a cardinal, as our clergy increase in number, perhaps down the road even becoming the pope of pets. I'm serious about all this," he insisted. "It isn't just a gimmick to get out of paying income taxes." But the government stood fast. The tax-exempt status was not allowed.

Bubbling Well Pet Memorial Park continued as one of the premier pet cemeteries in America but after the court ruled against the tax exempt status the Rev. J. Calvin Harberts placed less emphasis on his role as priest of pets. His 35-acre pet cemetery is on the slopes of Atlas Peak, overlooking Napa's exclusive Silverado Country Club and is surrounded by expensive homes.

Pathways lead from one burial section to another at various elevations in the pet graveyard. There are ponds with ducks, fountains with waterfalls, a zoo with living animals, Japanese gardens and statuary from various parts of the world. Each burial section is set aside for different kinds of pets. One is for birds, another for turtles and snakes, a Kitty Korner for cats, the Garden of Champions is for championship dogs. Great Danes and St. Bernards are buried in the Garden of Gentle Giants; Chihuahuas and miniatures are interred in the Garden of Mighty Midgets. Guide dogs and heroic dogs are in the Garden of Honors.

One section of the cemetery is a final resting place for 450 cats, birds and dogs exhumed from a pet cemetery that went bankrupt in Los Altos, 80 miles to the south. Funeral costs including coffin and marker, vary between $300 to $600. There are more than 5,000 individual graves marked with headstones. Other animals are cremated and their remains buried in a common grave in the mountains nearby for $25. More that 100,000 pets have been disposed of in this manner, Harberts noted. Each pet is remembered on a card file maintained on the outside altar in the pet cemetery.

ONE OF THE MOST EXCLUSIVE CULTS IN AMERICA

WHEN WE VISITED the century-old Esoteric Fraternity in the Mother Lode hamlet of Applegate, there were only two members. The prime reason for joining the group was "absolute abstinence from sexual activity." William J. Corecco, 89, was president. He and his brother, Steven, 91, were the last surviving members of one of the most exclusive religious cults in America.

"We knew the membership would be limited but never expected it to be as small as this," sighed William Corecco, who added: "Since the founding of the Esoteric Fraternity there has never been more than two dozen members at any given time. Very few have been willing to make the sacrifice."

At the time of my visit to the headquarters of the Esoteric Fraternity, Corecco and his brother said they had recently buried the last surviving female member, Luvenia Sublette, who was 83. The cult's headquarters was a four-story, 19th-century aerie at the end of a dirt road that spiraled up a 360-acre, heavily wooded hill owned by the group on the outskirts of Applegate, a tiny Sierra Nevada town 50 miles northeast of Sacramento. In the shadows of the faded yellow brick and frame headquarters building was a tiny graveyard containing the remains of 15 members of the sect.

Steven Correco explained during an interview in the headquarters' library, "To join it is necessary not only to live a life of a celibate, but also to give all of your money and worldly possessions to the fraternity. My brother and I are terribly disappointed there are not more members." The Esoterics believed they were to be the Order of Melchisedek as prophesied in Revelations in the Bible.

William Corecco, fourth president and 70 years an Esoteric, swayed back and forth in a creaky old rocker during the interview. He sat beside a pot-bellied stove that warmed the musty library. "The Bible says when 144,000 persons establish the Order of Melchisedek, the kingdom of God will be established on earth. That was our hope..."

Founding president and author of several books describing the sect's peculiar philosophy was Hiram Erastus Butler who died in 1916 and is buried outside the library window. "Hiram Butler was a Pennsylvanian," said William, "a simple, self-educated man who worked in a sawmill. He lost several fingers in a mill accident and became a hermit. For 14 years he lived in seclusion never speaking to another person. It was during this period of his life he received several revelations from God."

Butler revealed his revelations in a series of lectures in Boston. In 1889 the bearded mystic and a dozen followers—all single men and single women—pooled their resources and moved to the West Coast. Here they homesteaded the lonely hill overlooking the American River. They built the 18-room headquarters building and living quarters from timber cut on their land and made the furniture still used in the square yellow structure on top of the hill. They raised crops. They tended a small herd of stock. They meditated. And, they printed philosophical and religious books in their own publishing house at the bottom of the hill. Enoch Penn, second president, also wrote a number of books. He issued 1,000 copies of a magazine called Esoteric each month. The magazine ceased publication on his death in 1943. Next came the only woman president, Lena Crow, who for 17 years led what must be one of history's smallest cults to last any length of time. She was succeeded on her death in 1960 by William Corecco, a native Californian of Swiss descent. Although its membership was down to two very old men, mail continued to pour into Applegate (population 300) addressed to the Esoteric Fraternity, reported the local postmaster. And William kept busy filling orders for the 19 books and pamphlets published by the cult throughout its long history. One publication, "Practical Methods to Insure Success," written by Butler in 1893, was in its 45th printing.

"Although few have been willing to totally abstain from sex—the one requirement which is the foundation of our belief and absolutely necessary to achieve membership," continued Corecco. "Many are intrigued by our ideas. Esoteric publications are sold in bookstores across the nation, in England, France, Italy and Germany. We have German and Italian-language editions. Thousands of copies of our publications have been printed and sold since Butler published his first book in 1887." Throughout all 19 publications there is one central theme—to believe in and accept God, one must live the life of a celibate. Corecco said this would *not* result in no people left on earth. "Of course there would be no more children," he explained. "But there would be no more sickness. No more disease. No more death if man gave up sexual activity. When man gives up the sex act the kingdom of God will be established on earth. When that happens we all become sons of God."

He said an Esoteric Fraternity existed among the Jews years before the birth of Christ. "But it was lost. It was restored by Christ, but lost again by the Christians. That is precisely what we have been attempting in our group. We believe we were the chosen ones, that this time the Order of Melchisedek would finally be achieved...That we, the true believers would inherit and rule the earth for all eternity. Esoteric teachings are interpretations of the true meaning of the Bible. The Bible gives us to understand unless a man retains his seed—his substance of procreation and does not cast it forth as do other animals of the earth, he cannot achieve the more refined life, the holy spirit. Jesus said the kingdom of heaven will be established on earth when they neither marry nor are given in marriage, neither can they die any more, for they are equal to the angels. Christ's purpose is not that man should spend his existence in endless reproduction."

The cult preached reincarnation. "We have all lived on Earth hundreds of times before. The population of the world," Corecco maintained, "remains constant. Souls that leave at death reappear in the newborn. That is why when heaven on Earth occurs, it will no longer be necessary to die and be born again." He did not expect the Esoteric Fraternity to disappear with his death and the death of his brother. "I believe the time for the Order of Melchisedek is at hand," he insisted. "There is a younger man—35 is his age—presently living in Salt Lake City—a man who never married, who has visited here many times in the past. He knows our teachings better than anyone else. He has dedicated his life to the Fraternity. He is not yet a full-fledged member, but I believe he will make it. Perhaps in time this building on the hill and these grounds will become holy places for all the people of the world."

But for all that to happen, all manifestations of sexual activity will have to cease.

CHAPTER THREE

Walkin' George, 81, trudges desert highways collecting old bottles, cans, and trash.

FOUR PEAS IN A POD

WALKIN' GEORGE

T HEY CALL HIM "WALKIN' GEORGE" because for years he's trudged the highway that passes through Boron, an isolated desert town, collecting old bottles, cans and trash. You might take him for just another run-of-the-mill bum. Indeed, he does live in Boron in a roofless, trashy hovel, and when he goes to the big city he takes up residence in a Skid Row flophouse. But "Walkin' George" is not a bum. He's a bon vivant. He's an accomplished pianist, a gentle-man songster, a well-paid technician, a sophisticated weekend man-about-town who squires lady friends to some of the most lavish dining spots in Los Angeles. His real name is George Swain. He's Boron's beloved town character.

The year was 1978. Standing in the midst of the huge cache of trash he calls home (the heap of rags in the center of it all is his bed), the 59-

year-old pack rat explains with a laugh, "It has taken me thousands of hours to accumulate all this stuff. I'm just doing my bit for ecology." For 34 years "Walkin' George" had been an advanced chemical analyst for the big U.S. Borax & Chemical Corp. mine and mill, the mainstay of Boron, population 3,000. When he gets off work Friday afternoon, "Walkin' George" often hops a bus in his tattered clothes and heads for Los Angeles, 125 miles southwest of Boron.

He sleeps in cheap Skid Row hotels in downtown L.A. on Friday and Saturday nights. "I walk along Main Street hunched over, my hair disheveled, wearing my old clothes. I'm lost in the crowd. I look like just another one of the winos," explains Swain.

"I hate to spend money on hotel rooms. That's why I sleep in the cheap flophouses. But I like the good life, too!" He is a regular diner at many of the most expensive restaurants in downtown Los Angeles and Hollywood. "I enjoy a good aperitif and the best of wines with my meals when I eat out," confides "Walkin George." A lifelong bachelor, Swain has a lady friend he calls on when he goes to the city. "I keep decent shirts and a new suit at my girlfriend's apartment," he explains. "I lead a metamorphic existence. At times I am a caterpillar, at other times a butterfly..."

"Walkin' George" and his date go out on the town by taxi. They rarely miss a weekend performance at the Music Center. Sunday night he's back in his old clothes boarding the midnight bus for Boron and his desert lair.

Swain is an accomplished concert pianist and an opera buff since a teenager. His musical protégés number scores of children in Boron, boys and girls who have studied piano under his tutelage. "He is a fascinating person," said June Vickers, expressing the common sentiments of Boron residents. "He is a prime example of that old saw you can never tell a book by its cover.

"He refuses to take money for his music lessons. But he will take dinner. He never eats breakfast or lunch. But, oh my, is he a hearty eater at night! We have him at our house every Tuesday. He gives piano lessons to Debbie, our 10-year-old daughter." Swain spends at least three nights a week giving private piano lessons in return for good home-cooked meals.

"Walkin' George" is as unconcerned about the clothes he wears as he is about where he lives. He always wears an old pair of trousers, an old shirt, old shoes, no socks and his lab apron, except when he's out on the town.

Swain sings in two church choirs in Boron. He plays the piano for school plays at Boron High School. He frequently leaves the desert on long weekends to fly to San Francisco, Seattle and other cities to go to the opera. He has traveled by train and plane throughout the United States, Canada, Mexico, Central and South America.

He is an erudite, well-read man with an exceptional memory. He has many goals he hopes to achieve - to play Robert Schumann's "A-Minor Piano Concerto" with the Los Angeles Philharmonic, to ride the length of the Trans-Siberian Railroad, to go to the opera at La Scala and to attend a Wagner Festival in Bayreuth, Bavaria.

"We have Walkin' George Nights at the church from time to time," notes the Rev. Dick Seymour of Boron's First Baptist Church." Nearly everyone in town turns out. The kids flock around him. He's like the Pied Piper of Hamelin. The children sing out request after request for Walkin' George to play scores from their favorites—Beethoven's 5th Symphony, the introduction to the 'Holy Grail' the 'William Tell' Overture. He plays every request and more—and all from memory without any music," Seymour said. "This remarkable human being has introduced everyone in town to good music and opera. Boron is lucky, indeed, to have Walkin' George."

Early in 2000, some 22 years after my "Walkin' George" story first appeared and my segment about George Swain ran on the prime time NBC "Real People" show, I drove out to Boron to see how the fascinating old bum/ bon vivant was doing. He was now 80, retired after 44 years as a lab technician at the U.S. Borax plant.

Nothing had changed. His life style remained the same. He walked for miles every day picking up and recycling cans, bottles and trash tossed from cars along the roadside. "Americans are so wasteful," he sighed. His hair was disheveled. His clothes were tattered and stained. Yet, his metamorphic existence, continued as always. He frequently boarded a bus in Boron for the 125-mile trip to Los Angeles where he kept an expensive wardrobe in a girlfriend's apartment. For a half century he has always had a girlfriend in L.A. "My present friend is a beautiful 25-year-old blonde named Victoria," noted the 80-year-old, who accompanies her to one of the most exclusive restaurants in L.A. and an evening on the town each visit. He meets his lady friends at dance halls. He was still flying to cities across the country to see performances of Richard Wagner operas and traveling by train throughout Canada and the U.S., still maintaining his caterpillar-butterfly existence.

SELDOM SEEN SLIM

SELDOM SEEN SLIM, the last man in Ballarat, a tiny ghost town on the western edge of Death Valley, slipped out of sight behind the crumbling adobe wall. "You don't want to write a story about me," shouted the scrawny prospector as he ran up the dusty street in deserted Panamint Valley, 200 miles north of Los Angeles. Some time later Slim, one of the last of the West's legendary characters, had a change of heart and described what it's like to live alone for a half century in a town that died.

"I ain't lonely. Hell, I'm half coyote and half wild burro," spouted Slim as he sat beside his dilapidated trailer, thumbed tobacco into his corncob, gulped whisky and talked. "I'm a scientific prospector. Have been since the day I got in trouble with my first grade teacher, jumped out the school window and headed west." Slim said he had been a scientific prospector ever since.

"I got no people. I was born in an Illinois orphanage. Never did know my first name—just Slim. Slim Ferge is the only name I've ever had. That and Seldom Seen Slim." He said he came by his nickname in Randsburg, a mining town a few miles south of Ballarat. "Got stuck with it when one fella asked another if he had seen Slim. The other fella answered 'He's seldom seen here.'"

Slim settled in Ballarat when he went west and had been here ever since. Ballarat blossomed overnight during the gold and silver strikes of 1897. In its heyday 1,000 miners, a handful of families and camp followers lived in the riotous town. They all left except for the 27 buried in Ballarat's Boot Hill. And Seldom Seen. "There were buildings all over the place and I lived in every one of them after everybody pulled out," recalled Slim waving his hands across the deserted desert floor. Only a dozen or more adobe shells still stand today. Ballarat had a school, a jail, a two-story hotel, seven saloons, two blocks of stores, a post office, a Wells Fargo station.

"They closed the last saloon 48 years ago. I've been alone here ever since. Oh, now and then a drifter comes through and moves into one of the old places. But they usually don't last long. One fella came through here last year, spent several months in town, but we never talked to each other. I guess he got tired of the quiet. He finally pulled up stakes and left."

Slim didn't say how he managed to get by, other than that he was a scientific prospector and could tell what was in the rocks. "I know where the gold's buried," he insisted. He had a butane refrigerator, a wood stove and the old trailer. He claimed he hasn't taken a bath in 20 years and looked it: "I stand in the nude outside my trailer about once a month and splash water over myself," he said. There's no water in Ballarat.

Slim was taken to Trona, 30 miles away, a couple of times a month by prospector friends. He bought water and his supplies. The only time Slim left Ballarat was in July and August, when he slept in a bedroll in the High Sierra. "I have to leave. The sun gets so hot the rocks seem to curl up. It's 120 in the shade and there ain't no shade. That's the hell of it." Slim called himself the mayor, postmaster, chief of police, dog catcher and tax collector of Ballarat.

He stood in the middle of Main Street, waved his arms and declared, "I'm the traffic cop, too. Speed limit through here is 100 m.p.h. in low gear." He said he fell in love once. "But I put my hand on my gal's leg and got a handful of splinters. She never told me she had a wooden leg. That did it. I never fell in love again."

Slim was the last of his kind, or maybe the first. Inyo County records show that he had indeed been in the town 52 years and old-timers who visited Panamint Valley said he never left except for the summers. "Hell," snorted Slim, who said he was 78, "you put this in the paper and they'll be calling me Often Seen Slim."

SHOPPING CART DOUGHERTY

"SHOPPING CART" DOUGHERTY, the California walker, was on one of the longest hikes in history when I caught up with him on a remote stretch of high desert along Highway 395 near Little Lake in Inyo County. When we met he had been on a non-stop hike for 23 years. "It'll end when they find my bones along some lonely stretch of road," sighed the sandy-bearded, 60-year-old ex-middle-weight boxer.

His full name was John Patrick Dougherty. He came by his nickname because he traveled the state pushing all his belongings in a supermarket castaway. "I was a professional pugilist, fighting all over the state. When I quit the ring I took to selling rugs," he explained. "Then I got the urge to travel. I couldn't afford to travel. I couldn't afford a car. I didn't have money to ride a bus. I didn't like the idea of hopping freights—so, I started walking." Dougherty never stopped to figure how far he walked over the years. "Thousands of miles. I average 9 to 16 miles a day," he reckoned.

He was on a 222-mile stint from Bishop to Victorville. At the halfway mark, near Little Lake, he said: "I stay on the move. Sometimes I pause two or three days to mow lawns, wash dishes, do odd jobs to pick up scratch to keep going. But I never dilly-dally anywhere more than three days. I get itchy feet and have to move on. I avoid the big cities. I've been everywhere in California—up and down the coast, over the highest mountains, in the redwoods, in the deserts, in all the counties. But I've never set foot out of California. When I get to the borders at Arizonie, or Nevada, to Mexico or up to Oregon, I never cross the line. I turn around and head the other way. I was borned in California and growed up here and don't want to go nowhere but everywhere in this state."

"Shopping Cart" insisted he was about as well off as a man could get. "Ain't got no rent. I sleep in my pup tent off the road. I do my own cookin', my own laundry. I wash my clothes every other day. No bills. No taxes. No worries. Always seein' new spots. People knowed me from Crescent City to Calexico. What more can a man ask? Only expense is shoes. I go through a pair every two, three weeks. Only bother is ants and flies. But, hell, everybody gets flies some time."

His shopping cart was filled with jugs of water, tent, cot, canned food, clothing and tools. His tools were screwdrivers and crescent wrenches. "Lots of people break down along the road. I come by and help. I'm a good mechanic." Dougherty was quick to report he found his shopping cart in a Wilmington dump several years ago. "All the cops in California knowed it wasn't stolen. It was a mess—all bent, rusted, without wheels. I fixed it up and it's been with me ever since."

The above story about "Shopping Cart" Dougherty appeared in the *Los Angeles Times* and hundreds of newspapers throughout America, including the *Philadelphia Enquirer*. "Shopping Cart" Dougherty's elderly mother read about her son in the *Enquirer* and wrote me a letter. "I haven't seen or heard a word from him in 30 years," she explained. "How can I get in touch with him?"

"I'm not sure where he is now," I replied in a letter. "When I interviewed him several weeks ago in Little Lake he was headed south on Highway 395 pushing his shopping cart."

DR. TINKERPAW OF NITWIT RIDGE

W HEN ARE YOU GOING TO FINISH YOUR HOUSE, Dr. Tinkerpaw of Nitwit Ridge was asked. "Never! Never!" thundered Tinkerpaw, tugging on his pointed beard. "Time means nothing to me. The tide comes and goes. Time never returns. I'll worry about time when I'm in the marble orchard."

Dr. Tinkerpaw, whose real name was Art Beal, had been building his aerie for 45 years when we encountered him in Cambria, a small coastal town 250 miles north of Los Angeles. He was 77 and hadn't slowed a bit. "Everything you see I created," he said, waving his arms around him. "It's been all work and little rest." His "creation" creeps up a solid rock cliff for 250 feet or more, a room or two on each of eight or nine levels.

Beal's castle is built of the world's castoffs. "Everything in it is junk I picked up along life's travels," he said. Some of his rooms are made of driftwood gathered on the nearby beach. There are walls of concrete and abalone shells, of beer cans, old tires and rusted car wheels. "Pixies and gremlins didn't do it. I did it all with these two hands," he explained. At the outset, he noted "I had no more in mind of doing this than growing feathers."

"Nobody lived around here when it all began. The hill was hidden far back in the woods. So, I created my first one-room shack. But that wasn't enough. I put up another, and another and another. I can't stop now." His rooms are scattered over the slope. Some attached. Most not. "It never dawned on me to keep track of what I'm doing. I'm a member of that detergent club—work fast and leave no rings. That's why they call me Dr. Tinkerpaw. I tinker with my paws. Sometimes they call me Capt. Nitwit because I live on Nitwit Ridge." That accounts for the two names on his gate and mailbox.

Rooms and patios are crowded with chairs resurrected from city

CHARLES HILLINGER

dumps, with old couches spewing stuffing. But there's charm to the castle. Rock archways lead to gardens and orchards on every level. "I grow everything I eat," he said as he led the way through a bean patch. He had tomatoes, potatoes, avocados, oranges, lemons, apricots, kumquats.

Beal's bizarre bailiwick is no longer hidden in the bush. Handsome new expensive homes are rising all around him. A few of his neighbors have publicly called for "Dr. Tinkerpaw's monstrosity" to be bulldozed to oblivion. "They're all Johnny-come-latelys," boomed the lord of Nitwit Ridge. "I arrived in Cambria shortly after that first German fracas." Others who live close by look to Tinkerpaw as an integral part of the Cambria landscape. Said a note tacked to his top gate: "Dr. Tinkerpaw we love you."

Beal's roots go back to turn-of-the-century San Francisco. He lost his mother in the 1906 earthquake when he was a child. "My father? I never knew who he was or what happened to him. I've never known if I had any relatives. Never been married.

"School? I went through the front door and they pushed me out the back. As I was leaving someone said, 'Read a little. Maybe you will learn something.'" He said he worked at "practically everything there's a dime in—mostly pearl diving. That's dish washing." Yellowed news clippings note that Beal was one of the West Coast's leading long distance swimmers. Among his cherished possessions were five anthologies of verse with several of his poems published in each volume.

He was living on a small monthly stipend. Franklin D. Roosevelt and Will Rogers were his heroes. Their pictures hung from his walls. His dress was always the same—shirtless, grimy trousers, no socks, shoes without tongues. As for personal cleanliness, he winked, then bellowed: "Tinkerpaw takes a bath once a year, whether he needs it or not, to celebrate the coming of the rains."

CHAPTER FOUR

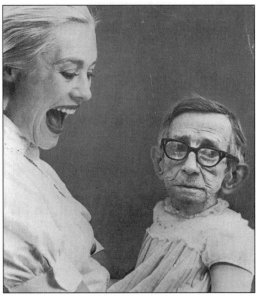

"You've got the sweetest little baby face"
—*Peachy Postcard published by* Wretched Mess News.
(Photo by A. Gescheidt.)

A WRETCHED MESS

MILFORD STANLEY POLTROON'S *Wretched Mess News* published in Oakland was not your ordinary, run-of-the-mill magazine. A typical issue carried the headline: "*CEMETERIES OBSOLETE, SAYS LOCAL TAXIDERMIST*" A photo accompanying the story purportedly showed the taxidermist's "entire family, all of whom he has skillfully stuffed and mounted after their decease." "It's much more fun to have the whole family together, though slightly stiff, than have them stuck out in some cemetery plot somewhere," the taxidermist, identified as Walter P. Funkle, is quoted as saying. "You can talk to them, change their costumes for the seasons, and everything, just so long as you dust them now and then." *Wretched Mess News*, sold for 59 cents a copy. It had a national circulation of more than 10,000 and was the zany creation of Dave Bascom. To his readers, he was Milford Stanley Poltroon (the last name is synonymous with coward).

Bascom headed one of the largest advertising agencies in the country up until the time he gave up his career to devote full time to humor. "I started Wretched Mess for the sheer hell of it," he explained. "Wretched Mess was much more fun than the constant stress of an ad agency, so I sold the agency and have been doing this ever since."

Bascom, 64 when we interviewed him, prepared all the advertisements but never lets advertisers see the ad copy until *Wretched Mess News* was printed and distributed. "Clients know they can expect the worst, but sometimes things get sticky and we lose an advertiser," admitted Bascom. "Like the Skippy Peanut Butter account. The ad advised readers to send in two slices of bread to Skippy Peanut Butter and Skippy will send you back a peanut butter sandwich. Many readers did just that. The peanut butter company failed to see the humor in the ad. As you might guess that was the last Skippy ad we had," laughed Bascom. There were timely illustrated features on such matters as fly swatting. How to properly execute shoulder swats, sidestrokes and back swatting, plus such advice as "Don't swat flies on rice pudding." Bascom maintained an office year round in West Yellowstone, but only spent his summers there. The rest of the year he was in Oakland, dreaming up wild greeting cards, crazy posters and other offbeat products. More than 50,000 persons each year bought Bascom's *Wretched Mess* calendars.

In the calendar each day of the year was a special holiday and each week an outlandish national observance. The days of the week and the months were all renamed. For example, one year April 6 was Pastafazoo Day; April 26, Non Your Sequiturs Day; July 1, Transcend Dental Meditation Day and Dec. 7, Remember Pearl Farber, the lady attacked by a Japanese gardener this day. Awshoot, Steptender, Oxsober, Nobetter and Dismember were the last five months of that year. Mudsdays were all the Mondays in Dismember. The symbol for all *Wretched Mess* enterprises was a bespectacled, wide-eyed, big-mouthed fish. "I invented a trout fly that looks like a wretched mess," explained Bascom. "You see, trouts are gullible and try to take anything from anyone out of a sense of obligation." One of Bascom's most successful posters shows a photograph of a Siamese cat sitting on a commode with the caption, "Nothing Is Impossible." "I get letters all the time from people saying their Siamese cats do the same thing," he noted. "If that's the case, all Americans should train their dogs to do likewise. It would help clean up a great urban problem."

He published bizarre photographs, like a dog's head on a pigeon's body with the caption, "I think I'm going to lay an egg," or a nurse holding a baby with the wrinkled face of an old man and the caption, "You've got the cutest baby face." His creations included elaborate personalized genius certificates and hippopotamus repellent "to prevent itinerant hippopotamuses from spoiling your barbecues." Bascom said he relied on "gullible, affluent people and other eccentrics" to buy his assortment of humor "People today take themselves altogether too seriously," he added. "I'm having a lot of fun and making a living, hopefully by enabling others to enjoy themselves."

Bascom's *Wretched Mess* philosophy was:

> When the road is rough,
> And the going is tough,
> And the future looks black,
> And you want to turn back,
> Give up.

CHAPTER FIVE

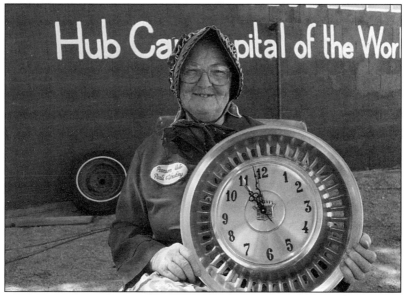

Hubcap Lucy Pearson, the Hubcap Queen, posing before the "Hub Cap Capital of the World."

DESERT DWELLERS

HUBCAP LUCY

THE SIGNS APPROACHING the tiny desert town proclaim: "Pearsonville—Hub Cap Capital of the World." This is the home of "Hubcap Lucy" Pearson, the "Hupcap Queen." She was 63 when we interviewed her in downtown Pearsonville. Hubcap Lucy had been collecting hubcaps since she and her husband, Andy, founded the tiny town in 1959.

Pearsonville is a wide spot in the middle of the desert on U.S. 395 in Inyo County, 60 miles north of Mojave. Hubcap aficionados all over America know about Hubcap Lucy. She has 80,000 used hubcaps all over the place in Pearsonville.

They hang from the walls in Mom and Pop's Café. They are in grocery store shopping carts, in huge drums, hanging on fences, piled high in the Hubcap Yard, on shelves in the Hubcap Shop, and stored in a huge Hubcap Trailer. "If I don't have them, nobody does. I ship hub-caps all over the country, as far as New England," Lucy said. She buys, sells and trades hubcaps. She is a walking encyclopedia on the subject.

Hubcap Lucy and her granddaughter, April Hamlin, 18, make hub-cap clocks that they sell for $35. "We will make a clock to fit any kind of hubcap," said Lucy. Lucy, Andy and their two children, Janice and Donald, came to California from Irvine, Kentucky. The Pearsons paid $8,000 for 80 acres in 1959, and that was the beginning of Pearsonville, population 100.

Because so many wrecks occur on the busy Los Angeles to Reno road that passes through Pearsonville, Andy, a mechanic, went into the wrecking business. "When Andy salvaged tires and wheels from wrecks, he'd throw the hubcaps away. I hate to see anything go to waste so I started collecting hubcaps and I've been doing it ever since," explained the Hubcap Queen. It became an obsession.

Pearsonville has come a long way. The Pearsons own all the busi-nesses—the wrecking company, garage, gas station, mini-mart, café, auto parts shop, hubcap shop and race track, where stock cars race every other Saturday night.

Cars throughout the United States sport "Where the hell is Pearson-ville?" bumper stickers. And, of course, most people don't have the fog-giest idea. The Pearsons have also sold thousands of T-shirts with drawings of hubcaps and the eye-catching message "Pearsonville— Hub Cap Capital of the World."

"I hope to still be doing hubcaps when I'm 100," mused Hubcap Lucy.

GASLESS GAS STATION

EARL HARVEY MAY HAVE BEEN OPERATING the only gasless gaso-line station in America. The old man's Arrowhead Junction Service Station was open every day—but he never sold any gas. He didn't have a gas pump.

"That's the problem," explained Harvey, 84, as he stood in torn and tattered clothes outside his dilapidated frame structure on the Mojave Desert 17 miles northwest of Needles. It almost seemed the slightest gust would blow the place down. "Three years ago a car plowed into my gas station, knocked over a couple of pillars, wiped out the only pump I had. The driver wasn't insured," recalled Harvey.

The accident was understandable. Harvey's station was a bull's-eye in the center of a target—right in the middle of the junction between U.S. Highway 95 and Old Route 66. He said the oil company he bought his gas from "isn't in a hurry for me to replace the pump because I never have done much business out here. Hell, I'd be lucky to make a profit of a few dollars a day. But it was a livelihood, that plus my Social Security. I'm anxious to get a new pump, but it will take about $1,000 and I just don't have that kind of money," he sighed. "At least not yet," he added with a ray of optimism.

But why, he was asked, the "OPEN" signs? He had "OPEN" signs plastered in windows on all four sides of the station. Yet he had no gas to sell. "The law of the desert!" the old man replied. "I've got to keep it open. They'd strip me blind if they thought it was abandoned."

So, Harvey was spending every day sitting on a stoop at the service station watching cars and trucks whiz by. "People stop, ask directions, I give them information. They know somebody is here. They see the 'OPEN' signs." The old man had lived on the desert 30 years. He wasn't alone. For the previous 10 years, Mrs. Catther Mostsenbocker, a widow, then 50, had also been a resident of Arrowhead Junction. Harvey lived in an old house. She lived in a trailer. "Catther cooks for the two of us, helps me take care of the place," said Harvey, a lifelong bachelor. They had no electricity, no running water, no indoor plumbing, no telephone, no radio, no television. It gets mighty hot in the summer at Arrowhead Junction—120° isn't uncommon.

The old man had a 20-acre mining claim at the junction. He was entitled to live on and use the land as long as he lived, then it reverted to the government under provisions of the Mining Claim Occupancy Act. He owned an acre of land at Goffs, 15 miles to the west, nearest neighbor to Arrowhead Junction. The acre was leased to store trailers. The person leasing it delivered 100 gallons of water a month to the old man as payment.

Harvey served in the Navy for 5 years when he was 16 to 21. He worked as a coal miner before coming West to prospect on the California desert. "People think it's lonely out here," he said. "Hell, it ain't lonely. There's beauty all around. In the evening, it's like looking forward to heaven after a long hot day. The mountains seem to grow in size at sundown."

CHAPTER SIX

Ruth "Spaceship Ruthie" Norman.
(Photo courtesy Unarius Academy of Science.)

THE OUTER SPACE CONNECTION

SPACESHIP RUTHIE

"**S**PACESHIP RUTHIE" stood on the mountaintop near Jamul in her flowing white gown and furs. "This is where the fleet of flying saucers will land," declared the 76-year-old high priestess of the Unarius Educational Foundation.

Signs on the mountaintop 35 miles east of San Diego proclaimed: "Welcome Space Brothers." "Spaceship Ruthie" stood beside a painting depicting a fleet of interplanetary vehicles arriving on the mountain. Ruth Norman ("Spaceship Ruthie") told how she bet $6,000 with a London bookmaking firm that at least one spaceship from another planet would arrive on Earth within the following 12 months. Her disciples wagered another $4,000 with Ladbrokes & Co. Ltd. that Ruth Norman's prediction would come true.

(In a phone call to the 75-year-old London firm, Bernice Richards, an official of the gaming corporation, confirmed the wagers. "We gave Mrs. Norman and her followers 100 to 1 odds at first. Then as they continued to send in more money we lowered the odds on later bets to 50 to 1," Miss Richards related. "Ladbrokes will bet on anything. We look at the 'spaceship from another planet' as a fun bet like the bets we take on the existence of the Loch Ness Monster.")

The Unarius Education Foundation was founded in 1954 by Mrs. Norman and her late husband, Ernest L. Norman. Unarius stands for Universal Articulate Interdimensional Understanding of Science. Norman wrote 23 books, his wife 22, all purportedly based on mental communications the couple had with leaders of 59 other planets. Thousands of the slick, hardback publications, selling from $10 to $20 lined the walls of the Unarius headquarters in El Cajon, a suburb of San Diego. "Followers of Archangel Uriel throughout the world buy our publications," said Vaughn Spaegel, one of the leaders of the psychic cult.

Ruth Norman was called the "Universal Seeress," "Archangel Uriel," and "Joshanna" by her disciples. But to nonbelievers locally the flamboyant cultist was best known as "Spaceship Ruthie."

"Spaceship Ruthie" paid $50,000 for the mountaintop in the hills of Jamul to serve as the landing field for a fleet of spaceships flying in from 32 planets in this and other solar systems. "I don't expect to lose my bet," insisted Ruth Norman, whose latest book was titled *Countdown!!! To Space Landing!*

"I have been in constant communication with other planets. I often make mental trips to other planets. Those who live on the other planets have the same human form as we do... Spaceships will be flying in for history's first interplanetary convention. The huge spaceships filled with visitors from other planets will land one atop another forming a giant tower on the mountaintop. I was directed by leaders of the other planet to buy the 65 acres in the hills of Jamul for the landing site and future world center of Unarius." Large futuristic models of underground cities on Mars, of solar systems and planets, of a 2,000-foot high power tower are on display at the Unarius headquarters.

Narrow, winding roads through the back country of San Diego County lead to "Spaceship Ruthie's" mountaintop. The last three miles are up a steep curvy dirt road ending at a locked gate. "Spaceship Ruthie" led the way in her chauffeur-driven Cadillac. "You think the astronauts landing on the moon was something," said "Spaceship

Ruthie." "That was a minor event when compared to the upcoming visit from inhabitants of the 32 planets later this year." But as you've probably guessed, "Spaceship Ruthie's" friends from other planets let her down. They were a no-show on her mountaintop landing site.

"LE GRAND PAPA" OF FLYING SAUCERS

I T WAS THE SPRING OF 1970 and by his own admission George W. Van Tassel, "Le Grand Papa" of flying saucer observers had come onto hard times. Not much was being heard about flying saucers at the time. After 21 years of investigation, the Air Force ceased evaluating reports of unidentified flying saucers. Dr. Edward U. Condon, the eminent physicist who headed the investigation, described the project as a "bunch of damned nonsense."

Van Tassel, each year since 1954, had staged an annual flying saucer convention at his remote Giant Rock headquarters in the desert 17 miles north of Yucca Valley. But attendance had been dropping markedly in the late 60s. He had serious thoughts about never having another get together of flying saucer aficionados.

"People see so many flying saucers, they're not a novelty any more," insisted Van Tassel, running his hand through his sparsely graying hair. "That's why no one's talking about them. Why, I just saw a monstrous saucer myself out here last September. It was 500 feet in diameter.

"Millions of people all over the world have seen flying saucers. Just look at all this evidence, all these photographs," declared the 60-year-old dean of saucer seers as he rummaged through a pile of crudely printed flying saucer publications. "The god damn people running the show in the publicity world won't let any more reports of sightings be broadcast. The government has ordered newspapers not to publish flying saucer stories. It's a national conspiracy." In better years Van Tassel attracted thousands to his Giant Rock restaurant where so-called photo evidence of saucers cover the walls. Many who came exchanged information about saucer sightings, about trips made to distant planets. Van Tassel repeated time and time again details of the flying saucers that landed at Giant Rock. Now, the five-mile dirt road leading to his 640 acres was seldom traveled. The restaurant operated by his wife, Eva, was generally empty.

Instead of devoting most of his attention and energy to flying saucers, Van Tassel in 1970 was concentrating on the completion of his "time machine" at the Giant Rock College of Universal Wisdom.

Auto Club maps and other maps of Southern California and of San Bernardino County in particular, indicated at the time the location of the college and pinpointed Giant Rock and the Giant Rock Airport all on Van Tassel's 640 acres. The college lacked one essential all other colleges have—students.

Van Tassel's college was a 35-foot high, 58-foot diameter silver dome—the "time machine," he called an Integratron. "This time machine will work on the same principle as the flying saucers from distant planets," reported Van Tassel. "There never has been a structure like this on earth before. It's a cyclotron backwards, designed to integrate energy into matter." He said he was going to install a primary 45-foot diameter coil and a secondary 18-foot diameter coil inside with an ion reflector at the top of the dome. "When completed as many as 10,000 people a day will be able to be rejuvenated by the Integratron," he explained. "The machine will bombard anyone walking into the building with ions. The body has a capacity like a battery. Every cell in the body will be charged simultaneously. A person will walk in one door and within seven seconds walk out the other door to begin a new life. 70 and 80-year-old people will be able to get up and run around like 20 years olds once they've gone through the machine. It will add 50 to 80 years to their lives. And 20 and 30 year olds will never grow old once they've walked through the Integratron. It will be the marvel of all ages." Van Tassel swore that it would work. "I've proved it out with experiments on mice," he claimed.

In his most recent copy of *The Proceedings*, the official publication of the College of Universal Wisdom, he detailed progress on his "time machine." A story in the same issue of *The Proceedings* called for the construction of a circle of seven pyramids equally spaced in the Los Angeles Basin, each crowned with 600-foot high masts connected by guy wires. "Smog will be eliminated once the pyramids are completed," proclaimed Van Tassel. On other pages he revealed that Neil Armstrong and Buzz Aldrin found spaceships from other planets "lined up in ranks" along the edge of a crater on the moon. "Why doesn't President Nixon let the astronauts tell the truth about what they really discovered on the moon?" he asked. Van Tassel, it must be noted, considered himself to be especially close to God. The College of Universal Wisdom was duly registered with the State of California as a branch of the Ministry of Universal Wisdom Inc. Van Tassel had moved into the religious business. As a church, the

Ministry was a non-profit, tax-exempt corporation.

"We have religious services every Friday night at Giant Rock Café," he said. "I am an ordained minister, a doctor of divinity." He reached into his wallet and produced a card bearing an inscription "Certification of Ordination into Christ Brotherhood." "I'm a full-fledged minister. I have performed marriages of earthlings and of aliens from outer space as well. I conduct funerals. I preach eternal intelligence." Needless to say Van Tassel never completed his "time machine," his college never had any students and the circle of seven pyramids to eliminate smog in the Los Angeles Basin was never erected.

PSYCHICS CONVENTION

INDIAN MEDICINE MEN, clairvoyants, mystics, reincarnation experts, crystal ball readers, palmists, "hollow earth" theorists and numerous other psychics from all over the West were holding a Psychic Fair in Landers, a remote slice of Southern California desert 40 miles north of Palm Springs. The fair was held on five acres surrounding a burned-out saloon, the new headquarters of Bishop Bea Winsor, 56, founder-leader of the Way of Life Psychic Institute. Several hundred believers in psychic phenomena and curious from near and far attended the three-day fair. Some, like Zephyr Lamarre, 23, arrived wearing pyramid coverings on their heads.

"I drove straight through from Lake Tahoe without stopping," said Ms Lamarre, "and I feel as fresh and wide awake as when I started. Wearing the pyramid did it. The energy generated by the pyramid keeps you from getting exhausted. Psychic phenomena leads me through life," said Ms Lamarre, who told of going several years without a first name. "People would ask my name and I would tell them I'm waiting for a new one. Finally the new name came to me. I have been known ever since as Zephyr, a name that means the gentle wind." "Reincarnation Ed" a fair attendee, claims to have regressed to 100 previous lives. He insisted that he lived "once as King Edward III of England. I was a Greek warrior at the battle of Themopolis in 512 BC and was Napoleon's nanny. Oh yes, in previous lives I have been both men and women at various times and lived on other planets too," continued "Reincarnation Ed." After a brilliant, glowing sundown attributed to energy generated by the psychics, everyone gathered around a huge bonfire. The Rev. Robert Short, 50, head of the Blue Rose Ministry, stood before the fire wearing a dazzling shirt covered with blue roses. A blue rose pendant dangled from his neck. His lapel held, you guessed it, a blue rose.

Rev. Short told fair-goers he often hears from his mentor, the president of the planet Saturn. "He's coming through now," excitedly declared the Blue Rose minister. As the crowd gathered around the fire, Rev. Short stood on a platform and began shouting one word at a time. Between each word he would shout "AND" and then "UMM."

"The president of the planet Saturn is speaking through my vocal chords!" shouted Rev. Short. "He's exhorting Earthlings to be prepared for a catastrophe. All the world will be experiencing a 15-degree tilt and California, Oregon and New York will crumble into the sea," the words blurted slowly between Rev. Short's "ANDs" and "UMMS."

Dr. George (Yin Yang) Yao, 50, told how the yin, the left, negative and female side of the body, has been becoming stronger than the yang, the right, positive and male side of every human body, "the reason for more homosexuals now than in the past," he observed. He sold a device he said would put the body into proper perspective. Gloria Perri, 50, gave readings with tarot cards. Can you really reveal a person's future by what the cards say, a skeptical reporter asked. "Honey, this thing is thousands of years old with people reading these cards since ancient times. The trouble is not enough people have been listening to what we clairvoyants have been saying," insisted Gloria.

Bill Cox talked about his latest communications from Agharta, the "hollow Earth" inside the Earth. "There are human beings like ourselves living inside the inner Earth. They have a powerful sun the size of a baseball that illuminates Agharta," he related. He said he has never been to Agharta "but I have been to one of the secret entrance shafts to the inner Earth, the one at the Gavea Stone in Brazil." Barbara Kossen read not only palms at the fair but feet as well. Swift Deer Ann Adaweihais (pronounced a-day-way-haas), an Indian medicine woman, told fortunes by "wrenching the secrets of tomorrow from crystals."

"I was lead to this remote quiet place on Earth by strange powerful forces," Bishop Winsor told the crowd. "This place is alive with vibrations. My home and headquarters was once a riotous saloon. I am transforming it into a psychic research center here on the Southern California desert, a center for psychics the world over to come to and tap the vast energies concentrated here."

CHAPTER SEVEN

Archer (Bus) Richardson, left, and his son, Arch,
in front of 1868 Stewart's Point Store.

SMALL BUT LIVELY

A STORE FROM ANOTHER CENTURY

I T'S THE 21ST CENTURY and the 19th century Stewarts Point General Merchandise store in a remote slice of Northern California is doing just fine, thank you.

"Yep, it's the same old place built in 1868 and in continuous operation ever since," said proprietor Arch Richardson, 52 in this turn of the century year. His great grandfather, Herbert Archer Richardson bought the store in 1881 and the Richardsons have been operating it ever since at Stewarts Point, a turn-back-the-clock hamlet perched on a bluff overlooking the rugged Sonoma County coast 110 miles northwest of San Francisco.

The weather-beaten frame store is a classic relic of the past, jammed floor-to-ceiling with thousands of items. "If we don't have it, we will get it for you," is the motto of Arch Richardson as it was with his father, grandfather and great grandfather who ran the store before him. Arch has been working in the store since he was 6 years old. He took over from his father, Archer R. (Bus) Richardson when he retired at the age of 67 in 1986.

Like his son, Bus started working in the store when he was 6. The old redwood shelves are piled high with canned goods, clothing, sports equipment, lanterns, nuts and bolts, tools and other hardware, cast-iron cookware, fresh vegetables and fruit, you name it. Hanging from the ceiling are rubber boots and other modern items for sale and a sampling of Richardson family heirlooms, like the 1888 Studebaker baby buggy, a 170-year-old wheelbarrow, and 19th century fish traps, horse collars and oxen yoke.

Top shelves are cluttered with dust-covered high-button shoes, home remedies, old wagon lanterns, buggy whips, candle molds and numerous other items of the past still in the store's inventory, but no longer for sale. Hornet and yellow jacket nests, stuffed fish and colorful abalone shells hang from the ceiling. The floors squeak with age. Shopping carts purchased in 1948 are still used by customers, many of whom have charge accounts and pay their bills monthly. Patrons of the old-fashioned general store are 500 ranchers and rural resident within a 30-mile radius, and people just passing through.

Stewarts Point is a collection of marvelous old barns, lichen and moss covered houses, an old hotel, saloon, schoolhouse, no longer used for their original purposes, and the general store. Many of the buildings date back to the early 1850s.

It's a one-family town—the Richardsons of Stewarts Point, descendants of Herbert Archer Richardson who arrived here from Franconia, New Hampshire, in 1876 with a new bride and 40 cents in his pocket. Herbert Archer quickly became a timber baron, and as the years passed he bought 25,000 acres, including eight-miles of shoreline. He ran cattle and sheep and employed more than 300 lumberjacks cutting and processing redwood shipped out of Stewarts Point on his nine sailing vessels.

Lumber was hauled on the nine-mile Richardson Railroad to where the old store is located. Logs were carried the last half-mile to Richardson Harbor on rail cars mounted on wooden tracks. Brakemen gingerly guided the cars down a steep slope on a gravity run to the edge of the cliff. From the cliff, the logs were loaded onto a chute and carried to the decks of lumber ships tied up at the Richardson Wharf. Oxen pulled the empty rail cars back up the steep slope. In 1926, when Highway 1 was finally pushed through to Stewarts Point, the lumber ships were replaced by trucks. Lumbering actively slowed considerably during the Great Depression.

Herbert Archer Richardson also ran the 19th-century Stewarts Point Hotel and Saloon. "Grandfather was a stubborn New Englander by nature," said Bus Richardson. "When the Volstead Act went into effect in 1920 and Prohibition became the law of the land, he said if he couldn't sell liquor it meant he wasn't going to make any money. That's when he closed the hotel and saloon. The building has been standing vacant ever since." The family patriarch died at the age of 91 in 1942. Members of the Richardson clan still run sheep, cattle and a small timber operation on the 25,000 acres now owned by the descendants of the original timber baron. Bus Richardson, his father and his grandfather were postmasters at Stewarts Point from 1876 to 1984.

The second story of the store was a dance hall for nearly a century. "We had to knock off dancing because every time dancers would whirl around and do a John Paul Jones (change partners) the whole building rocked back and forth," Bus Richardson told me during my first visit to the store in 1976. "Almost shook her down, so we had to call the dancing quits," he explained. The second floor is now used for storage. The Richardsons, like Stewarts Point, are throwbacks to yesteryear. Their life-styles have changed little since the days of their grandparents. All are hard working, unpretentious, living in 150-year-old homes filled with century-old furniture. "We love the simple life," insisted Julia Richardson. "We could have sold our land to the developers and become very wealthy. But we never had the heart to. To do that would destroy Stewarts Point. We could have built modern new homes, but we treasure these old places. In essence we are sentimentalists." And, to this day, the heart and soul of the community is still the 1868 Stewarts Point General Merchandise Store.

SMALLEST FREE REPUBLIC IN WORLD

THE SIGN AT THE DIRT ROAD leading into the forest proclaims: "Smallest Free Republic in the World. The Republic of North California. Population 2." The road winds through the woods and dead-ends where a footbridge crosses a stream. On the other side

CHARLES HILLINGER

of the stream is an archway. At the archway is the "republic's" flag—a white star on a blue field, four red stripes, three white stripes, a pine tree, a bear, a buffalo. The archway bears the inscription: "REPUBLIC OF NORTH CALIFORNIA. SELF-DEFENSE FOR SELF-SURVIVAL. RENEW EVERY HOPE! YE WHO ENTER HERE."

Valentino D. Baima, 77, self-proclaimed president of the 10-acre, 25-year-old republic welcomed us at the archway. He was wearing his pith helmet as usual. "Come along," he said. "Governor Lilly Belle has been expecting you." Governor Lilly Belle is Lilly Belle Baima, 83, a retired schoolteacher and the president's wife of 38 years.

"Welcome to the Republic of North California, our magnificent obsession," said the governor. A flag of the republic hangs from the dining room wall above a photograph of Thomas Jefferson and a banner that reads, "Let this republic stand." On another wall hangs the Great Seal of the Republic, showing a mountain range, a lake, a forest, two deer, a house, a stream and the figure of a man tilling crops and wearing a pith helmet. The seal bears the words, "Peaceful, cooperative, co-existence for survival."

The president and the governor declared their 10 acres a republic after several years of disputes with a local irrigation district over water rights on their property. "There was no justice in the courts for us. We became disillusioned with the United States, the state of California and Nevada County for not affording us the protection to which we were entitled under the law," Baima said. "So Lilly Belle and I declared our land an independent republic with our own set of rules and regulations."

They stopped voting in local, state and national elections. "But we never quit paying taxes. People would resent us if we didn't pay taxes. Isn't that right, Sweetie?" said the president to the governor. "I am a pacifist. I spent 3½ years in conscientious objectors camps during World War II," the president continued. "Governor Lilly Belle was my pen pal when I was in the camps. When I was released in 1945 we were married, moved up here on the outskirts of Nevada City and bought this property." Few are aware of the republic's existence. The Baimas' "magnificent obsession" is on a seldom-traveled country road in the foothills of the High Sierra 50 miles northeast of Sacramento.

Baima is an artist and sculptor. He and his wife support themselves mainly from selling vegetables and fruit they grow on their property to local hospitals and restaurants. "You know, we take this republic business seriously," chimed in the governor. "We have lived it 25 years. We follow the precepts of Tom Jefferson to a T." Correspondence is conducted on Republic of North California stationery that carries the Baimas names and titles. Their cars bear both California and Republic of North California license plates.

The "republic" consists of four acres of farmland, a lake, a road, a grove of madrona trees and lush gardens tended by Baima and his wife. A flume that carries the stream over part of the land was built by Chinese in the 1850s. When the Baimas first moved here there were no telephones, no electricity and no indoor plumbing in the area. But now everything is up to date in North California. Baima mentioned a letter he received some years ago from a commune in Maine, explaining the commune established a kingdom in the state of Maine and elected a queen as its ruler. The kingdom wanted to establish diplomatic and trade relations with the Republic of North California.

THE PEOPLE OF PEANUT

THE PEOPLE OF PEANUT sighed with relief when word was received that a quicksilver mill proposed for the hamlet was to be located elsewhere. "It's not that we Peanuters are against progress," said Mrs. Ralph Patton as she and her husband sat on their patio eating peanuts (what else!). "We just like being out of it. We favor the quiet life."

There's only one Peanut in the nation. It's in sparsely populated, mountainous Trinity County in the northwest corner of California midpoint on State Highway 36 between Eureka and Red Bluff. In 1968 when I visited Peanut to do this story Highway 36—150 miles of winding mountain road nearly all one lane—was perhaps the narrowest highway in America. A few miles on Highway 36 and most people turn back. It was that bad. That's why Peanut had few visitors. The town was settled shortly after the Civil War by a caravan of pioneers in covered wagons from Missouri. Gold mining in the Trinity Mountains raised Peanut's population to 200 by the turn of the 20th Century. "It was then that my dad and a committee of men met to give this place a name," said Ralph Patton, then 60, a rancher and lifelong Peanuter.

"They started at 6 o'clock in the evening with the postal directory at hand to make sure they didn't choose a name already in use. It wasn't easy. Everytime someone came up with a suggestion, a post office with that name was found in the directory. By 4 the next morning they finally got to the nuts. Pecan, Chestnut, Walnut—hell, even all the nuts were taken. Except peanut. To this day our town, as far as we know, has been the first and only Peanut in the United States."

The town had its own post office for half a century. But it burned to the ground, so now Peanuters call for their mail at Hayfork. 10 miles to the north. "Peanut's been running out of steam lately," said Patton, who, like the dozen Peanut families in this rugged mountain wilderness, talks like a Vermonter—slow and deliberate.

"The Peanut school closed. The old Peanut sawmill burned. The Peanut general store went broke. The Peanut Bar tossed in the towel. The Peanut bridge over Peanut Creek is gone. It washed out in the December 1964, flood. Even our Peanut city limits sign is gone. Somebody swiped it from the big oak it was nailed to," sighed Patton's wife. "There once was a Peanut Dairy known for miles around for its Peanut butter and during Prohibition days Peanuters were reputed to have the best stills in Trinity County."

Peanut has seen better days, but Peanuters like it the way it is even if the Peanut Women's Club along with nearly everything else has moved to Hayfork, a town of nearly 1,000 people on the other side of the mountain.

CHAPTER EIGHT

Turnoff to Zzyzx from Interstate 15, the Los Angeles to Las Vegas freeway.

A ZEST FOR Z'S

ZZYZX AND THE "OLD-TIME MEDICINE MAN"

THE 71-YEAR-OLD, pudgy, blue-eyed, ruddy-faced, thin-haired promoter called himself the "last of the old-time medicine men." To radio listeners in 50 states and scores of countries Dr. Curtis Howe Springer was a friendly philosopher who played religious records, quoted from the Bible and peddled miraculous cures for everything from sore toes to cancer on daily half hour programs broadcast from his resort in Zzyzx, California.

Zzyzx—pronounced zeye-zix—is one of the most out-of-the-way places in the state. It's at the end of a five-mile dirt road on the shores of Soda Dry Lake in the heart of the Mojave Desert, 200 miles east of Los Angeles. Millions have passed the Zzyzx turnoff sign on Interstate 15, the busy Los Angeles to Las Vegas freeway—but few passing by had

CHARLES HILLINGER

any idea of the unique community carved out on sand by Dr. Springer. The Zzyzx vista is the same for miles—heat rays spiraling from Soda Dry Lake, huge sand dunes and barren desert mountains. At Zzyzx was a 60-room hotel, a lake, a castle, church, radio station and several structures. Average temperatures in summer at Zzyzx are 110 during the day. Those living in Zzyzx were mostly old people, cripples and shut-ins from all over the United States and Canada. They heard about Zzyzx from Dr. Springer's radio broadcasts. For those who came here there were mineral baths in the shape of a cross, swimming in Lake Tuendae, shuffleboard, daily church services and travelogues at night.

"We offer fundamental Christian services in Dr. Springer's church," explained Ed Burns, lay evangelist and chaplain at Zzyzx. "It's all based on the living grace of Christ. We're not a cult. Just a Lord-fearing community." Dr. Springer and his wife, Helen, occupied a suite of rooms in the rambling two-story Zzyzx Hotel. When asked if the doctor title in front of his name signified a Ph.D. or MD, Dr. Springer told this writer, "Just between us, man-to-man, I'm self educated. I call myself doctor because of my many honorary degrees, also because I am a minister of God. I've had churches all my life. I have this one here at Zzyzx. No, I can't truthfully say I am an ordained Methodist minister. A licensed Methodist minister would be a better way of putting it. Actually, I'm basically a salesman. I use the Gospel, mix in my brand of philosophy, sell a line of natural foods and promote the hotel in my radio broadcasts."

Dr. Springer said he had the longest continual program on radio. "It began in 1924 over KDKA in Pittsburgh, the world's pioneer radio station. I sang a solo the first day of commercial broadcasting anywhere on earth. I've been on the air ever since." For 30 years in his studio at Zzyzx, Dr. Springer cut tapes used to broadcast his daily programs over 221 stations in the U.S. and 102 stations in foreign countries. He claimed his listeners numbered in excess of 14 million. "My voice," he continued with obvious pride, "is on the air every minute of the day, every day of the year somewhere."

He said he operated health resorts in six states before coming to California to retire in 1944. "I happened to pick up a book on mineral springs in Los Angeles and read a chapter on Old Fort Soda Springs on the Mojave Desert near Baker. My wife and I went out there, found the springs, set up camp and I filed claims on the land. I filed for 12,000 acres, a parcel 8 miles long and 3 miles wide. I am buying it from the government. I have money in the bank to pay for all of it," he insisted.

He said the government hadn't seen fit to sell the land to him "at least not yet. But everything is going to come out all right. I am on the best of terms with the government. I have taken all proper legal steps."

On checking with the Bureau of Land Management office in Riverside, however, the area manager said one of its biggest files was dedicated to Curtis Howe Springer, described as a "super squatter" who laid out a town on federal land to which he had no claim. "Dr. Springer made a placer mining claim to hunt for gold on the property when he first went out there. We have always held the claim is not valid, because Dr. Springer by his own admission never worked the claim," noted Roy Davidson, the BLM area manager who had spent years working on the Zzyzx matter. "He should have been evicted years ago," said Davidson. "Springer has never been given any authority to be on the land, to live on the land, to operate a business on the land. The BLM repeatedly through the years has turned down his applications to purchase or lease land at Zzyzx," reported John Peavy, BLM's chief of resource management in Southern California.

But despite all the attempts over the years to evict him from the federal land since he arrived at Zzyzx in 1944, nothing had happened by the time I did a feature story on Zzyzx and Curtis Howe Springer that appeared in the July 14, 1967 *Los Angeles Times*.

Dr. Springer said all he found when he first moved to the desert in 1944 were remains of Fort Soda built by the Spanish in 1787. "There were crumbling walls of the old fort, a blacksmith shop and jail. I erected my hotel around the historic monument." He said the day he came to the old fort he gave the site a unique name. "I called it Zzyzx, coining the last word in the English language. Many think it's an old Indian word. But it's a word I invented, copyrighted and patented." He began to develop the community immediately. "I planted 7,000 shade trees, 2,000 palm trees and 4,000 flowering bushes. The lost Mojave River surfaces at Zzyzx. I tapped the river and built Lake Tuendae from the 2 million gallons of sparkling mineral water that flows out of the ground every hour."

Zyport was his private airstrip. Boulevard of Dreams was the divided parkway leading to his oasis on Lake Tuendae, which contained a tiny endangered fish called the Mojave chub. Dr. Springer claimed over 1 million guests had stayed in his 60-room hotel, that he had sold his 36 different food supplements to millions of people throughout the world, one of his products alone to more than 18 million radio listeners. He referred to Dr. Curtis Howe Springer Foundation in his literature as a tax exempt, nonprofit corporation.

"The foundation has helped support hundreds from Skid Row who have come to Zzyzx through the years," Dr. Springer related. "I have proved to the government that I am helping humanity—that is why my foundation is tax exempt." The Internal Revenue Service reported that although Dr. Springer filed each year for a nonprofit, tax-exempt status with the federal government, it never had been granted. The State Board of Equalization, San Bernardino County Assessor's Office and the State Franchise Tax Board, however, did grant a tax exemption. "We know he has brought men out there from Skid Row and rehabilitated them. That is why we granted Dr. Springer a property tax exemption. We consider his foundation in the same category as a church," said Robert Herbin of the San Bernardino County Assessor's Office. At one point the BLM finally was given permission by Dr. Springer to audit the Zzyzx Hotel business records.

"He claimed to keep no books, to have no bank account, that all money was cash, handled out of pocket. His hotel records for the year we did the audit was a suitcase filled with slips of paper indicating names of persons staying at the hotel and what they purportedly paid," noted Roy Davidson.

Dr. Springer motored to Los Angeles every week, staying in his suite at the Alexandria Hotel from Monday through Wednesday. "I take care of my business in the city—order ingredients for my food products, ship out radio tapes and take telephone calls from throughout the world," he explained. There were no telephones at Zzyzx. Dr. Springer said he received calls from people from all walks of life, from all continents. "Just recently, for example, I had a call from Bombay, India. The party at the other end identified himself as Sir Charles Maltby. He told me: 'Dr. Springer, I picked you up on my transistor while up in the Himalayas looking for the abominable snowman. You came through loud and clear. I like the sound of your place out there at Zzyzx. Do you have room for me?'" Dr. Springer said he did, indeed, have room. He said Sir Charles arrived four days later and spent a week at Zzyzx, thoroughly delighted with the resort.

In his booklet, "Eat Your Way To Health," Dr. Springer noted that "here at Zzyzx you find thousands of acres devoted to teaching folks how to get a greater joy out of life. The Dr. Curtis H. Springer Foundation is a nonprofit, charitable and tax-exempt institution operating Zzyzx Mineral Springs for the benefit of all who are seeking health or a restful vacation. You will be interested to know that each year any profits resulting from the sale of products are turned over to the Dr. Curtis H. Springer Foundation to further our work in offering a helping hand to others. Send as a contribution the amount God has made possible because we want to help."

Dr. Springer urged his radio listeners to send donations for miraculous cures for everything from minor ailments to maladies as serious as cancer. He claimed he could restore hair and rejuvenate body cells. His magic potions—concoctions of celery, turnip, carrot and parsley juice—were shipped to all 50 states and overseas. And the money rolled in. Many residents of the Zzyzx Hotel were older men and women who contributed their life savings for the privilege of staying in spartan quarters until they die. Dr. Springer did not want his picture taken for the newspaper story. He said it would hurt his business, that millions of his listeners think of him as a virile, athletic man, that they would be shocked to see Dr. Springer as he truly is, a thin-haired man in his 70s. He finally consented and was photographed.

One of his products was a hair restorer, made of "secret French ingredients." In his radio broadcasts he told how he "once had a bald spot, then used the product and now had a head of hair like an 18-year-old." Each day he broadcast testimonials from across the nation, often from film actors and actresses "who must remain anonymous because of the prominence of their names in pictures—you understand." His appeal was always for a particular price on each product or a "contribution as God makes possible for you to send."

Why had the government permitted Dr. Springer to be in trespass all those years? "During much of the time Dr. Springer was at Zzyzx, the BLM administered one third of all public domain in California with a five man staff," replied Peavy. "It was virtually impossible to keep up with the paper work, let alone crack down on squatters. The BLM issued trespass papers on Dr. Springer for years, but unlike many federal agencies, it had no direct police power. Hopefully your story will get the Justice Department to take action," said Peavy.

My front-page Los Angeles Times story about the super squatter brought public attention to Springer's illegal activity. Federal marshals finally arrested Curtis Howe Springer for alleged violations of food and drug laws and unauthorized use of federal land. Zzyzx and all the improvements erected by Springer were confiscated by the Bureau of Land Management. The old "medicine man" was found guilty and spent

CHARLES HILLINGER

several months in jail. He died in Las Vegas in 1986 at the age of 90.

Since 1976 Zzyzx has functioned as the California State University system's Desert Studies Center, a teaching and research station. The university system has free use of the land and facilities under a 25-year cooperative management agreement with the BLM. Scientists from the system's 20 campuses and other educational institutions come to the center to do research. NASA and Jet Propulsion Laboratory scientists, for example, conduct satellite imagery studies at Zzyzx. Cal State Los Angeles professor emeritus Donald Lowrie was doing research on desert spiders when I was in Zzyzx recently. Geologists from Cal State Fresno and Cal State Bakersfield make it their base while researching Mojave Desert earthquake faults. The research and teaching center can house as many as 80 persons at once. University classes make field trips here. Every weekend from October through May, special desert-related extension courses convene at Zzyzx, administered by Cal State San Bernardino, the closest of the state campuses. Each session is devoted to a particular topic. Claude Warren, chairman of the anthropology department for the University of Nevada, Las Vegas, and his anthropologist wife, Elizabeth, for example, have conducted courses about historical camp sites along the Old Spanish Trail. Upward of 3,000 scientists, researchers, students and members of the public use the Desert Studies Center each year.

"You can thank me for one of the premier desert research centers on Earth," allowed Curtis Howe Springer matter of factly a few years before his death. That observation by the "last of the old medicine men" was right on the mark, as Zzyzx did indeed emerge from its shady, colorful past to become a significant scientific desert research station.

ZEST FOR Z'S

ZACHARY ZZZZRA is no longer unhappy. Vladimir Zzzzzzabakov canceled his telephone. It's part of the continuing zany Z battle in San Francisco for the last listing in the local phone book. For years Zzzzra had been listed in Guinness Book of World Records "for the most determined attempt to be the last personal name in a local telephone directory."

"It really upset me when the phone book came out last year with this name Vladimir Zzzzzzabakov below my name," said Zzzzra. "I phoned this guy Vladimir and asked him how come he put so many Zs in his name. I demanded he tell me his real name." Zzzzra said Zzzzzzabakov responded, "That's none of your damn business" and promptly hung up. Zzzzra didn't know Zzzzzzabakov had canceled his phone until the new San Francisco directory was published last week.

"Had I known, I would not have changed my name—if only for the listing in the new phone book—to Zachary Zzzzzzzzzzra," explained Zzzzra.

Zzzzra added six more Z's to his name to outsmart Zzzzzzabakov. "Zzzzra is my real name. It's no nom de plume," insists Zzzzra, who says it is pronounced Z-z-rah.

"My name is colloquial Dutch, meaning smooth sailing down the Zider Zee. There are quite a few in Holland with that name. It was my father's name, my grandfather's and many grandfathers' way back." Zzzzra, 60, a painting contractor, admitted, however, that he added an extra "z" to his name when Zelda Zzywramp aced him out many years ago in the San Francisco directory. "I never met Zelda, but we talked to one another over the telephone several times," said Zzzzra.

Zzzzra first made Guinness when he out-zeed Zeke Zzypt (zipped) of Chicago, who had pushed aside Zero Zzyzz (rhymes with fizz) of New York, who replaced Vladimir Zzyd (zid) of Miami.

Poco Myers, a secretary for a San Francisco publishing firm, got caught up in the zany Z-business when she had a new phone installed recently and got Zzzzzzabakov's old number. "My phone began ringing off the hook the first day I got it," said Poco Myers. "People call me all hours of the day and night, many simply saying, 'How do you pronounce your name? Zzzzzzzzzzz?' Then they hang up."

She said she would ask the phone company for a new number, but she has already mailed the "Z" phone number to relatives and friends all over the country. "It would be just as much of a hassle to get another new phone number and mail out a whole batch of new announcements as it is to listen to the Zzzzzz calls," she figures.

And anyway, Poco Myers expects most of the Zzzzzzabakov calls will stop coming now that the new phone book is out. As for Zzzzra (or is it Zzzzzzzzzzra?), his pride added six more Z's to his name, at least until the next new phone book is published.

CHARLES HILLINGER

CHAPTER NINE

One of the people-powered "works of art" in the Frenetic
Kinetic Crazy ContraptionCross-Country Sculpture Race.

A CRAZY SCULPTURE RACE
& PROPHET OF SOAP

PEOPLE-POWERED SCULPTURES

THE ANNUAL Frenetic Kinetic Crazy Contraption Cross-Country Sculpture Race culminated in a frantic, frenzied finish on the main street of Ferndale, a 19th-Century Victorian, Northern California village. One of the official timekeepers, Gayle Loomis, 29, a school teacher by trade, forgot to bring her watch. It was expected. It was that kind of a race.

Forty-one marvelous machines, animated sculptures ingeniously fashioned from pipes, plywood, polyethylene, bicycles, garbage cans, oil drums, crab traps, baby playpens, fiberglass septic tanks and miscellaneous junk, competed in a wild, woolly, wacky three-day thriller.

People-powered sculptures rolled, wobbled, spun and crept along a perilous 34-mile course over land, sand, sloughs, mudflats, river and sea.

It's one of the nuttiest races in the nation. Thirty-four of the contraptions finished the race. Three sank crossing Humboldt Bay, however, all the racers were rescued from the chilly sea. Winners in 6 hours and 39 minutes aboard the sculpture entitled The Flying Galumpkie Brothers were John and Eugene Hrynkiewicz of Covina. Finishing last were Aly and Michael Krause and Peter Folks driving The Double Egret II in 48 hours and 52 minutes.

The Frenetic Kinetic Sculpture race began on a Friday with the sounding of the noon whistle on the square in the town of Arcata, 30 miles north of Ferndale. Intrepid racers and crazy contraption pit crews were assembled around the President William McKinley statue in the center of the square on their marks for the start. When the noon whistle sounded, bands played, dogs barked, people cheered, jugglers juggled. April Hayes ("People think my name sounds like a weather report"), the race's Rutabaga Queen, who was dressed in a gay 90s costume, danced an Irish jig.

No one is sure why the race queen is called the Rutabaga Queen. Rutabagas are not grown anywhere near Ferndale. The Rutabaga Queen confessed she had never seen a rutabaga. "It's something you put in soup, isn't it?" the queen coyly inquired.

The Arcata town square was jammed with hundreds of spectators. Balloons filled the air. And the racers dashed madly to their contraptions when the whistle went off.

KRUNCHHHHHHHHHHHHHH!!!!!!!!!!!! The marvelous machines smashed together on the opening downhill run. What else could be expected? To avoid being run down, Sue Williams, race chairperson, hurled herself across the hood of an official car, her top hat flying off in the brisk wind. "I'm all right," shouted Sue to the stunned crowd. The race chairperson who lives in the valley of the Giant Redwood Stumps, was mildly struck in the left leg by the Thunderbolt Grease Slapper, but luckily she escaped with minor bruises. The race doctor sent for a strawberry daiquiri to soothe the ruffled official.

There was a deafening crescendo of aoogaas from the Frenetic Kinetic Sculptures as the racers untangled themselves. Racers pedaled their contraptions down country roads, across the Mad River, through Manila and Samoa, two small towns, and onto a five-mile stretch of sand dunes.

The rolling sand dunes were the scene of a mighty struggle. It was impossible to propel the statues by pedaling. Racers spent hours dragging, pushing and pulling their mobile works of art through the sand. For larger entries like Hobart Brown's Bigger Better Ball Bearing Banana, 20-foot-long yellow contraption pedaled by Brown and four others decked out in top hats and tuxedos and with an all-female pit crew dressed in white togas, it was no easy matter. Bogged down was the norm, not the exception, in the sand dunes where signs warned: "Beware of Dune Goons!"

It was Hobart Brown and Jack Mays, metal sculptors in Ferndale, an art colony with a population of 1,400, who came up with the idea for the race.

All but three entries managed to make it through the first day, even to descend a 97-foot, steep sand dune cliff known as Dead Man's Drop. This was accomplished by holding fast to ropes and easing the contraptions down the steep precipice. Some of the kinetic statues weighed nearly a ton and a half.

Saturday's leg of the race started in Eureka at daybreak. At Fields Landing, racers quickly regeared their rigs. It was wheels up, pontoons down with chains removed from bicycle wheels and connected to propellers and water paddles. Three Whitworth two-pound Civil War cannons were fired, the Marching Male Chauvinist Pig Band struck up "Beer Barrel Polka" and the crazy contraptions entered the water one at a time down a boat ramp. Most floated. Some sank.

Those crossing the bay included the Yellow Submarine, a cleverly sculpted 750-gallon fiberglass septic tank; the Last Rite, a pedaled, sailing 15-foot coffin with rubber corpse; the Baby Machine, a baby pen built around two bicycles with pink and white gingham bumper pads and operated by Kris Douglas and Sandi Case decked out in baby clothes, booties and bonnets. The Baby Machine was one of three all-female sculptures.

Racers, pit crews and others had an enormous chili feast prepared by Abra (Mother Jugs) Vargas around a giant campfire Saturday night on Crab Island where everyone slept in sleeping bags. Sunday the race course followed a sand spit, spanned the Eel River, and crossed Cock Robin and Cannibal Islands. From there, the brave racers and their marvelous machines plodded through two feet of muck in icky mudflats before finally finishing, worn, weary, mud-splattered but saturated with deep feelings of achievement.

Winners received such appropriate prizes as five gallons of chocolate frosting, a tap dance course, a used tuxedo and a case of toilet paper. "It's not the prizes, it's not where you come in, finishing is what's important," vowed Bob Iorg, 35-year-old creator of the Fuzz Buster, echoing the sentiments of all.

Hobart Brown summed up what the Frenetic Kinetic Crazy Contraption Cross-Country Sculpture Race is all about when he declared: "It's a chance for an artist or anyone to sense a total experience with his own creation. It resolves a need for the release of human tensions and emotions without hurting anyone."

PEACE PLAN ON SOAP LABEL

HE'S A SELF-PROCLAIMED RABBI, self-proclaimed doctor and a successful soap maker. "Dr. E.H. Bronner, Soap Maker, Master Chemist, Rabbi, SMMC, DD. Working to help all mankind free in All-One-God-Faith, Inc.," proclaims the huge sign outside Emil Bronner's 3-acre soap factory in Escondido. The sign continues: "All-One. We live to love, teach, unite friend and enemy in All-One-God-State. Eternally-One. All-One! All-One! All-One!" Bronner's "magic" soap is sold in health food stores throughout the United States, Canada, England and Australia. Bronner was a wiry 69-year-old when we met him. He dismissed his blindness as "no handicap."

He was in his aerie, a three-story tower on the roof of his hilltop house above his soap factory. "The soap is important," Bronner said, "but the label is the key. The 1,700-word label on my quart-size bottle of liquid soap is my peace plan. For years I tried to get my message to the people, but the newspapers refused to print my stuff. So, I began bottling my soap in 1967 and putting my peace plan on the label." The wrappers on the soap containers spell out the soap maker's philosophy. It has got to be one of the oddest labels on any product sold in America. "Dad changes the label every month, sometimes oftener. He is constantly changing the wording on the bottle," explained Jim Bronner, 37, a retired Navy chief machinist mate and fourth-generation soap-making son. "Dad has a singleness of purpose to bring people to understand his philosophy. He uses the soap as a vehicle for his philosophy."

"1st perfect thyself! 2nd work hard! 3rd win victory, teach All-One and overnight we're all free. All-One! All-One! All-One!" is one line on the label. Words of Thomas Paine, Jesus, Hillel, the rabbi and teacher who lived at the time of Christ, and many others are part of Bronner's rambling peace plan. Does anyone read the small type on the soap bottles? "Yes they do," insisted the soap maker. "My home phone number is on every label. They call all hours of the day and night. They call from everywhere the soap goes, Australia, England, New York, Florida, Canada. Half the calls are collect. I accept them. The callers are people who need help. They call about the peace plan. They call about the soap."

Bronner has at least two phones in every room of his large home. He even has two phones in his rooftop perch where he goes to think, to dictate his philosophy and to sunbathe in the nude. "Guaranteed since 1848!" says the label on the quart bottles of soap. Bronner explained that his grandfather was the first soap maker in the family, that it is a tradition handed down from grandfather to father to son and now grandson.

The original family name was Heilbronner. They were one of the biggest soap manufacturers in Germany until Hitler's rise to power. "I got out early and came to the United States," Bronner recalled. "Because of Hitler, I changed my name from Heilbronner to simply Bronner. You know, the Heil Hitler stuff."

Bronner worked as a chemist with major U.S. soap companies for years. He has several soap patents. "The first couple of years dad started bottling his own brand, he sold less than 2,000 gallons of his peppermint soap," said Jim Bronner. Suddenly, the soap caught on among the hippies of San Francisco's Haight-Ashbury district, and in communes across the country. "Sales skyrocketed because of the product, because of my unusual label," Bronner related. "The hippies liked the peppermint smell of the soap, the cooling effect of it on their body. They liked the 'No synthetics! None!' notation on the label.

"Most of the hippies were for socialism, for burning the place down. But they read my peace plan anyway. And they bought my soap." Now those who shop in health food outlets from coast to coast continue to buy the soap with the funny label.

And Emil Bronner continues to refine his peace plan. "I must keep changing my label to get it perfect," he explained. "Mark Twain said the difference between an almost-perfect word and a perfect word is the difference between a lightning bug and lightning.

"We sell more than 100,000 gallons of peppermint soap a year, all word-of-mouth, no advertising, no sales force," Bronner said. As the label says: "Absolute cleanliness is Godliness. Dr. Bronner's soap cleans body-mind-soul-spirit, uniting one, All-One!..."

CHAPTER TEN

Poet Cornel Lengyel in an inspired mood amidst his 80 woodland acres. (Photo by Don Cormier)

A COUPLE OF POETS

EVERY POET SHOULD HAVE A FEW ACRES

"I hold no mortgage on the great world's goods, no deeds or bonds or due collateral. I'll need no lawyer to prepare my will: my earthly baggage is ephemeral."—CORNEL LENGYEL

"I ESCAPED A QUARTER OF A CENTURY AGO, a refugee from the city," said Cornel Lengyel (Len-jell), pensive, lean; a pipe smoker wearing a woolen scarf. "Every poet should have a few acres. Keeps you in touch with the elementary things. Everybody should have a half acre of worms, if nothing else."

Lengyel's 80 acres are deep in the woods of El Dorado National Forest near the Mother Lode hamlet of Georgetown. He lived a solitary life with his wife, Teresa, and an assortment of dogs. The couple's four children were all grown and gone. Lengyel's poetry has been published since he was a teen-ager. He is said to have "mastered classical forms to an extraordinary degree."

George Santayana on reading a book of verse by the poet in the woods wrote Lengyel from Rome: "You have invented a new form of verse, the blank-verse sonnet; and from the beginning you have made it a natural and powerful instrument."

Lengyel won the Alice Fay di Castagnola Award ($3,500) for his "Latter Day Psalms" given by the Poetry Society of America. Among other honors are the Maxwell Anderson Award for poetic drama for his play, "Atom Clock" and the Huntington Hartford Fellowship in Literature. He has written other plays and historical books as well. "Four Days in July," an acclaimed hour-by-hour recreation of the men and events behind the Declaration of Independence, has been reprinted in 14 languages. "Presidents of the U.S.A." sold more than 200,000 copies. "I Benedict Arnold: Anatomy of Treason" and "Ethan Allen and the Green Mountain Boys," have done well. But Cornel Lengyel's first love is poetry.

> *In green and candid youth I told the truth, I told my truth:*
> *They closed their ears, they shut their eyes,*
> *   they turned from me in sad surprise.*
> *In lean and cautious age I told them lies, I told but lies:*
> *They heard me out, they learned my name,*
> *They pressed me in a book of fame.*
>
> —from FOUR DOZEN SONGS

Moments after the visit began in the poet's rustic old farmhouse embraced by a forest of pine, black oak and mesquite, Lengyel leaped from his chair and went directly to his "terribly poor piano purchased from a secondhand store. I like to play a little Bach. I seldom have a captive audience. It puts me in harmony with the universe," he said, playing two favorites, "Chaconne" and "Chromatic Fantasy." "The man behind this music still speaks to you after all these years," he mused. Then came the long walk through the woods, hiking a few of the many miles of trails Lengyel and his family created over the years, pausing briefly at his favorite places. "This was solid jungle when we first came," said Lengyel. "We cleared tons and tons of thick chaparral. It's still solid jungle. I built four cabins back in here, to get away from my family. It sometimes takes a certain amount of concentration...one has to escape from little noises. Even a good plumber has to have it quiet." On his walks in the woods he carries a notebook. "Poets are persona non grata in America," he sighed sadly, stopping to tap his pipe against his hiking boot. "Gresham's law applies. The most improbably, impractical thing I can think of is being a poet. Yet I am still writing poetry. It's like an adolescent vice. It persists through life."

He stopped to rest on an old backless couch with stuffing spewing out that he had hauled into the woods a long time ago. "All you do is sit here long enough to hatch a whole nest of field mice," he laughed. "But sometimes you get an idea among the trees. A refreshing walk in the woods gives you ideas you don't get in city streets."

> *These have been given you: Low clouds, gray pines,*
> *autumn-colored hills, changing lights of a rainy day,*
> *smell of wet leaves in the silent woods;*
> *a gray-green boulder, a gnarled black oak*
> *half-hidden by flowering manzanita;*
> *moonlit puddles of water to hold a thousand stars;*
> *and dawn hours fresh with the scent of vanishing gods.*
> *These have been given you, undeserved yet given,*
> *given with love, by love that, mute and mortal, walked by your side*
> *awhile in the woods, familiar as the mist*
> *yet ever a smiling stranger:*
> *Love that remains a stranger, unseen, unheard,*
> *yet speaks at times of old immortal things.*
> —"Gifts From the Forest" from, A DOZEN POSTSCRIPTS

Hands in his pockets, notebook under his left arm, dead leaves crunching under his footsteps, Lengyel talked of poetry: "The poet tries to translate the buzzing confusion that surrounds him from birth to death. He strives to interpret his particular pains and pleasures, to appease his private fears, and hungers, to give form and meaning to the more permanent and perplexing facts of life.

"The acorn that sprouts today," said Lengyel, walking through a grove of rust red madrones, "will outlive the strongest man, may outlast the laurels of most living artists. At the same time the tallest oak can be ground into sawdust in less than an hour, while the odes of Horace have remained green to perceptive eyes for 20 centuries." He thought about the first poet: "Adam, perhaps, who according to the report in *Genesis*, gave names to the birds and beasts in the Garden. The second poet, we surmise, was the Serpent, an avant-gardist who complained to Adam's wife: 'So, he's given names to everything! How dull and conventional! Why not try something new? Why not taste the fruit of the Forbidden Trees?'" The trail led past his wife Teresa's garden.

> *Consider how the violets you smell this spring*
> *in your forest-bound garden of rocks*
> *convey the same surprising scent that Sappho*
> *sniffed some twenty centuries ago.*
> *While empires crumble and epics fade,*
> *the scent of the violet drawn from the indifferent dust,*
> *proclaims the same enduring news:*
> *the mute and fragrant gospel of the grass.*
>
> —from *A DOZEN POSTSCRIPTS*

"If you're a stick in the mud, then the mud around you has some significance," said Lengyel, who said of the walk that it was "keeping in touch with the elementary things."

THE GRAVY POET

SHE IS KNOWN AS THE GRAVY POET because her poetry is about everyday people and everyday things in Tulare, a small Central California farm town. And she has even written an ode to gravy called "Gravy Tells a Lot":

> *You can put your trust in gravy*
> *the way it stretches out the sausage*
> *the way it stretches out the dreams*
> *from payday til tomorrow*
> *slipping exquisitely down the throats*
> *of toothless visionaries eating with a spoon...*

Wilma Elizabeth McDaniel, poet laureate of Tulare, has been writing poetry since she was a young child living in sharecropper houses in and around Stroud, Okla. Her parents were poor dirt farmers. She picked crops along with seven other children in the family. "They were hard times. We never had a decent roof over our heads," recalls Wilma McDaniel. "Every time it rained we moved the pots and pans around to catch the leaks."

The family moved to California in 1936 as part of the massive Dust Bowl migration. And Wilma kept writing and tucking away her poems in shoe boxes and dresser drawers so no one would see them. "I've always been shy. You might say I'm a recluse. I never expected to be published, to be public," she says. Since 1973, a dozen books of her poetry and short stories about life in rural San Joaquin Valley have been published in printings of 250 to 1,000 copies.

She writes her poems and stories longhand on lined notebook paper. "I can create these people I write about," she explains. "But they're just as real as they would be living next door." Her poetry and stories, she adds, are "about poor people who don't know such a thing as being poor. People who struggle to make it. Always have a dream. Hope things be better. If didn't get too much better in this world, be better in the next."

She writes about Bessie Barker who has been to 447 yard sales and, about that good old boy Obie Crenshaw who runs a small garage and wears his trousers very low and baggy. And about Zar-Eta in Thrifty Drug:

> wearing only two bath towels
> seamed up the sides
> one slit for her neck two for her arms
> dangling earrings that looked exactly like
> little red balls of gum from the Kiwanis dispenser
> she searches for cologne
> takes a bottle from a black and gold box
> tiger patterned and sprays herself
> all the way to the counter.

Wilma McDaniel writes about the public sale north of town, about the local cemetery, the dog catcher, the Tulare water tower and blue bib overalls. Her first published book, "The Carousel Would Haunt Me," begins with the title poem:

the carousel would haunt me
as its tunes turned in my brain
on little painted horses
round and round again...

She writes about things she knows about in poems like "The Fearless":

John Bow stayed in Ahwahnee Sanitarium
two full years, his lungs gone, the doctors said
and no one visited him except Yellow Eyes and one
colored man named Archie White
who weren't afraid of TB...

And:

the soap was harsh and left us clean
to crawl between the sheets
of innocence.

MECHANICS' INSTITUTE LIBRARY
57 Post Street
San Francisco, CA 94104
(415) 393-0101

CHAPTER ELEVEN

Medie Webster, age 87, the last speaker in the world of her tribal language.

LAST SPEAKER OF
ANCIENT LANGUAGE

TINY, FRAIL MEDIE WEBSTER, 87, of Montgomery Creek, was the last of her people speaking an age-old language. She was one of just 200 Atsugewi (at-su-gay-we) Indians, whose ancestors for centuries hunted and gathered food in what is now Lassen Volcanic National Park. And, she was the only Atsugewi still fluent in her tribal language. "Sometimes I think about the old days when I was a little girl and all of us Atsugewis spoke our own language. We took life for granted and thought we would always be here living as our people did from the beginning of time," sighed the old woman.

She told how her generation was "sent to the white man's school and forced to learn the white man's language and to forget the Indian ways. I only went as far as first grade. As I grew older I learned English but I kept speaking Atsugewi as well."

Gradually, all the other older members of the tribe who spoke the language, including Medie's husband of 60 years, Daniel, have died. Two years earlier when Ramsey Blake, in his late 80s, died, Medie was the only Atsugewi fluent in the tribal language left, although other tribe members know a few words.

She lived with her grandson, Warren Conrad Jr., 24, in a modest cottage built 50 years ago by her husband at the end of a mile-long dirt road on the outskirts of Montgomery Creek. Her home, 61 miles north-west of Lassen Park, was the only dwelling on the road. "She talks to me in Atsugewi all the time," said Conrad. "I have to interrupt her and say: 'Gram, I don't understand what you are saying. Please speak English.'"

Conrad said his grandmother "is like a person of another time. She tells me stories about the wagon days before cars, about old-time medicine men, about what it was like when she was a little girl, about the old ceremonial dances no longer performed. She sings to me in Atsugewi."

Meanwhile, other tribal members tried to keep their culture alive. For example, every summer for 16 years Medie Webster's niece, Lillian Snooks, 61, had presented a program about the Atsugewis twice a day, five days a week, at the natural amphitheater behind the information center at the Manzanita Lake entrance to Lassen Park.

She always mentioned the Atsugewi language. Snooks and her sister, Laverna Jenkins, 58, had been National Park Service rangers since 1972. "The Indian ways of the Atsugewis are dying fast. That is why I give the programs about my people, a little-known Indian tribe, to help perpetuate what is still known about them before all is lost," Snooks explained.

She said that Atsugewi means pine tree people, a name that comes from the forests where the Indians have always lived. The lakes and mountains in Lassen Park, she says, were the spiritual lakes and mountains of the Atsugewi. There were an estimated 2,000 Atsugewis when non-Indians first came to this area 150 years ago.

"We are losing our Indian ways so quickly. Another generation or two and the lasts traces of Atsugewi culture may vanish from the face of the Earth," said Snooks.

CHAPTER TWELVE

Portrait of Leopold Wrasse (by R. Reynolds), "hermit of the vineyard," who endowed scholarships for aggie students.

HERMITS

ODD DUCK

THE OLD MAN was laughed at and ridiculed on the rare occasions he came to town. It was his unorthodox manner, the way he dressed. He would wear dirty, ragged trousers, a pajama top instead of a shirt, a little visor with his hair sticking out in all directions.

Leopold Wrasse lived alone in a 20-acre vineyard he owned on the outskirts of Caruthers, a small town 15 miles southwest of Fresno. Everyone who remembers the old man says he was a strange one, "an odd duck," "a real kook." But Leopold Wrasse has been one of the greatest benefactors agriculture students in California have ever known. When Wrasse died in 1945 at the age of 96, he left a scholarship fund of $500,000 to California State Polytechnic, San Luis Obispo.

The hermit of the vineyard had never been a student at the school, but he liked what was going on at Cal Poly. By the year 2000, since the

Leopold Wrasse scholarships were established, 5,740 ag students at Cal Poly had received $4,170,000 in grants and through prudent investments the fund was now valued in excess of $5.7 million.

Not bad, when you consider the most the man ever earned for a day's work was $8. Wrasse had no electricity on his farm. He had no knives, forks, spoons, plates or cups. He had one little bowl. He filled it with water and dunked stale bread in it. He bought a sack of stale bread regularly from a bakery—cost him 50 cents a sack. The old man's diet was the stale bread, plus raisins, grapes, tomatoes and apricots that he grew.

He had a house but slept outdoors on a cot every day of the year except when it rained. Then he would push the cot inside his barn. He couldn't have slept in his tumble-down house even if he wanted to. There wasn't any room. The farmhouse was filled with junk he had scavenged from dumps, with old clothes and old newspapers, filled floor to ceiling. It was unpainted and looked as though it would collapse any minute. The windows were all broken.

Wrasse was a nudist. "You people in town. You don't know how to live," he'd shout at people on the streets of Caruthers. "You wear clothes. No air gets to your body. You don't eat right. You don't know how to breathe. You live in stuffy houses."

Wrasse was born in Pomerania, Germany, in 1849. He said he came to America to get away from his father, who was a drunkard. He worked as a carpenter and saved practically every penny he earned. He invested in first mortgages and in savings accounts. He bought insurance policies. Later in life he purchased the vineyard.

In 1938 Julian A. McFee, president of Cal Poly (enrollment at that time was 130 students, today, 13,000 students) heard about the hermit in the vineyard. "Mr. McFee suggested that a German-speaking instructor named Henry Figgy and I drive over to Caruthers and visit Wrasse," recalled Les Vanoncini, a Cal Poly ag teacher. "I was a student at Cal Poly at the time. We drove over to the vineyard in Henry's old Model T Ford. First time we saw Wrasse he was naked as a jaybird, hoeing in his vineyard. We just sat around and talked with him about his grapes, about the little ag school at San Luis Obispo. Figgy got along fine with the old man. They spoke German to each other.

"In time, president McFee visited Wrasse. McFee told the hermit about some poor farm kids who were bright students and hard workers but could not afford to attend school." That year, Wrasse set up a $20,000 loan fund for needy ag students at Cal Poly. After the fund was set up, McFee invited the old man to visit the school.

"Henry and I drove out to pick him up," Vanoncini recalled. "Wrasse had never worn a suit in his life. He went into town and paid $2 for a second-hand suit at the Salvation Army, 25 cents for a shirt, a nickel for a necktie and a nickel for a hat. He wore socks for the first time in years. Wrasse told the professor and the student he paid two bits for a dozen socks. "They're full of holes, but the holes ain't all in the same place," said the hermit. "I'm wearing two socks on the same foot. None of the holes show."

Wrasse stayed on the campus three days. He insisted on sleeping in a hay barn. He removed his shoes almost immediately on arrival. "We took him out to the school dairy where he watched students milking cows," said Vanocini. "He saw students working a herd of cattle on the school ranch. He really loved that. His whole philosophy was wrapped up in a hard work ethic. President McFee introduced Wrasse to the student body at an assembly and called him California's No. 1 farmer."

The hermit never forgot that day. Besides the scholarship fund, Wrasse made four bequests of $10,000 each in his will:
—To a little old farm woman down the road from his place. She brought him a quart of milk once in a while.
—To a German-speaking woman who talked to him no more than a dozen times.
—To the banker who handled his account.
—To the late Arthur L. Selland, who befriended him, advised him on many of his investments and visited him regularly as a friend. Selland later became mayor of Fresno.

When Wrasse died, his estate was tied up in litigation for 11 years because he had nephews and nieces living in Germany. Finally in 1957 the courts ruled his entire estate—except for the $40,000 in separate bequests—would go to Cal Poly for the scholarships as stipulated in his will. Scholarships are granted based on need, scholastic standing, school and community activity. A student must have at least a C average to apply. The scholarships were for $500 a year until recent years when the amount was increased to $1,000. Wrasse's will also required proof that a scholarship recipient had earned at least $250 the previous year. Several student body presidents and other outstanding Cal Poly students have been Leopold Wrasse Scholarship Fund recipients over the years.

HERMIT OF HARDROCK GULCH

I NFORMED THAT RONALD REAGAN was the new governor of California, Christine Love, the 94-year-old hermit of Hardock Gulch, retorted: "Never heard of him." Governor Reagan didn't need to be concerned. The old prospector hadn't paid much attention to the ways of the outside world since moving to her miner's shack in 1931. By the time we caught up with her she had lived all by herself in the same tiny shack 36 years, seven miles up a jeep trail from the nearest paved road. She had no electricity, no running water, no radio. Her closest neighbor was 10 miles away in Oro Grande, a hamlet north of Victorville.

For years Christine left her place once a month, walking 20 miles round trip with her burro "to get water and grub" at the Oro Grande general store. Since her burro died 10 years before our visit she never wandered far from her shack. She had a dog. The dog also died years ago. Died in his dog bed a few feet from where Christine sat in her rickety rocking chair. The dog bed was still there. So was the dog still in the bed. His bones collapsed in a heap where he died.

Famed Western painter Bill Bender, his wife, Helen, and two other couples had been "looking after" Christine Love ever since her beast of burden went to burro heaven. "One of us takes a four-wheel drive truck up there at least once or twice a month to make sure Christine's all right, that she has enough food, water and wood for her stove," explained Bender.

She had enough water to sink a ship. Stacks of five gallon bottles filled with water. "Christine insists we always bring a jug of water each time we come up. She has this great fear of running out of drinking water," continued Bender. "She's an individualist. She doesn't like to be disturbed. We don't intrude. We don't wear out our welcome by going up there too often."

According to old-timers, before the burro went belly up no one was welcome at the hermit's shack, built by Christine with her own hands. The story goes she had a cache of ammo and fired at anyone who came near. "She never fired at me," said Bender. The artist urged Christine to come down off the mountain and live in town where she'd be more comfortable.

"Too many livin' off the government as it is. Let me be," snorted the hermit of Hardrock Gulch, her stubborn streak reflected in an icy stare from her sharp blue eyes. "Don't want anybody worrying over me," she snapped. "I can take care of myself. Always have. Will till I die." Christine had never seen television. "Don't want to. Had enough of radio when it first came out," she declared.

Christine Love was born in Denmark but left there at an early age. She married Rufus K. Love, who, she explained, "Hired the talent, provided the costumes and produced vaudeville shows all over the West for years. We had a good life, but no kids. Rufus died in Los Angeles in 1920." Christine remained in the city 10 years, working in a restaurant. In 1931 she chucked her job to prospect in the hills north of Victorville.

"Lots of 'em came up here in the Great Depression. I had a claim; mined talc, limestone, calcium aluminate. Hauled it out by truckloads. Had three, four men up here working for me. Claim jumpers swarmed all over the place like a bunch of hornets. Took this and that. Now, all I have left is the house." The stone and board miner's shack sat on the side of a mountain a few feet from a pile of old tailings. Its soot-filled interior, charred from years of cooking and heating with cast-iron, wood-burner stove, was furnished with an antique bed, an ancient rocker, pots and pans hanging from nails.

Lonely? "Hell, no! I like it this way," allowed Christine. "I've got enough to do. Cook my meals. Keep up the place. Feed the quail. Still get paid, you know, caretaker, $100 a year, for watching over mining interests up here." As to her health, Christine claimed she'd never been to a doctor in her life. "Oh, I saw a doctor about 20 years ago," she laughed. "Passed him on the street when I was down in town getting groceries."

"TO HELL WITH EVERYBODY"

THE OLD HERMIT of California's northeastern-most corner was mad at the world. "To hell with everybody," was his favorite saying. But the people of sparsely populated, mountainous Modoc County—nearly everybody within 50 miles of the Old Hermit at Willow Ranch—had a warm spot in their hearts for recluse Glenn Rogers.

CHARLES HILLINGER

Women bake cookies and cakes and put up jams, jellies, fruits and preserves for him. A dump he frequented was surreptitiously "salted" by Modoc County men with tobacco, coffee and the "goodies" prepared by their wives.

Rogers, 67, lived in a 13-by-15-foot shack he built on the edge of Willow Ranch, an abandoned timber town on the shores of 18-mile-long Goose Lake, half in Oregon, half in California. Few people had ever seen Rogers or his shack, hidden in a gully on a mile-high valley with stands of pine, juniper and apple trees. Rogers' nearest neighbors lived 5 miles to the north across the state line in the tiny town of New Pine Creek, Oregon, and 33 miles to the south in Alturas, population 2,800, seat of Modoc County.

When we met him, Rogers had devoted his last 11 years relocating the old Willow Ranch Dump, scavenging a few items each day. "It's my exercise," he explained, describing his mile walk to the dump and another mile walk back home. He was gradually filling his shack from floor to roof with pots, pans, toasters, old clothing, stove pipes, broken furniture, bottles and cans. He left space inside his dwelling for only a narrow aisle that led past his wood stove to his bed—an old mattress and blankets. "I'm gonna clean out the place one of these days," he said. But why relocate the dump into his home?

"Fifteen cents a pound, that's reason enough," he explained. "Peddlers are eager for this old stuff. But no peddlers have been through these parts lately. One of these days..." he winked. When the Old Hermit saw anybody coming to his place—his benefactors or anyone else—he vanished into the trees. Only Modoc County Sheriff Lynn E. Harris and Alturas postal employee Bob Rush stopped by his shack from time to time.

They discovered Rogers living in one of the old houses in the abandoned town. Rush was a deputy sheriff at the time. "We were told someone was hiding out in Willow Ranch," recalled Harris. "It was in the middle of winter. Bob and I snowshoed to the old town and there he was, cold, dirty and hungry—existing on apricot seeds, breaking open the pits and eating the seeds." Ever since, Rush and Harris visited Rogers at least a couple of times a month to make sure the Old Hermit was OK.

"Those apricot seeds kept me goin'," said Rogers who stood but 5 foot 3 and weighed only 85 pounds on a scale he resurrected from the dump. "I just eat fried taters and such. Maybe a pancake now and then. I only eat once a day, but I drink 100 buckets of coffee a week."

He was born on a Minnesota farm, quit school after the sixth grade. "My last job was a gandy dancer. Workin' on the railroad ain't no fun—all those oil cans around. I walked the country—four round trips Frisco to New York all on foot. Never took to the rails once. Walked through 35 of the states. Oh, I thought about a job, but durin' the Depression you couldn't sweep up enough work to keep a canary." He said he had always been a loner, mostly because of his size. "The old man and old lady had 11 kids. I was No. 9, the runt of the litter, picked on and shoved around by older kids."

Ever in love? Last time he dated a woman? "Seems like 100 years, the last time I spoke to a woman. She was a peroxide blonde. She called me Shorty. I walked one way, she went the other."

Rogers said he finally settled down 11 years ago, first in the abandoned house, then in his own shack, hidden where "I'd never be bothered with people again. I was walkin' through here. Like the country, gettin' old and thinkin' I better hang my hat on the same hook for a change." He had a dog for a pet until a few months ago when the animal "got mange and turned up his toes. This is livin'," he insisted. "I've always been an under $600-a-year man. Never got ulcers. Don't have to worry about nothin'."

Harris and Rush tried to talk the Old Hermit into coming into town and signing up with the Welfare Department to get a decent place to sleep and three regular meals. But he would never have any part of it. "It's a good life up here," he maintained. "Out in the open. Don't have to smell the gas buggies or look at those high, narrow buildings. I lived in the city twice—in New York for a coupla years. In Chicago. Damn near blew my lungs out. Theater district was the best in New York. Go in and sleep in those movie houses all night." The Old Hermit liked to throw out sayings he'd picked up over the years, such as one that goes back to his railroading days:

"Throw coal in the stream engine, keep the world warm. That's all there's to it." As he cut wood for his stove with a rickety saw, he growled: "Harder than the rocks of hell to saw." He never bathed. "What's the use." His only medicine was a package of Smith Brothers cough drops. "Couldn't get TB up here if you hammered it in with a pile driver," he allowed. The Old Hermit lived in California's coldest corner.

Temperatures often drop to 25 below zero in winter. Snow drifts against his shack 5 or 6 feet deep. The wind whistled through the knotholes.

But the Old Hermit—though he never admitted it—wasn't ever really alone. Modoc County people went to the dump in all kinds of weather to throw away just about anything they figure Glenn Rogers might need.

DESERT FATS

IT WAS MIDDAY and the temperature was 116 degrees when "Desert Fats" Jack Copley began his rounds. Desert Fats was mayor and sole resident of Bonanza Springs, four miles up what passes as a dirt trail into the heart of the Clipper Mountains, just north of a Santa Fe Railway siding called Danby, midway between Barstow and Needles off Old Highway 66.

Fats was like scores of other pensioner prospectors, holing out in old mining camps in the California deserts and mountains. When we visited Fats, his "rounds" included feeding his catfish and bluegills in three fair-sized ponds near his shanty. "Surprised to see water out here in the middle of all this dryness, ain't ya?" Desert Fats said as he hurled huge handfuls of horse meat to his fish. His spring-fed ponds were stocked with hundreds of catfish and bluegills.

Bonanza Springs is an abandoned Santa Fe camp. In the days of steam Danby was an important stop for the thirsty engines. Water was siphoned from Bonanza Springs to Danby.

"Planned to make a fortune on a catfish-bluegill resort out here. You know, like a big trout farm. Figured people would come from miles. It'd be like an oasis in the middle of the Sahara. But this is government land and the Bureau of Land Management said uh-uh—no soap." The portly prospector continued: "Suppose you wonder why the sun doesn't dry me out? Last time I weighed, the scale said 370. Hell, it might be nearer 400 now. The sun doesn't dehydrate me—just makes more of me."

Desert Fats said he'd been living in Bonanza Springs 15 years. "Look as far as you can see—50 miles of nothing. You can't see a thing, just raw desert, the mountains and that big sky. It beats them dingy apartments in L.A. It ain't lonely. I always find plenty to pass the time. Never made a dime out of the desert, but I ain't quit tryin'" He went into the frog business for a time. "Frog legs bring good money. God, a pair costs an arm and a leg in a fancy restaurant. Just when the frogs were getting nice and fat, wildcats and hawks wiped 'em out."

He had been poking around the Clipper Mountains unearthing rocks. His camp was littered with prospecting samples. "I look for gold, silver, copper, nickel—and anything I can find. But I've never found nothing worth a damn. Give up? Hell, no! You gotta think positive. It's like shooting dice. I still think I'm going to get rich. Why give up now?"

Bonanza Springs sometimes had a population of three, all prospecting pensioners. Sam Mellow divided his time between here and Los Angeles. Al Stangberg, the third Bonanza Springer, was vacationing in "Lake Tayhoe" said Desert Fats."Once there were four of us holed up out here. We had a guy named Sparky for awhile—an old railroad telegrapher. The sun got to him. One day he just started out alone across the desert. We found his bones six months later, 10 miles out."

Desert Fats hung his head, lowered his eyes, and his thoughts turned to his dead companion. "You got to learn to respect the desert. If you don't, it'll never respect you."

A coyote howled. A jackrabbit shot across the main street of Bonanza Springs, dodging between its clutter of old cars, the 8-ton 1925 Federal truck, the four prospecting shacks and rubble of rocks. Desert Fats excused himself. He went about the rest of his afternoon "rounds"—checking out a likely vein in what he hoped was a legendary lost mine.

CHAPTER THIRTEEN

"Sweetwater Clyde" Foster taking it easy at his Sweetwater Gold Mine.

MINERS

SWEETWATER CLYDE

SWEETWATER CLYDE was 50 years behind times. He drove a faded white, rusted, beat-up 1937 half-ton Mack truck. He operated the Sweetwater Gold Mine his dad bought in 1933 with the same mining equipment that his father used. The year was 1988. Sweetwater Clyde was 77. His real name was Clyde Foster.

"This old mine has been worked continuously since 1862. Never abandoned. A few got rich here. A lot went broke. I've done both, hit it a few times and other times it's been a long time between drinks," recalled Sweetwater Clyde. His father was a lifelong California gold miner. So was his grandfather, and so was he. For 55 years he had worked the Sweetwater Mine, except for time out for a couple of wars. He was an Army sergeant in the South Pacific in World War II, and later in Korea.

"Wouldn't swap this life for anything," he allowed, his sharp blue eyes brightening with excitement. "If I struck it rich, I'd never leave. I'd just keep digging deeper and deeper and further into the mountain plowing all the money into the hole lookin' for more. It's the lure of gold that keeps me goin', and the thrill of findin' it."

Sweetwater Clyde had a solid copper tombstone among the clutter in his 1896 gold miner's shack of weathered boards and corrugated tin roof. The inscribed tombstone, ready for the moment he gasped his last breath, read: "Clyde T. Foster. Sweetwater Clyde. 1911 - Not Yet! It wasn't the gold he wanted so much as just finding the gold. Future miners, as this place you pass, turn down an empty glass."

"My friends will chisel off the 'Not Yet' and bury me under the lilac bushes over yonder," said the 5-foot, 6-inch, 150-pound miner. "But I'm not leaving soon. I've got 20 years of planning already doped out for developin' the mine." He noted that the Sweetwater's best years were in the 1880s and 1890s, when more than $500,000 in gold was recovered. His own best years, he recalled, were the early 1950s, when for four years straight he pulled out more than 1,000 ounces of $35-an-ounce gold. "That was only $35,000 a year then, but it would be $450,000 at today's prices. I'd like to do that again," he mused with a mellow grin and dreamy eyes.

Sweetwater Clyde took a 15-ounce bar of gold (worth $6,750) from one of his pockets and told how it was a recent recovery from 30 tons of crude. To get to his mine at the 4,000-foot level in a remote region of the High Sierra—about 10 miles from the tiny town of Midpines in Mariposa County—required navigation of three miles of bumpy, one-lane dirt road. At the entrance to his 10 claims on 200 acres of Sweetwater Ridge was a sign proclaiming: "SWEETWATER MINE. SHOOTING WILL BE RECIPROCATED."

"Sign's been there 20 years. Nobody shot a hole in it yet. I haven't had to shoot back at anybody," he said. His mine shaft was a horizontal hole, half a mile into the mountain, with 2,000-foot shafts branching in four directions. He entered and left the mine in his tiny ore train. Some of the track led out of the mine and over a 40-foot-high, 125-foot-long trestle he built out of trees to carry his waste material to a dump site.

Sweetwater Clyde had his own sawmill for cutting shoring timber. He processed what he dug from the mine through a 90-year-old machine called a Chilean jaw crusher. Its three stone wheels, each weighing 3,000 pounds, could grind a ton of crude to fine sand. The crusher was driven by a 1926 Studebaker automobile engine.

An American flag fluttered from the porch of his sturdy old shack. The shack was heated by an ancient pot-bellied wood stove. He cooked his beans and other grub on a 1925 gas range. His floor was covered with a layer of filth dragged in over the years and never swept away. The windows were so heavy with dirt that they could not be seen through. Spider webs dangled from the ceiling. Rusty old mining equipment was all over his diggings. "I don't throw anything away. Never know when I'm gonna need it," said Sweetwater Clyde, a throwback to the 1930s, one of the last of the West's old-time, hardrock gold miners.

DOWN THE ROAD DUGAN

"DOWN THE ROAD" DUGAN is on the endangered list—one of the last of a vanishing species. He's whiskered. Grimy. Wears a dirty old flop hat. His tools of trade—pick, shovel and pan. "I've had a lust for gold all my days," declared Dugan, who was 72 when we caught up with him. "My God, I hope the Good Lord gives me another five years. I think I'm getting close." "Down the Road" had been getting close all his life

For 52 years he'd been working the hills of El Dorado County, mostly around Georgetown, a roaring camp of the 1850s and 60s in the Mother Lode. They call him a river rat, sniper, pocket hunter, gopher, prospector. He came by his peculiar name logically enough. Trudging through the hills with determined gait. Pick and shovel slung over his shoulder. Pan hanging down his side, gripped in one hand. Heading down the road each new day hoping to strike an enrichment.

"Man without hope ain't got nuttin'," said Dugan. He's a latter-day Argonaut. "Hell, this is where it all began," he allowed. "Coloma, where Jim Marshall hit it in 1848. Hangtown. Pilot Hill. Smith's Flat. Lotus. Kelsey's. They're all close by. Thousands of quartz seams all over these hills. Quartz is where the glitter is, boy."

You've been getting by all these years fooling around with gold? Dugan was asked. "Fooling around! You don't fool around with gold," he retorted. "It's a dangerous occupation. Through the ages gold has been sought. Miners kill each other for it. That's why I've always been a little afraid. That's why I keep to myself. If you do get any gold, you don't tell anybody about it. You can't afford to trust your fellow man. Partners are honest as long as you don't find anything."

Dugan said his rightful name is Roy Arling—that he was born in Bureau County, Illinois. "My daddy died when I was two. My mother took in washing. I'd always watch the sun settin' in the West. That's what did it. That settin' sun. At 14 I quit school, left home and started to ramble. I've been ramblin' ever since except for a couple years in the Army. They've been callin' me 'Down the Road' Dugan since I came west. I picked it up in Nevada. It was out of order to ask a man his true name. I'll tell you, boy, I've seen the seamy side of life and I've seen some glory holes. Gold has been good to me. Good enough to keep me in beans. I've hit it a time or two, I'll tell you," Dugan winked, reminiscing: "Biggest hit was a place the old Chinese called Rucky Chucky. Filled up several sacks of high grade— some of the prettiest gold I've ever seen. Had blood red stain in it from hematite iron. Oh, did I have a time for myself. Got on a Santa Fe, went to Chicago—to New York, back to Frisco. Ate in the diners. Didya ever eat in a diner car?"

As Dugan was going down the road to his current diggin's he waded briefly in a stream, shaking a few samples in his pan. "When you've got a lust for gold, you use your pan every chance. You never know. There's never a moment of routine in my life. Every day I look forward to what tomorrow brings." On his way down the road Dugan stops by the bar in the old Georgetown Hotel. "I'm a man of the truth," he insisted. "I enjoy a little libation now and then. I like to sing the old songs."

The boys at the Georgetown Hotel look forward to visits by Dugan. A few years back he asked the organist if he knew "I Can Hear the Hungry Coyote." Told no, the old miner searched his belongings and came up with a faded, tattered music sheet of his favorite number. It's now the saloon's theme song. "It's a song you never hear on the radio," sighed Dugan.

"Down the Road" has never married. He's a lifelong loner. He lives in old shacks or sleeps outdoors. Lately he's given thought to the hereafter. "I've been thinkin' when my time comes, I'd like to be buried in Spanish Dry Diggin's, in the old cemetery there alongside those forgotten miners of the 1850s and 60s. I'm not a religious man, but I want to be buried with benefit of clergy. My mother was a true believer." Under his name on the tombstone, Dugan continued, "I'd like it to read—He Had a Lust for Gold."

"Ever eat a lilac, Lu?" shouted Ray Bush over the deafening clatter of the jackhammer. Alleghany Lu brushed smudge from her face, yelled to Bush that she couldn't recollect she ever had. "You ain't missed nuttin'," Bush shouted. "Lilacs taste terrible." Alleghany Lu, 62-year-old lifelong gold miner, and Bush, 48, her hired hand, were engaged in small talk as they worked in Lu's diggin's at the San Francisco Mine on the south face of a hill overlooking the tiny hamlet of Washington in Nevada County.

Miners have called Luthena Caston "Alleghany Lu" for 30 years or more, eversince she operated the Seven Acres in Alleghany, a gold mine a few miles north of her present location. "Lu's got gold mining in her blood. She will never call it quits," said Bush. How long she'll last is anybody's guess. But the days of Alleghany Lu's mining career seemed numbered.

Lu Caston admittedly sank over $200,000 of her own money and money she's promoted from others—her partners—into the San Francisco. She's scarred a wide swath of mountain, moving thousands of tons of dirt looking for the elusive rich vein. She's built a mill, spent money on bulldozers and expensive equipment.

"I know there's at least a million in cold cash somewhere in here. I can't stop now. I got 10 years and my life savings at stake," she sighed. Lu sees all the indications of a high-grade vein. "Solid gold right behind the mariposite," she claimed. "See that white rock up there? I'm getting close...getting so close I can smell it.

"This is one of the richest spots in the state. Several geologists have looked at this thing. They agree. Formations here are identical to those at the Sixteen-to-One just over the hill. You know the Sixteen-to-One— $35 million in gold taken from it." She reached into a bulging attaché case and grabbed an old dirt-stained copy of the Mineral Information Service published by the State Division of Mines and Geology.

"Come on up here. Let me show you something," Lu said as she grabbed a small pick and pan. Bush laid aside the jackhammer as he finished the last of a series of holes he and Lu drilled for blasting and reached into a portable cooler for a beer. Lu hoisted herself up the steep mountain side, and chipped away at a rock to demonstrate a show of color. "This is pocket country. A big outfit could hack it. I had hopes I could. I'm not giving up yet," she said. "Everybody said I'm an idiot for sticking with her all this time," Bush chimed in. "But this country is what it is because of people like Lu. She's got guts. Determination. Stubborn as a mule, by God."

"Who the hell is going to find all the stuff? It's the jackass guys like Ray and me that made the West, that made the nation," said Lu, a childless widow. "Abraham Lincoln said he believed the mineral wealth of the nation inexhaustible. Said as long as there are prospectors, this country would prosper. Instead of promoting mining, this country's been tearing it down ever since old Roosevelt spoiled everything.

"We depend almost entirely on foreign imports when there's plenty of stuff right here in the ground in America. We've got all kinds of chrome, yet we import two-thirds of our chrome. Now, doesn't that make sense? Get gold back in the hands of the people and the people will regain control of the government. This country's in bad shape. Gold's only in the hands of the government—not in the hands of the people. All we get is fluke money, today."

How long Lu will last isn't certain—but Lu's out of a grubstake. "I want to learn to play the piano again," Lu said. "I want to be out of debt again. I don't know how long I've got. I know I can't last forever. I have a feeling I'm going under. If I could only hit it. There's at least a million in cold cash waiting just a few feet below the surface. I know there's gold in here. I'm getting so close I can smell it."

"WE'RE GONNA STRIKE IT RICH BEFORE WE DIE"

T HE TWO PARTNERS were walking across the open desert headed for their diggin's, she with a shovel over her shoulder, he with a pick over his. "We're gonna strike it rich before we die. I've never been more certain. It's gonna happen," mused the younger partner, Pearl Smock, 73, as they plodded along. "Money doesn't mean a damn to me. High livin' doesn't mean a damn," allowed Pearl's partner, Glen Deyo, 84. "But I think we're onto somethin' big out here." The two lifelong hard-rock miners have been holed up together at the Jewel Box Mine in a remote slice of the Mojave Desert 200 miles east of Los Angeles for the last seven years.

It is 15 miles by dirt road they have blazed over raw desert from their mining camp to the nearest pavement. Their closest neighbor, another miner, is 25 miles away. "We both hit this spot the same time comin' from different directions," Deyo recalled. "I had just come up out of Mexico. My partner had been prospectin' to the north of here."

He stopped suddenly, knelt to the ground and picked up a rock. "Look at this. It's silica gel. Mother of all jewels. This whole area is alive with silica gel, a deposit rich in topaz, sapphire and diamonds. That's why we call our mine the Jewel Box. See those hills," the old miner continued, waving his right arm in the direction of distant purple mountains. "Those hills are full of copper, silver, gold. Oh, my partner and I know where the treasures are buried out here. It's only a matter of time now. I know what it is to strike it rich. I've made it and spent it several times in my life. When I've been rich, I traveled the world.

"Went everywhere, Europe, South America, Africa, all over the 50 states. Had fancy cars. Lived in expensive homes. Now, I'm old, but hell, I'm not ready to quit. Not yet. I have the best partner I've ever had in my life. She does her share and then some. That's why I'm glad it's gonna happen again, for my partner's sake."

The two partners paused to catch their breaths. The old man rested his left foot on a boulder, his right hand on his pick. The old lady leaned on her shovel with both hands. "I was born in a minin' camp in Ideeho," said Pearl as they paused. "I hardly took my first steps when my daddy took me out pannin' nuggets. Been at it ever since. Minin' always kept me goin', always kept me in grub. Never been broke. Not even in the darkest days of the Depression. Durin' the Great Depression I carried bat guano out of caves in sacks on my back. When my partner and I hit it big, I'm gonna give all my riches to poor kids orphanages. Hell, I'm too old to spend it on myself. Even if my partner and I don't get rich, we got no complaints. Seven years together in this camp. I have my livin' quarters. He has his. He's old. I'm old. So hell, there's nothin' wrong bein' cooped up here together without gettin' hitched. Miners trust and respect each other."

"We get along just fine, my partner and me," Deyo declared with a mischievous grin. "Damn few times when we agree. Argue all the time. That's why we get on so well, because we argue all the time. I won't deny that." Deyo likes Pearl's cooking. "She makes the best damn pot of beans I've had anywhere."

Their shack is warm and comfortable, equipped with stove and refrigerator and electric lights powered by a small generator. *Thirty* dogs share their grub in the mining camp. A crank telephone hangs in a corner. "It works," Peal assured. "But there ain't no telephone lines up here." About once a month, when supplies run low, the two partners drive an old truck to the nearest town, a desert hamlet 50 miles away. "We're both tough as nails," added Deyo. "That's why we've lived so long. We're from two of the oldest families in America. Her ancestors and mine were here before the Revolutionary War. I'm Nordic French. My partner, she's part Nez Perce Indian. The rest of her is Big Greek and Dutch."

"I wouldn't trade my life for nothin'," Pearl insisted.

SALMON RIVER STEVE

"OF COURSE, I DREAM OF HITTING A BONANZA. Otherwise I wouldn't be here," snorted "Salmon River Steve" Huntington, 83, as he worked the gravel in the stream, looking for color. For 65 years Huntington has been following his hunches, searching for gold throughout the West. "Hell, old prospectors like me are always chasing rainbows. But my nine claims up Specimen Gulch ain't rainbows," said the blue-eyed, flop-hatted miner.

Like Down the Road Dugan, Alleghany Lu, Pearl Smock and Glen Deyo, Salmon River Steve insisted he was so close to a big hit he could smell the gold. His gray beard was stained with tobacco juice dribbling from his Optimo cigar. Huntington's home was an old weather-beaten trailer on blocks, topped with a corrugated iron roof. A clutter of rusting mining equipment embraced the trailer, situated in a dense forest of alders overlooking the North Fork of the Salmon River.

His trailer was six miles from Forks of Salmon, a remote Northern California hamlet. His nearest neighbor was five miles away. Salmon River Steve had a million-dollar view. The back end of his trailer hung out over a hill, where giant boulders covered with brilliant green moss spilled into the roaring, crystal-clear Salmon River. Spectacular snow-capped mountains towered over his campsite.

"At my age, with my resources, if I wasn't mining I'd probably be holed up in some God-awful flophouse in L.A., Frisco or Seattle," said the miner. "Instead I'm living in this paradise. Most people have never seen country this beautiful, let alone live in it."

He drank the river water, bathed in it, washed his clothes in it, swam in it, found specks of gold in it. The miner's companion for 17

CHARLES HILLINGER

years, his dog Tessie, died a few months earlier and was buried nearby. Huntington was married twice, both times for 13 years. His first wife died. He divorced the second one. "I like women, but I don't plan to get hitched again. When I get lonely I go to a dance. I don't get lonely often. I'm too busy pursuing gold," he explained. Mining, he said, had been good to him. "There's something fascinating about gold mining. I've enjoyed working whether I've made money or not. It's kept me in grub most of the time. I've never struck it rich, but I've hit little pockets. What I've made, I've put back in equipment. Oh, I've been flat busted many times. So broke I didn't know whether I was ever going to eat again. But somehow I've always pulled out of it. You got to take it on the chin like a fighter. You get hit on the chin time and time again. But you don't want it to knock you out."

When the gold failed to show Salmon River Steve relied on what he called "those Social Insecurity checks" to keep him afloat. He didn't wear glasses. He had his own teeth. He chopped his own wood for his stove. He didn't know a doctor and didn't plan on knowing one. He hiked 10 miles to his "diggin's."

The old miner said he was born in Cody, Wyoming, that his father Hallam Huntington was "one hell of a cowboy. When he threw a rope I never saw him miss." His father, he recalled, was a friend and hunting companion of Buffalo Bill Cody, and he remembered sitting on Buffalo Bill's lap when he was 3 years old.

"If I found the kind of gold I've been searchin' for all these years, I would travel the world," mused the miner. "First place I'd go would be to Cody. I left there in a horse-drawn wagon when I was four. Never been back. I'd like to see Cody again."

Three months after my story about Salmon River Steve appeared I had a phone call from Cindy Baldwin in Cody who related that the people from Huntington's birthplace wanted to fly him "back home for a week-long sentimental journey."

"Someone in Southern California sent a copy of the *Los Angeles Times* story to a relative in Cody," later explained Bruce McCormack, editor of the Cody Enterprise. "The story was passed around. Folks in town got to talking about that old fella and decided to pitch in and bring him back here, let him see Cody again before he died." Led by Mark Baldwin and his wife, Cindy, owner-operators of the Caroline Lockhart Bed & Breakfast, townspeople chipped in enough money to make Salmon River Steve's dream come true.

Huntington, with a cigar dangling from his lips and a gap-toothed grin creasing his face, drove his rusty old pickup with 186,000 miles on the odometer to the nearest airport in Medford, Oregon. Photographer Gary Friedman and I met him at the airport to accompany him to Cody. The first leg of the trip was a jet flight to Denver, followed by hop in a vintage 1950 propeller plane. In Cody, Salmon River Steve emerged from the airplane chomping on his cigar, wearing a sweat-stained floppy hat, a lumber jacket, a new pair of pants he bought for the occasion, and carrying a small suitcase with a big rip and change of clothes. "Welcome back to Cody, the place you were born," said Peg Shreve, Cody's representative in the Wyoming Statehouse, as a crowd of townspeople cheered. The old prospector replied: "This is the highlight of my life. I'll never forget this as long as I live." Driving through town, Huntington was greeted with signs on business marquees: "WELCOME HOME SALMON RIVER STEVE!"

Cody boasts that it is the only place in the world with a rodeo every night of the week all summer and Salmon River Steve was the honored guest at the first rodeo of the year. He stood out in the arena and tipped his hat to the grandstand crowd as he was introduced. They loved it. He loved it. Asked how he kept in such great shape by the rodeo's master of ceremony, he explained: "Well, I do a lot of walking and a lot of pick and shovel work on my claims." He was asked if he was a religious man. "My religion is a simple formula. If I know something's wrong, I don't do it," he replied.

The old prospector visited the Buffalo Bill Historical Center (named for Wild West showman Buffalo Bill Cody, who founded the town), stopped by the grave of famed mountain man "Liver Eating" John Johnston, portrayed by Robert Redford as Jeremiah Johnson in the movie. He saw Eric Sorg's one-man show on the life of Buffalo Bill at the theater in the Irma Hotel, which Buffalo Bill built in 1902 and named after his daughter.

Huntington was given a new outfit of clothes, including a $100 Stetson hat, by Wayne Lundvall, who runs the local sporting goods store. He went horseback riding at the Rimrock Dude Ranch and danced to tunes like "This is Where the Cowboys Ride the Range" at Cassie's, a cowboy bar. At the dude ranch Huntington described his old home to foreman Ryon St. Clair. His description was so vivid St. Clair

CHARLES HILLINGER

knew exactly where the old Huntington place was located.

"It all adds up. There's an old irrigation ditch up there called Huntington Ditch. It was built by and named after your daddy," St. Clair told the prospector. St. Clair drove Huntington to the old homestead. "I guess everybody ought to go back to where he was born sometime in his life, Salmon River Steve told St. Clair as they bounced over the rough country in a pickup.

Tears welled in the gray-bearded prospector's sharp blue eyes when they arrived at the site of his birthplace and he walked among the ruins of the log cabin and barn he hadn't seen in 80 years. Across the lush meadow against the side of a hill stood the cream-colored rock walls of a root cellar where his mother once preserved home-grown strawberries. A brisk walk up the narrow canyon by Roaring Paint Creek brought him to "the old cave where my brothers and I played." A flood of memories came back:

"Old Zip, our dog, would come up here with us. Zip lost a leg in a bear trap. I fell in Paint Creek and got all wet one time and my mother spanked me...Time changes everything. I thought of this place often all through life. I never knew whether I'd ever see it again. I never knew if I did get to see it if anything would be the same as I remembered it." He reached over and plucked three wild roses off a bush near the crumpled wall of the log cabin, one for his sister, Iris Martin, in her 90s in Bryn Mawr, California, one for his brother, Corey, 100, in San Diego, and one for himself.

Salmon River Steve Huntington, 83, the lifelong gold prospector from Forks of Salmon, a remote Northern California hamlet in the mountains of Siskiyou County, had come home to his birthplace in the equally remote Absaroka Mountains near Dead Indian Pass 25 miles north of Cody.

ANTI-AMERICAN, PRO-RUSSIAN SHRINE

HIDDEN IN A RUGGED RANGE of Mojave Desert mountains 150 miles northeast of Los Angeles is a mysterious anti-American, pro-Russian shrine. It is a corrugated-iron miner's shack, covered inside and out with well-preserved, penciled messages about the "noble Russian people," "our great leader Stalin," "Democratic dogs," "worthless American women" and astrology.

"I am certain no more than a dozen people have ever been back in here and seen this cabin," said Tom Chapman, who acted as a guide on a 10-mile hike over steep cliffs and rocky gullies in the scorching desert sun to the remote site. Chapman had lived in the desert 30 miles from the cabin since being released from a Japanese prison camp in the Philippines in 1945 when we met him. He found the shrine while hiking through the area. He had returned to the shack many times during the 30 years since he discovered it.

The writings on the walls are one man's diary of the war years and his reactions to the events of the times. Accurate dates and descriptions of many World War II battles are penciled on the walls. "I have radio. I listen all the time," notes one entry. Scattered among the chronicles of the historic events are accounts of the man's successes and failures as a miner. An entry dated September, 1943, reads: "This was a good summer picking gold out of kreeks and rivers." Three months later, he wrote: "I work claims for weeks for noting. I dont find more gold." The following spring he wrote, "In the five winter months I spent $70. In the citi I would spendt $350 in five monts."

Examples of his anti-American, pro-Russian feelings include the following: "Russia is goliath of world. Stalin dont take orders from U.S. United States needs threshin from Japs. Heil Stalin. I dont care if I die on road, in ditch or kreek, I will always be with you Stalin. Russians are good people. Stalin is good ruler. My mother and grandmother always say world needs bigger Russia. Amerika will be Russian colony. Soon world have one language, Russian language of Communists."

One of the many puzzling entries on the wall is "Thank God Russia kaptured Ruegen. Ruegen was one of the German sekret agents in the United States." He also wrote, "U.S. people all crucks. United States born rats comme here pesterin and stealin. I had money in banks. U.S. confiscated it. I had property. U.S.A. confiscated it."

Another entry tells about the "Democratic dogs" who came to his cabin in April, 1943, and stole a bottle in which had had hidden $400. A later entry dated February, 1944, tells how he found the lost bottle with the money intact. There are several disparaging entries about American women. "Amerikan women are whores," he wrote. "I dont want a woman in United States." He also mentioned his early years in Russia and told of fathering a child by a Russian woman.

Ralph Hevener, a retired miner, had lived since 1934 in a canyon eight miles from the Russian's shack. "I remember him well," Hevener said. "He was an enormous man. He had a long, full, black beard. He was a loner. I never knew his name. There were only three of us miners living in this area when the Russian was here. To my knowledge, I was the only one he ever talked to. The Russian would walk 20 miles to town for supplies now and then. I had an old car and gave him a lift part of the way a number of times. He had a heavy accent and said he had several claims up the canyon. He never told me anything about himself. He would sometimes sit in the car in silence. I never could pry any information out of him."

Outside the Russian's cabin are rusted bedsprings and a stove, some mining equipment, a pile of food cans. The door to the cabin is seven feet high, much taller than entries commonly found on old mining shacks. Several tons of unworked ore are piled up around the cabin, as well as tailings that were worked. But there is no evidence of a mine in the vicinity.

A legend among the few people living in this part of the desert is that the mysterious miner was a "7-foot tall defrocked Russian nobleman, who was hiding out in the desert in the guise of a gold miner."

Because of its remoteness, there has been no vandalism to the cabin. "The writings have faded somewhat," Chapman noted. "But other than that, what you see here today is exactly what was here when I first saw it in 1950, five years after the Russian disappeared. If it were easy to find the cabin, I'm sure vandals would have torn it apart long ago. But it's impossible to get in here with trail bikes or four-wheel drives. No trails lead here.

"What all this means is hard to figure. What brought the Russian to this remote spot at the beginning of the war? Why did he vanish at war's end?" mused Chapman. "Who he was and where he went is a mystery. I sure would like some answers to it in my lifetime."

CHAPTER FOURTEEN

Patricia "Bat Lady" Brown-Berry, holding a dead silver-hair bat, travels the world to study bats.

SCIENTISTS

BAT LADY

PATRICIA BROWN-BERRY has dedicated her life to turning around people's attitude toward bats. "Bats have a bad rap," she insists. "There are many myths and fears about bats that are totally untrue. Exterminating bats is big business for pesticide companies in this country."

Known to many as the "Bat Lady," Brown-Berry is an internationally renowned bat advocate, bat biologist, bat behaviorologist and bat communications expert. She has been fascinated by and working with bats since she received her doctorate in neurophysiology at UCLA in 1973.

"Bats are vital to the well-being of mankind," says Brown-Berry. "They enrich the whole biomass, are an integral part of the ecosystem. Bats are nature's way of controlling mosquitoes, moths and other insects. Bats pollinate half the fruit in the tropics, fruit like bananas, papayas, mangoes, avocados."

The "Bat Lady" travels the world to study bats and has followed them all over North America, as well as in Japan, Australia, Europe, the Mideast, Mexico and Central and South America. "Bats are said to have rabies, to carry diseases. There are only 10 cases of people getting rabies from bats in all of the U.S. public health records. Household pets are rabid in much greater numbers than bats," she explains. "Bats are no Typhoid Marys. They are a minuscule health hazard. Yet pesticide companies make millions every year wiping out bats whose populations are in great decline because of chemical poisoning."

Brown-Berry has written numerous scientific papers on the biology of bats, especially on vocal communication and echolocation. It is her research on various species of bats—there are about 1,000 species on Earth, 24 recorded in California—that has taken her around the world. Through scientific grants from the National Science Foundation, National Geographic and other agencies and organizations, she has studied bats in ancient Egyptian tombs and bats with enormously long claws and feet that gaff fish in the waters of Panama.

"We're just beginning to understand bat sensory systems. Bats are dolphin-like, with extraordinary navigational systems. They fly in total darkness, sending out high-frequency, high-intensity sounds that bounce back to them on striking objects," noted Brown-Berry. "Bats' sophisticated echolocation systems enable them to find insects. Echolocation also informs bats of texture, size, shape and those insects edible and those not."

She talked about Bracken Cave in Texas, home of a colony of 20 million Mexican free-tailed bats that fly from the cave after darkness, consuming 250,000 pounds of mosquitoes and other insects each night. Bats vary in size from the bumblebee bat of Thailand, weighing a third less than a penny and the world's smallest mammal, to Chinese flying foxes weighing 3 to 4 pounds with wingspans up to six feet. In China, the bat is revered. The Chinese word *bien-fu* means both good luck and bat, said the Bat Lady. *Wu-fu*, the Chinese design of five bats in a circle wingtip to wingtip, is a symbol of long life, health, prosperity, happiness and painless death.

"It's time to turn around the bats' bad rap in America. People should be blessed having bats," maintains Brown-Berry, one of a handful of bat experts in the United States. She is also director of the Maturango Museum in Ridgecrest, 175 miles northeast of Los Angeles, a museum dedicated to the natural resources of the Mojave Desert.

ANTS IN HIS PANTS

R OY SNELLING, one of a handful of myrmecologists on Earth, returned home with a pocket full of *nobomessor cockerellis*. It wasn't easy. Snelling had been looking for nobomessor cockerellis for two years. He finally found them on a remote mountaintop 50 miles southwest of Needles. Once he spotted the elusive *nobomessor cockerellis* he stayed awake all but four of 48 hours lying on his stomach, observing them.

Nobomessor cockerellis are shiny black, slender, quarter-inch termite eating ants never before seen in California. Snelling was just the man to track them down. At the time he was 30, a Los Angeles County Museum entomologist and the only bona fide myrmecologist (ant scientist) in the West, one of four in the nation and one of only 10 in the world.

His 600-mile round trip to Old Woman Mountains marked a milestone in his eight years of cataloguing ants. "I've always had a hunch *nobomessor cockerellis* existed somewhere in California," said Snelling. *Nobomessor cockerellis* made an even 300 different species of ants he had found and catalogued to date.

Before Snelling came along nobody ever bothered much about California ants except finding ways to keep them out of the kitchen. He is one of a handful of humans who ever heard ants clicking and squeaking. "Only a few species of ants make audible noises," he explained, "but those that do can be heard from as far away as six inches." He's heard rare Mexican ants snap their jaws together, making a clicking clatter. And he's listened to other species squeak as they rubbed their stomachs together.

Snelling is a walking encyclopedia on ants. "Non-workers live only three or four days. Workers have a life expectancy of 60 to 90 days. And a queen ant lives as long as 15 years," he noted. In his search for ants, Snelling has climbed to the top of 14,494-foot Mt. Whitney to collect the highest-living ants in continental U.S.A. He was constantly alert for any sign of imported fire ants, deadly insects that have killed thousands of chickens and turkeys and a number of humans in recent years in Southern states. Fire ants, native of Brazil, were first seen in this country in 1915 in Mobile, Alabama. Since then they have spread throughout the South. Snelling's ant collection at the Los Angeles County Museum was one of the finest in the world—40,000 specimens, 600 different species, the largest an inch-and-a-quarter long, the smallest $1/21$ inch.

Many species of ants are beneficial, feasting on termites and other destructive bugs. Many others, of course, such as the common Argentine ant, cause housewives no end of trouble. Some species nibble at fruit, vegetables and flowers, causing farmers and florists headaches. The ant, one of the most common insects, is still a big mystery to man. "We know very little about the ant," said Snelling. "Scientists have been studying them for only about 150 years. A male ant's life is pretty shabby. Big healthy ants are always females. Scraggly miserable looking ants are always males. It's strictly a female's world. The biggest day in a male ant's brief life span is the day he mates. When the act of mating is completed in a matter of seconds, the male drops dead."

Snelling talked about a species of a California desert ant that goes out early each morning and cuts leaves from a shrub. "The ants chew the leaves, make a mulch, then wait several days for fungus to develop on the mulch. These desert ants live on fungus," he related. "Another California ant is a pal to aphids and a pain in the neck to gardeners. These ants protect aphids from all enemies, encouraging rapid aphid reproduction. Aphid-loving ants wave their antennas over aphids, causing the aphid to secret a droplet of honey dew, a nectar that has much the same effect on ants that martinis have on humans."

WORLD'S OLDEST OOLOGIST IS A RARE BIRD

As THE WORLD'S OLDEST OOLOGIST, Wilson C. Hanna was a rare bird, indeed. There are only about 50 bird egg collectors in America, no more than twice that number on Earth. As far back as Hanna could remember he'd been collecting eggs. "My first recollection is climbing a tree as a boy of 4 and finding a bird's nest with eggs in it. It completely fascinated me," Hanna said as he strolled through his 100 by 50 foot bird egg house.

The fascination had never dulled for the oologist who was 84 when we met. He roamed the world in pursuit of common, rare and unusual eggs. His collection numbered more than 200,000 eggs all perforated with a small hole to remove the white and yoke.

"They're fragile. They wouldn't last if the insides weren't removed," said Hanna. For years Hanna kept his eggs in bureau drawers at his

Colton home, but now they're housed in 200 display cases in the Bird Egg Wing of the San Bernardino County Museum. Eggs on display were collected throughout the world by Hanna and scores of others during the last 200 years.

"Many who travel to remote parts of the world pick up all sorts of things, including bird eggs," said Hanna. "When I get wind of someone returning with eggs, I let them know of my collection. Very often they add to it." The collection includes Guira cuckoo eggs collected by Teddy Roosevelt on one of his South American expeditions.

To make the collection interesting for the uninitiated all eggs in Hanna's collection are identified and described. Included are eggs of extinct birds such as the passenger pigeon and eggs of birds as rare as the whooping crane.

Daniel W. Anderson, ornithologist from the University of Wisconsin, did a study of 4,500 eggs in Hanna's collection. Anderson measured and weighed eggs of North American birds to determine appreciable change in shell weight and thickness. He was especially interested in 23 species of birds that have declined in numbers in recent years.

The study, supported by the U.S. Fish and Wildlife Service, was an effort to determine cause of decline and possible effects of pesticides. "Man has been decimating birds indiscriminately for years," said Hanna. "Many birds I knew as a boy in Southern California are no longer found here."

FLAT-FOOTED FLIES

SINCE THE EARLY 1800s, the scientific world has had only four flat-footed fly experts. The most recent was Dr. Edward L. Kessel, who was 67 when we encountered him, the reigning authority on that species of flies for the previous 40 years.

When dipterists—scientists specializing in flies—happen to catch flat-footed flies, they mailed them to Dr. Kessel who followed flat-footed flies as far away as the Arctic. He chased them all over America and Canada. He caught an awful lot of them in California, even in his own backyard in the woods where he lived in Marin County. Most flies have rounded feet. "If you spent all your time catching flies, you might not catch a flat-footed fly in your life.

"They're rare," continued Kessel. "You have to know where to look." He knew where. He had thousands of the tiny platypezidae—flat-footed flies—mounted on pins in file cases in his office at the California Academy of Sciences in San Francisco. "I can spot them 20 feet away," he explained. "They run around in circles on large, horizontal leaves. They run. Then they suddenly stop. Then they go again."

There are about 175 species of flat-footed flies. Some have special markings on their feet, like the flag-footed, flat-footed flies that flash in the forest like sparklers on the Fourth of July. Like all flies, the flat-footers have six feet. But the flag-footed, flat-footed flies have tiny silver flags on their hind legs.

"The flags are sort of stiff, like the flag the astronauts placed on the moon," Kessel noted. "The silver flags reflect the filtered sun rays in the forest, flashing during the mating dance. Female flag-footed, flat-footed flies can't resist the flashing," Kessel said "They lose their inhibitions. The females fly to the males. Females take over flying during mating, towing the males. Males have two big red eyes. They remind me of a boat trailer with big taillights being pulled along."

Kessel is the first person in history to describe the mating and the egg-laying idiosyncrasies of these types of flies. The gray-haired dipterist observed egg laying in his own yard. "I saw several flat-footed flies walking on top of a mushroom, then disappearing over the side. Well, it's not easy to see what's going on under the lid of a mushroom."

He fetched a shovel and dug a hole for his head. "I got my reading glasses, then lay on the ground with my head in the hole to watch. A neighbor spotted me and came dashing over to see if I had had a heart attack." What Kessel learned that day was the female flat-footed flies drop their eggs in spaces between gills on mushroom stems.

"I think I discovered why these flies have flat feet—and, incidentally, females have bigger and wider flat feet than males. It seemed the feet spread across several gills (fine flutings) to keep the female from slipping when she lay her eggs, to give her support on the mushroom. Up to that time I had a hunch the flat feet served as snowshoes on over-ripe mushrooms. But I later learned the flies do not lay eggs on over-ripe mushrooms."

The world's only flat-footed fly expert was a professor of entomology at the University of San Francisco. He also was assistant curator of insects and editor of scientific publications at the California Academy of Sciences. Kessel said flat-footed flies are neither pests nor beneficial insects, they are sort of neutral. He said you don't have to worry about flat-footed flies coming in to dinner. They prefer the outdoors.

OLDEST LIVING THING ON EARTH

WHAT WOULD YOU do if you discovered the oldest living thing on Earth and nobody cared? That was botany professor Frank C. Vasek's dilemma. "I'm just sick about this. It could be as important as the pyramids of Egypt. But it could also vanish with the snap of a finger," sighed Vesek, 55.

The University of California, Riverside, professor was standing in the middle of what he had identified as the world's oldest known living organism, a ring of creosote bushes. He said the 70-foot-long, 25-foot-wide, irregular ellipse of scraggly desert shrubs began with one seed approximately 11,700 years ago.

"This outer ring of creosote bushes is comparable to the outer layer of living bark on a redwood tree," Vasek explained. "The inside wood has long since rotted away. The entire distance to the center of the creosote ring was at one time solid wood. The creosote bush starts with a center stem and grows outward with the inside dying and rotting away, and the circle keeps getting bigger and bigger."

What concerned Vasek was that King Clone, the name given the 11,700-year-old ring of creosote bushes, was on private, undeveloped land in Johnson Valley in the Mojave Desert 150 miles northeast of Los Angeles. The professor had tried to get the federal government, the state and San Bernardino County to buy the land on which King Clone is located and set it aside as a park "to protect the world's oldest living thing."

"But I can't get anybody interested. To the layman, King Clone is just another uninteresting, commonplace bunch of creosote bushes," Vasek lamented. "To make matters worse, if the subdividers don't destroy the oldest living thing on Earth, the motorcyclists and off-road vehicle people may well do it for them."

Allen Redden, a Lucerne Valley real estate agent, was subdividing 320 acres of desert in Johnson Valley into 20-acre parcels. King Clone was on one of those parcels. "Maybe the professor is right. Maybe those bushes are the oldest living thing on Earth, but when you have millions of creosote growing all over the desert and they all look alike, it's hard to get too excited about it," Redden said.

Redden thought someone would buy the 20 acres and bulldoze King Clone for a homesite, horse pasture or farm land. Vasek winced at the thought. "You know I hate to even stand inside King Clone. I have such a reverence for this champion of survival that has been in continuous existence in this harsh environment since the Wisconsin Ice Age," he mused. "It is dear to my heart. It predates anything historical. I can't believe I haven't been able to interest someone to set aside, protect and preserve something twice as old as the oldest bristlecone pine (until now believed to be the oldest living thing), something three times as old as the redwoods."

The find is well known to the scientific community. Vasek has had papers published about King Clone in the prestigious American Journal of Botany and other scientific publications. Ten years earlier, Vasek noted that in some areas of the desert creosote bushes grew in rings and he set out to learn if these clumps came from one seed or from several. "Using isoenzymes as genetic markers, I discovered in King Clone all of the bushes in the ring had identical genotypes, all came from the same seed," he explained.

Creosote, like humans, can be "fingerprinted." The individual bushes outside the rings all have different isoenzyme combinations. Creosote bushes, like trees, have a ring of growth each year. The living segments of King Clone are 100 to 150 years old. Vasek radiocarbondated old wood dug from within the circle and extrapolated the age of the desert shrub. He pinpointed creosote rings he had studied from aerial photographs. He had studied the bush throughout the Mojave Desert.

The harsher the environment, the older the bush. Vasek said the clonal clumps of creosote in Johnson Valley were the oldest he had discovered anywhere. Another ring half a mile from King Clone was found by Vasek to be only 9,500 years old.

"Outhouse Nate" Asaro has an acre filled with portable toilets. (Photo by Frank Q. Brown).

ODD JOBS

OUTHOUSE NATE

WHEN THE HOUSING INDUSTRY BOOMED in Southern California "Outhouse Nate" made a fortune. Nate Asaro, known to his friends as "Outhouse Nate" was in the portable toilet business. His firm, Arbor Sanitation Co., was one of the biggest in the state.

When times were good, Asaro had 1,500 portable toilets on building sites. When times were bad he had an acre filled with his outhouses waiting to be rented. Asaro was in the Navy during World War II. When he was discharged he became a butcher in Redondo Beach. But after seven years of cutting and selling meat he was ready for something else.

"I was looking for a better business to get into, something I would enjoy more, and the prospects for outhouses were great," he recalled. At first his outhouses were barn red on the outside and blushing pink inside. "As I grew older I became more conservative. I changed the colors to green inside and out," he explained.

Prices varied, the cheapest renting for $37.50 plus tax a month. "It's a state use tax. Whenever someone uses an outhouse in California they have to pay a tax. Imagine a tax just for using a toilet," Asaro sighed. He built his own portable rest rooms and rented them primarily to builders. "We rent outhouses to many other individuals and organizations as well," said Asaro. "Every year we have some out on Christmas tree lots. The Rose Parade is a good client for portable toilet companies—400 to 500 outhouses are used along the parade route.

"Portable rest rooms are put up at golf tournaments, auto races, all sorts of special events including private parties, weddings and bar mitzvahs. State law requires at least one at every building site and at least one on every other floor in high rise structures under construction." Some of the companies have personal identities stenciled on outhouses like the daisy on A & B Sanitation units accompanied by the slogan: "Clean-fresh as a daisy." Casey's Chemical Toilets are marked with a half moon for the "C" in Casey.

There is a national organization of the nation's 400 portable rest room companies called the Portable Sanitation Assn., headquartered in Washington, D.C. "We have a heck of a time at our meetings," confided Asaro. "Some hotels refuse to post the name of our organization and meeting rooms on lobby bulletin boards. They use the initials PSA instead, insisting it offends guests to see the world toilet in a hotel lobby."

My story about "Outhouse Nate" appeared in newspapers across America. Johnny Carson referred to it in one of his monologues on his popular TV show. When Nate Asaro died I delivered the eulogy. He was a close personal friend for 50 years.

CLEANING UP AMERICA

CLEMERT (BABY BOY) LEE was walking along Interstate 15 "cleaning up America" in the middle of the Mojave Desert near Zzyzx, the tiny town with a funny name. The year was 1975 and Lee, 80, was spiking empty aluminum beer and soft-drink cans tossed out of cars and trucks along the busy Los Angeles to Las Vegas freeway.

"Ain't people nasty the way they throw junk all over the roadside," Lee declared as he filled a cardboard box with cans. His wife, Grace, 72, was sitting in the family camper a half-mile down the road, guarding 15 large sacks and boxes brimming with empty cans.

"Nobody wants to hire a man my age," said Lee as he spiked another can. "This is better than sittin' at home twiddlin' my thumbs. I make $15 to $20 a day stabbin' the empties. It don't do me any good to bend over. That's why I use the stick. And, I'm not a gonna get hurt by a snake as long as I have the stick. I'd whomp any snake that comes near."

Lee said he and his wife had seen most of the West, the last couple of years, constantly on the road cleaning up the countryside. "When I was your age," the old man drawled, "I was a reporter on the *Denver Post*. I had a full life. Played sax and clarinet for a number of different orchestras. Was a court reporter for years. Worked as a guard for the Navy 15 years until the government decided I was too old."

Why does your wife call you Baby Boy? Lee was asked. "Gracie's been calling me Baby Boy all 52 years of our married life," Lee laughed. "My friends all call me that, too. It's no nickname. It's the real thing. I'll tell ya how I come by it. I played with the Army Band all during World War I. When I joined the Army I had to show my birth certificate.

"That was the hell of it. You see my name is officially Baby Boy Lee. That's all they ever called me in the Army. It was tough to take at roll calls. And, that's what I've been called ever since, Baby Boy Lee. My father was in Europe when I was born. My mother wanted to wait until he came home before she named me so the doctor put Baby Boy Lee on the birth certificate." Lee said his parents named him Clemert when his father came back from the trip. They forgot about the birth certificate until he went off to war.

The old man walked back to the camper with another load of empties. When Mrs. Lee found out her husband was accompanied by a reporter and photographer, she blurted: "Isn't that nice. My Baby Boy used to be a reporter just like you. Now he's cleaning up America. When we first started driving all over the map to pick up cans we were embarrassed someone would recognize us," she said. "But heck, the cars whiz by so fast we're just a couple of blurs along the highway."

HE RIDES THE RAILS IN A BRIGHT YELLOW BUG

FROM THE AIR it looked like a bright yellow bug creeping across the vast desert emptiness. It inched over miles of rolling sand dunes, clung to shoulders of barren mountains and spanned

"Tinker Toy" trestles. Charley (Roadrunner) Mendez had one of the loneliest jobs in the West. He was a Santa Fe Railway track supervisor, responsible for patrolling 250 miles of track in the middle of Southern California's big sand pile, the Mojave Desert.

Mendez rode the rails in his two-cylinder motor car—the bright yellow bug. He saw no roads, no cars, no houses, no towns, no people—just tracks, mountains, sand and sun. All he heard was the steady putt, putt, putt, putt of his motor car—and the quiet. He sang and whistled to himself as he rolled along.

"You got to do something to keep from going crazy," he said. "It is lonely. Real lonely out here. And at night all alone in this little motor car, it's a bear cat—especially during thunderstorms." Mendez patrolled the Santa Fe single track from Ripley and Blythe across open desert to Amboy and the mainline Los Angeles-San Francisco to Chicago tracks from Rice to Parker, Arizona. If all went well he ran a 100-mile-a-day schedule, staying overnight in a Parker motel or a house in a remote desert railroad community called Cadiz.

In emergencies, particularly during storms, the Roadrunner—as Mendez was called by fellow railroaders—troubleshooted his territory at night making sure it was safe for trains to go through. "Flash floods play hell with the tracks out here," he explained. "Rainstorms are fairly common in the high country of Turtle, Little Maria, Big Maria and Old Woman mountains. There's nothing to hold back the water on the dry slopes. It comes whooshing down over the desert floor, frequently wiping out miles of tracks. When I see dark clouds forming or get a forecast for rain, I take off in my motor car."

A six-foot antenna stuck up out of the aluminum roof of the yellow bug—Mendez's link to the outside world. He talked to engineers operating trains along his stretch of track and to dispatchers in Blythe and Parker. When he reported track was out, trains were rerouted around the trouble spots. He summoned his two section gangs, one based in Blythe, the other in Cadiz to make repairs. When high water threatened a remote trestle Mendez stood by around-the-clock to pass the word on whether it was safe.

During his patrols he traveled 10 to 20 m.p.h., always on the alert for trouble. Over the noise of his motor car and his singing he was tuned in to the sounds of the rails. "I can tell when a track is loose just by the ring," he explained. "There's a different ring when something's wrong." He slammed on the brakes when he heard or spotted trouble—

when a spike needed driving with his sledge hammer, a broken bolt needed replacement or the track was higher or lower than it should be. Minor problems he repaired. For major jobs he summoned his section gangs, pinpointing trouble by mile posts along the rails.

He was alert for all trains in the area, getting off the track by lifting his 700 pound car out of the way with handles that slid out from underneath the car. Another danger was sidewinders. "If I don't kill them, they will kill me," he said. "Sidewinders strike fast. If one strikes me, I'm sure it would be fatal. I'm so far from any help." As his car moved along lizards by the hundreds sunning themselves on the rails jumped off the track, desert hawks soared overhead and coyotes and jackrabbits scurried across desert terrain. "I like it out here. The clean air. The beautiful flowers. Everything. I like my job. I like the money." Mendez was born in the desert. His patrol passed his old one-room school, now boarded and abandoned, in Rice, population 10.

He traveled through ghost towns like Chubbuck, skirted two operating salt mines and a long-forgotten graveyard at Danby Dry Lake. It was not only one of the loneliest jobs there is but one of the hottest—under the aluminum roof of his bright yellow rail car. That's why Mendez carried a 5-gallon jug of water and had reserve water stashed all along his track. But when the air cooled and desert flowers bloomed he gathered spectacular bouquets when homeward bound for his wife and two young boys in Blythe.

WOODEN INDIANS

A SIGN ON CHIP FYN'S DOOR PROCLAIMED "It's the 1880s again!" Fyn chucked Manhattan for the California woods. He was carving "segar" store wooden Indians out of sugar pine logs in tiny Pollock Pines, 60 miles northeast of Sacramento. "That's the way we spelled cigar in the 1880s," Fyn explained.

Fyn, 36 when we bumped into him, was John Tramposch. He had been an aero-space engineer in New York City. "I was into aircraft and helicopter design. Top-notch money," said Fyn between whacks at the bigger-than-life Indian he was carving with mallet and chisel. "But it was a drag. That lasted four years. Then I went into the florist business. Business boomed. I opened up one shop, another, another. Soon I had six.

"I also had a whole bunch of people I had to pay each week. The inventory got bigger and bigger. So did the taxes. Finally I had it. I quit.

CHARLES HILLINGER

I said good-bye to Manhattan and became a free soul. I fled the East Coast and moved to the California mountains."

The carver sprouted a handlebar mustache and mutton chops to look like a typical 19th-century wooden-Indian carver. "If a guy gets older and changes into another person, it's only natural he changes his name. That's how I became Chip Fyn," he related.

He had always sculpted for fun and been a "19th Century nut. Storefront figures are a lost art," he said. "It flourished from the 1860s and died out by the turn of the century. But wooden Indians actually got started 300 years earlier, in the 1600s after Sir Walter Raleigh introduced tobacco to England from America." When steam replaced wooden ships in the mid 1800s, figurehead carvers along New York's waterfront switched to wooden Indians and other trademarks to identify shops.

"There were gunship figures and special ones for dressmakers," Fyn said. "Figures for segar stores, druggists, Yankee notions, umbrella shops, tea stores, theaters and banks. All kinds of other figures, too, like Uncle Sam, George Washington, race track touts, miners and baseball players." And Chip Fyn was carving them all. As fast as he finished one he started chipping away at another sugar pine log. It took him roughly 100 hours—two weeks—to "hack out" a wooden Indian that he sold to restaurants, businesses, private individuals—all sorts of people. Business was brisk.

Chip lived in a frame house in the forest with his family. His home was heated with a stove fired by Chip's wood chips and scraps. "You won't believe this," said Fyn as he chiseled a wrinkle in a wooden Indian's forehead, "but I often get the feeling the old-time storefront carvers are looking over my shoulder, making sure I don't let them down."

KING OF QUEEN BEES

"HONEY PUTS PEP IN YOUR STEP and I eat a lot of it," said Clarence Wenner, who was known by beekeepers around the world as the "Grand Old Man of Queen Bees." Wenner was 79 when I visited him at his "beehive" in Glenn. He was shipping 40,000 queen bees from his apiary in Northern California every year all over America, to South America, Europe. Asia, Canada and Mexico.

His queens were eagerly sought by beekeepers because of their gentle dispositions and because their hives are good honey producers. "Some queens can be nasty. They'll sting you every time," said Wenner.

"The world doesn't need nasty queen bees. Those are the kind you don't want to propagate. My queens lay there quiet. They don't fly up at you. Gentle queens are the result of years of selective breeding."

Wenner had been propagating queen bees since he was 15 some 64 years ago. During that time he had been stung thousands of times. "I get stung every day, but my stings are from workers, not from my queens," he insisted as he spotted a queen bee among thousands of worker bees, picked her up and let her crawl on his hand. As gentle as the queens are, he never permitted two queen bees to get close to one another. "They'll fight to death. One gets a vital hold on the other and then it's good-bye," he explained.

The queen bee, he related, flies from her hive on her seventh day of life and mates up to 12 times with drones, who explode and die on contact with the queen. "She never mates after that day. She'll be away from her hive about an hour, then flies directly back to her hive after mating," continued Wenner. "From the 10th day on and for the rest of her life, she produces thousands upon thousands of eggs from the sperm of those drones. She's capable of laying 3,000 eggs a day." Queen bees will live three years, while worker bees last about 40 days during a busy summer. The workers die when their wings are destroyed by friction.

"The whole story is incredible," Wenner said. "A queen can lay eight times her weight in eggs in one day. The colonies are well organized. The bees are industrious. But it is the queen who holds it all together. She is the key to the whole works." Wenner shipped his queen bees by air mail in tiny pine boxes. Accompanying the queen are half a dozen worker bees who feed and care for her during the trip. He was charging $6 for each queen when I did the interview. The beekeeper's fascination with the winged, stinging insects hadn't waned. "There's something about bees. You get your nose into a beehive and it settles you down, makes the worries go away," he mused.

CHIMNEY SWEEPS

IT WAS A SCENE RIGHT OUT OF MARY POPPINS. Thirty-two professional chimney sweeps, in top hats and tails and armed with the brushes of their trade were crawling up ladders, dancing across roof tops and dusting out the chimneys on a Hans Christian Anderson cottage in Solvang, a quaint Danish town in Santa Barbara County. It was

CHARLES HILLINGER

the annual convention of the Golden State Chimney Guild whose members come from shops with colorful names, such as, "Chim-Chim Chere," "Damper Dan," "Cinderfella," "Chim Chimney Sweep," "Mr. Chimney Cricket," "Top Hat and Brush" and on and on.

"There has been a resurgence of chimney sweeping with the energy crunch, skyrocketing fuel prices and wood fire," said Jeff Aadnessen, who with his wife, Rosie, runs the "His and Her Chimney Sweep" in Folsom.

There was a sprinkling of female sweeps among the 46 members of the statewide guild, including Suzy Howard, owner with her husband, John, of "Clean Sweep" of Petaluma. Suzy was a beauty operator before she became a sweep five years earlier. "I love it," she said. "It's like being a kid again. I get dirty and nobody cares. If I'm not dirty, I'm not doing a good job."

Dale Eberhardt had been a Red Bluff fireman 12 years. He was also sweeping chimneys on the side and was successful at it. He swept 600 chimneys the previous year. "This industry has really taken off since people started burning wood in their fireplaces to heat their homes," noted Eberhardt. "I keep fighting more and more fires caused by faulty and unsafe fireplaces. I could see the need for a chimney sweep in Red Bluff and so I went into the business."

Dean of the California Chimney Sweeps was Jerry Marx of North Hollywood who learned his trade in Germany. "Europeans believe chimney sweeps bring good luck," said Marx. "Some sweeps would walk through towns in Germany in their top hat and tails and all the girls would run up and kiss them. That got me started."

The 46 members of the California guild were also members of the National Chimney Sweep Guild headquartered in Merrimack, N.H., an organization with 800 sweeps throughout the nation. "Sweeping" is a quarterly magazine of the National Guild. As the sweeps walked over the roof tops of the convention motel for the fun of it, Don Leavitt of San Diego remarked: "The one problem with chimney sweeps is we're so formal."

The convention was held, of course, at the Chimney Sweep Inn in Solvang. "When we learned there was a motel named after our industry," said "Chimney Cricket" John Cline in his opening address, "we knew immediately Solvang was going to be the site of our convention. And, so, here we are." On that note, the sweeps all raised their brushes high over their heads and sang their theme song "Chim-Chim Chere!"

CHAPTER SIXTEEN

Virginia "Stagecoach Ginny" Fellingham loading passengers for a ride.

STILL MORE ODD JOBS

STAGECOACH GINNY

STAGECOACH GINNY held onto the reins as she drove the Wells Fargo stage down Main Street in the typical small-town, hands-in-pocket parade at the 66th annual Red Bluff Round-Up. Virginia Fellingham, aka "Stagecoach Ginny," was 64 at the time. It was her 30th year as a full-time stagecoach driver for the San Francisco-based banking company. She had driven a Wells Fargo stagecoach in more than 3,000 parades and rodeos.

Fellingham and her team of horses were as calm as the quiet sea as they headed down Main Street. She didn't scream or crack her whip or jump up and down. She had a way with her horses. The gentle tug of the lines with her sturdy hands gave the animals all the directions they needed.

"Driving a stagecoach is like playing a piano," she explained. "With the lines you have your hand on every horse. You feel each horse individually. You got to have a certain rhythm, a certain beat. The horses know me like a book. I know them." The 5-foot-4, 115-pound stagecoach driver had appeared in parades and rodeos throughout the West, at the Calgary Stampede and at President Richard Nixon's second inaugural in Washington. She had driven the stage in several Wells Fargo television commercials.

Riding shotgun beside Stagecoach Ginny in her 26th Red Bluff parade was Jay Lambert, 72, one of the nation's best-known authorities on the stagecoach and builder of nine replicas of 1860s Concord stages for Wells Fargo. Concords were the Rolls-Royces of their day, a coach Mark Twain described as "a cradle on wheels." Lambert said Fellingham "is the best stagecoach driver alive, man or woman. I'm sure she ranks among the best all-time stagecoach drivers in history."

Fellingham operated a ranch near Livermore when she wasn't driving a stagecoach. She appeared in an average of 120 parades and rodeos each year driving original stagecoaches dating to the 1860s and the replicas made by Lambert. She transported the stagecoach and horses to her appearances in a big red 55-foot truck and trailer with Wells Fargo & Co. stenciled in huge letters. To get to Red Bluff she drove the rig 210 miles from her ranch.

Her horses in the Red Bluff parade were Albert, named after Prince Albert in the tobacco can, Ellie and Nellie named after two old friends, and Lady. "I've been drivin' horses all my life. I never tire of it," Fellingham said with a big grin and bright eyes. "Why, when I was 5 on our farm in Kansas, I drove a team of horses down a lane while the rest of the family pitched corn into the wagon. I drove a horse and buggy to the one-room school I attended." She moved to California and married rancher Al (Sport) Fellingham, who died 23 years before our interview. She had a son, Paul, 36, and a daughter, Patsy, 32. Paul helped her run her ranch. Stagecoach Ginny carried on a tradition dating to 1852 when Wells Fargo was founded in San Francisco, a tradition of running the bank's stagecoaches in parades. For years, in addition to banks, Wells Fargo operated stagecoach lines throughout the West, carrying money, passengers and mail.

PAID TO WATCH TV, ALL SHE SEES IS FISH

BARBARA BOGNER was paid to watch television eight hours a day, five days a week in her hometown, Red Bluff, but all she saw was fish. "It's the most exciting thing I've ever done," she insisted.

Barbara Bogner, Carol Carpenter and Herb Myer all watched king salmon, steelhead trout, carp, shad, suckers, squawfish, lamprey and other species swim by their television screens in a trailer on the shores of the Sacramento River. At the same time three other fish counters for U.S. Fish and Wildlife Service were earning their livings watching fish swim across television screens in a trailer on the banks of the Columbia River near Portland.

They were keeping tabs on fish populations, a method conceived and put into operation for the first time anywhere at Red Bluff. Main concern was the Pacific salmon returning from the open ocean to fight its way upstream to spawn and die. "We came up with the idea of monitoring fish negotiating our two fish ladders at the Red Bluff diversion dam by using closed circuit TV," explained Dale Schoeneman, leader of the team that came up with the idea. Before television sets were installed two men were stationed at the bottom of 30-foot-deep concrete "holes" on either side of the dam adjacent to the fish ladders. "It's impossible to heat a concrete hole in the winter," said Schoeneman. "Counting fish in an air-conditioned trailer is much more comfortable."

Sven Johnson, ichthyologist, noted that the Sacramento River is the only river system on the Pacific coast where Chinook (king) salmon run year-round. The Red Bluff Diversion Dam is 190 miles north of the Sacramento River Delta. "Female salmon come up here filled with 5,000 to 6,000 eggs they distribute in redds (nests) they dig on the river bottom," explained Johnson. "When the eggs are dispersed, a male salmon fertilizes the eggs, then both female and male complete their life cycle and die."

The record count for one hour monitoring by TV was 1,101 fish. The daily record was 5,557 fish passing the dam. Most fish in a week were 14,484. For a one year period the three counters at Red Bluff recorded a total of 116,678 adult salmon over 28 inches in length, 14,593 jack salmon under 26 inches and 6,388 steelhead trout. Each day, seven days a week, counting by television was made from 6 a.m. to 10 p.m. Television cameras pick up fish swimming by windows in the concrete holes next to the fish ladders.

"There is very little movement of fish at night—less than 4% our studies show," noted Barbara Bogner. "We shut the gates at 10 p.m. and hold the few active fish back." The television fish watchers count for 50 minutes, then push a button that closes underwater steel gates holding

Charles Hillinger

the fish back for 10 minutes. "We don't even have a lunch break. We gobble our food down in one of the 10-minute rest periods," said Bogner.

DRAWBRIDGE BLUES

P EOPLE CUSS OUT HAL MENZEL every time he goes to work. Sometimes they toss beer cans and bottles at him. "It's an occupational hazard," sighed Menzel, 60, veteran drawbridge operator. Menzel was one of four operators of the Henry Ford Drawbridge leading to Terminal Island, half in Los Angeles, half in Long Beach. "People lean out their car windows and swear at us—not the bridge. They sit on their horns thinking that's going to help matters," explained Menzel, continuing: "They blame the drawbridge operator as if it's his fault a boat or ship is going by." When large ships pass through, as many as 100 cars are kept waiting as long as 25 minutes. Windows have been broken in the bridge control house by bottles tossed from cars. One night an angry motorist took a shot at a drawbridge operator. Luckily he missed. But it left a bullet hole at heart level in the window by the operator's control station.

One woman left her car, burst furiously into the control room, and whacked an operator several times over the head with her purse. The driver of a catering truck walked to the control room while the bridge was up and blurted: "Why is it every time I come this way you lower the gates and raise the bridge?" He returned to his truck, then suddenly darted back, shouting: "Now look what you did. While I was talking to you someone stole the cash box out of my truck."

The Henry Ford is one of the most famous drawbridges in America. It has appeared in scores of movies and television shows. "Every time the bridge is shown in a film or TV show there's a chase sequence with cars bursting through the gate, speeding up the part-opened bridge and flying into the drink," Menzel noted. One Emergency TV segment showed a car making it to the top of the half-open Henry Ford and winding up teetering from the end of the raised bridge. The old bridge shows its age. It creaks, groans and vibrates as it goes up and down. "She's cold and stiff in the joints, especially when it's foggy and chilly," said Menzel.

To give the bridge a rest to prolong its life after 50 years of daily ups and downs the drawbridge was given weekends off. "Pleasure boats were wearing the bridge out on Saturdays and Sundays. It was like a yo-yo on weekends—200 to 300 lifts a day," Menzel explained. So, from 6 p.m. Fridays to 6:30 a.m. Mondays the two leaves of the bridge are frozen straight up at 90 degree angles. Boats and ships whiz back and forth at will on weekends, sailing by the 200-foot-wide bridge over Cerritos Channel. Vehicular traffic was diverted to the newer and larger Commodore Heim Bridge on the Terminal Island Freeway. The Henry Ford Bridge is Southern California's only bascule (counterbalanced) bridge. Suspended from iron girders on each end of the bridge are 1,500 tons of concrete blocks.

"People get sore at us because they think we open the bridge too soon," said Menzel. "Sometimes a ship is three or four blocks away when we raise it. But we can't help that. Once a ship gives us three long blasts, up the bridge goes. We have no choice. The big ships give us the signal when they are quite a distance away because they can't stop on a dime and they want to be sure the bridge is open. We catch hell every time the bridge opens. A thin-skinned person could never hack this job..."

BACKYARD GEYSER

HOWARD CREAM AND HIS WIFE OLGA were buying their geyser on the installment plan. It's in their backyard. It erupts every 30 to 40 minutes during winter, every 40 to 50 minutes during summer. It's the only regularly spouting geyser in the state. California's "Old Faithful" is on the outskirts of Calistoga at the upper end of Napa Valley, 75 miles north of San Francisco. It rumbles, gurgles, bubbles and blasts off steam minutes before a huge column of boiling water bursts 50 to 150 feet into the air.

"Man! Look at that!" exclaimed Cream ecstatically as the geyser erupted. He marked the time down on a log he keeps during his waking hours. "Hear the power coming out of it? I taped the noise of one eruption from inception to expiration. You should hear the tape." The column of steam and water shot 80 feet into the air. A brilliant full rainbow appeared behind the towering fountain. Rainbow and blast lasted a full four minutes. Cream, an electrician, and his wife, a schoolteacher, paid $150,000 for the geyser, a house and 25 acres in 1971. They gave their life savings as down payment. "We're originally from Bridgeport, Connecticut," Cream related. "The wife and I looked all over the United States for something worthwhile to invest in.

CHARLES HILLINGER

"We believe God or some supernatural being directed us here. My God, man, we're sitting on a gigantic pool of hot water. Everywhere we dig on our 25 acres we hit scalding hot water less than 20 feet down. There's an underground river flowing over hot magma and lava beneath our property. That's why we have the geyser. Why, I could build a huge powerhouse and tap all that energy for the rest of my life."

The Creams charged $1.00 for people to come onto their property and see their geyser blow its top every half hour or so. One of the nation's geyser experts, geophysicist John S. Rinehart of Santa Fe, said he almost bought the Creams' geyser from its previous owner. "I studied it a number of times over the years," he said.

"The former owners gave me all their records of eruptions. It is a very faithful geyser. We know it has been erupting at regular intervals for at least 70 years. But I didn't buy it because you never can be too sure about geysers. They're not predictable. I wasn't sure it would keep going." If it keeps going, the Creams have a good thing. At least 30,000 people a year have been paying to view it for a long time.

CACTUS GROOMER

GILBERT H. TEGELBERG combed the long, stiff, silvery haired Old Man Cactus plants. "Watch out for the dandruff," Southern California's "Cactus King" cautioned with a grin. "I try to keep these fellows well groomed," he went on. "It's characters like these that have kept my wife, my son and me in groceries for 50 years." The Old Man Cactus was one of 1,500 species of desert plants grown by Tegelberg in three huge hot houses in the sparsely populated high desert above Lucerne Valley.

Cactophiles across America call Tegelberg the "Cactus King" because his collection is considered one of the finest. There are roughly 2,000 known species of cacti and the Tegelberg had grown nearly all of them. He is believed to have developed more hybrids than any other grower. Several cacti now owned by collectors throughout the world carry his name— plants like the *ferobergia gil tegelberg* and *mammillaria tegelbergiana*.

Collectors pay from $500 to $2,000 for one of his rare cactus plants. "I've got a few in here I wouldn't sell for any price," he allowed. The Tegelberg family at the time was one of less than 50 commercial cactus grower in California. "You know, cacti are native to the western hemisphere," said Tegelberg as he walked from table to table describing one rare plant after another. "Most species come from the tropics of Mexico, Central and South America. That's why, even though our gardens are on the desert, we grow them in hothouses under controlled atmospheric conditions. They're all so different. Look at this bishop's cap. A dead ringer for the cap bishops wear."

Stories about the "Cactus King" appear in Cactus and Succulent Society of America's journal mailed to more than 3,000 society members across the nation. British, German, Dutch and Japanese cactus society journals often carry features on his work. Cactophiles from around the world visit the Tegelberg place on a lonely desert road 130 miles northeast of downtown Los Angeles.

CHAPTER SEVENTEEN

Yolanda Delgado-Garcia, present owner of Juanito's. The original owner,
her father-in-law, Juan Gomez, was known as the Menudo King.

SOUP & TORTILLAS

500 GALLONS OF SOUP EVERY SUNDAY

THERE'S BEEN A SOUP LINE on the east side of Los Angeles for years. Nothing to do with the economic situation. It's the menudo. People come from miles around—from as far away as Long Beach and Santa Ana—to stand in line with empty soup pans. They start lining up shortly before 6 a.m. each Sunday waiting for Juan M. Gomez to open his small corner stand in a quiet residential neighborhood at 4160 Floral Drive, East Los Angeles. Menudo is a Sunday morning breakfast tradition with most Mexican-American families in Southern California.

It's a unique soup—or stew—made of the light-colored, rubbery lining of a cow's stomach (tripe), a calf's foot, white hominy, plus a fiery blend of spices, including garlic, chiles, onions and oregano.

Scores of tiny food stands in Mexican-American neighborhoods feature menudo on Saturday and Sunday mornings. Juanito's, owned and operated by Juan Gomez and his wife, Cleo, is particularly popular. Every Sunday morning Juanito, as everyone calls Gomez, sells upwards of 500 gallons of his soup to as many as 1,000 customers who line up outside his small stucco establishment.

"I open at 6 o'clock Sunday morning and stay open as long as the menudo lasts—usually about three hours," explains Gomez. But why do the crowds drive so far when they could buy menudo at food stands much closer to home? "Lots of other places sell menudo," concedes Manual Villalobos of Monterey Park, one of the first in line on a recent Sunday. "Near my house there are three different stands selling menudo in one block alone. But the flavor isn't the same as Juanito's."

Villalobos has been driving 24 miles round-trip every Sunday morning for five years just to buy a pot of menudo for his family. "There are twelve in our house—eight kids, my wife, my mother and my aunt and myself. We all love menudo from the littlest baby on up. Every Sunday we have menudo and French rolls for breakfast. And, I'm a cook myself. I earn my living cooking. Sure I can make menudo, but not like Juanito. Nobody makes menudo like Juanito."

Gomez explains the reason for his popularity: "My wife taught me everything I know about making menudo and tamales. And Cleo's mother taught her everything she knows about cooking." He also sells 12,000 homemade tamales from the small stand each week. He cooks the menudo in big 20 gallon pots for six hours before the big Sunday morning rush. To thousands of Mexicans in Southern California, Juanito Gomez is the Sunday Morning Menudo King.

TORTILLA QUEEN

H ELEN LUGO oversees the making of 1,320,000 tortillas a day. She's Los Angeles' Tortilla Queen. "Never in my wildest dreams did I ever think I would be making so many tortillas," the 62-year-old Mexican-American community leader said. She was founder-president and 51% owner of the city's largest tortilla factory, El Dorado, in Lincoln Heights.

When we visited Helen Lugo on Cinco de Mayo—a big Mexican holiday—she was busier than ever filling orders. "More tortillas are consumed in Los Angeles than in any other city in the world outside Mexico City," she noted. Los Angeles County has more than 2 million Mexican-Americans. "But it isn't only Mexicans. Anglos, blacks, Chinese, Japanese—everybody in LA eats tortillas," said the Tortilla Queen.

Mrs. Lugo and her 75 employees were producing 1.2 million corn tortillas and 120,000 flour tortillas every day of the week. And, El Dorado was but one of 400 tortilla factories in the Los Angeles area.

Bernardo Gutierrez, vice president of El Dorado, and Luis Fonseca, treasurer and sales manager, estimate that there are in excess of 12.5 million tortillas sold in Los Angeles every day. The other corporate owner of the big tortilla factory is Alice Salazar, Mrs. Lugo's sister. Many tortilla factories are small, neighborhood, family operations. That's how the Tortilla Queen started 30 years ago—in a modest way, making a few dozen of the thin unleavened tortillas in a little "around the corner" shop.

Her factory grew and grew and grew as more and more Angelenos came to enjoy Mrs. Lugo's tortillas."The secret of El Dorado's success is the quality and flavor of Helen's tortillas," noted Luis Fonseca. "Even in something as simple as tortillas made of corn, water and a little lime, a method of preparation makes a difference."

Tons of high quality shelled large kernel California white corn are purchased by the tortilla factory each month. The corn is cooked in huge vats for three hours, then ground into dough on stones called metates. The metates are imported from Mexico.

Every day trucks from Mrs. Lugo's factory make deliveries through-out the city—plus a fleet of 100 independent jobbers who pick up "the bread of Mexico" and deliver hot tortillas in their small trucks. Hundreds walk, drive or take the bus to the big tortilla factory in Lincoln Heights every day to buy packages of tortillas "hot off the griddle."

"Most Mexican-Americans eat an average of a dozen tortillas a day, a family of four will consume about 50, a family of eight about 100," according to Fonseca. Tortillas are eaten in an endless number of ways—plain with melted butter or melted cheese, as tacos, tostadas, quesadillas, enchiladas and as part of many other Mexican dishes.

CHAPTER EIGHTEEN

Frank "King of the Windmills" Medina (left) in his yard full of windmills, with author Hillinger. (Photo by Con Keyes).

OF WINDMILLS, GOATS, A SKINFLINT'S MEMORIAL, AND A "MOLE"

KING OF THE WINDMILLS

"I CUT MY TEETH ON THESE SUCKERS," shouted Frank Medina over the raucous symphony of squawking, squeaking, spinning windmills. Medina, 73 when we caught up with him, called himself "King of the Windmills" and had 102 of them in his front yard on the outskirts of Stockton to prove it.

"I have been nuts about windmills since I was a kid. I love to hear them go around. I love to sit and watch them spin," he said. "This is something relatively new with me. I just started collecting windmills eight years ago. This is just the beginning. I hope to fill my 20 acres with at least 2,000 windmills before I die."

Medina's life hadn't always been filled with windmills. "I worked my butt off bailin' hay for 66 years," he explained. "Now I'm takin' it easy watching windmills." He was running ads in rural newspapers throughout the Midwest looking for windmills. "It ain't a cheap hobby," he confided. "I've spent over $50,000 buying up the old windmills you see here. But it's worth it. It gives people something to talk about. People drive by my place out here in the country and can't believe their eyes. Never again will they see anything like this."

Medina was once mentioned in "Ripley's Believe It of Not," but not for his windmills—for his teeth. The old hay bailer had all of his own teeth, including his wisdom teeth, never had a cavity. Never been to a dentist. He attributed this marvel to "exercising my teeth by squeezing them together, drinking a gallon of milk a day, chewing on bones and never smoking."

His oldest windmill was made in 1874. Most of the others were out of the 1920s and 1930s. Many were riddled with bullet holes. All were on stub towers. "Farmers used to buy them on stub towers," he explained. "Then farmers would put on legs to whatever height they desired." Some windmills were bent, rusted and beat up when he bought them. Some were in tip-top shape. None was newer than 40 years. Just about every windmill on his front lawn had a bird nest. "Most of the time I keep these suckers tied down so they don't spin. I untie them on special occasions. I don't want them to wear themselves out," he observed.

Verrill Fell, 76, of Wellington, Nevada, stopped by Medina's house during the interview to look over the collection. "Are ya usin' all the water you're pumpin'?" asked Fell with a quizzical look. "Naw, none of 'em are pumpin' water," replied Medina with a sparkling grin. "These windmills are out-to-pasture, retired windmills. You're lookin' at nothin' like you never seen nowhere before, no how," Frank Medina, "The Windmill King" told the old-timer from Wellington.

GOAT LADY IN THE VALLEY OF GIANT REDWOOD STUMPS

IN RUGGED NORTH COAST BLUFFS within sound of the sea lies the Valley of the Giant Redwood Stumps—home of California's "goat lady." To get to Grace Bauder's place, near Trinidad, you drive a winding dirt road through miles of enormous redwood stumps—remnants of a forest of 2,000-year-old cathedral-like trees felled by lumbermen at the turn of the 20th century. When we met Grace Bauder she had been grazing goats on her 361 acres for 31 years.

She was 77 then and had tended thousands of goats among the redwood stumps over the years. Her herd numbered more than 200. Married twice, the white-haired goat lady was divorced from her first husband, widowed from her second 25 years.

How can you stand living out here all alone, friends have asked. Why don't you find yourself a man and marry again? "If I were to find a man," she replied, "who would stand on a stack of Bibles as high as one of my redwood stumps and swear my billy goats smell like a rose, I might consider." Then she added: "I'm never going to get another man. I'm not looking for one. When my goats talk back to me I don't know what they say. They know what I say when I say get out of here. Goats have more personality, are truer than human beings. They won't try to do you any harm. They come to you when you call them." She had a name for each goat and summoned them in her high-pitched voice.

"If my goats go to chasing around, I can tie them up, shut them up. What'cha gonna' do with a husband?" she asked. "If one of my goats gets sick, I can doctor him. If a goat dies, I bury him. What would you do with a man? Look at the funeral expenses."

Grace had raised goats ever since she was a girl of 4 in the tiny town of Rohnerville, south of Eureka. She had lived in Humboldt County all her life. "I don't have to do this—to feed and care for these goats," she said. "I get sufficient money to live on from property rentals I have. This is my hobby. I enjoy being around these animals."

She milked her herd by hand and sold the milk as well as goat butter and goat cheese. She clipped wool from her angoras twice a year. "Santa Claus whiskers and women's wigs are made of mohair, you know," she said. "There's a big demand for goat meat. Italians, Mexicans, Spanish and Greeks are fond of goat meat." She said she couldn't keep up with demands for goat milk.

For Grace Bauder, a petite 5 foot 1 inch in height, there was no fear in living alone. "When we bought this place in the redwood stumps, it was alive with bobcats. They killed the goats, chickens, everything. Humboldt County had a bounty on bobcats at the time—$2.50 a skin. That was a lot of money in those days. In a little over two years I

CHARLES HILLINGER

trapped and killed 330 bobcats. Killed five bears on my property during the same time."

She lived in a rough-hewn home she built and expected to be running her goats in the Valley of the Giant Redwood Stumps for years to come. "I saw a doctor in town last week," she confided. "He said I was tough as nails—said if I didn't meet up with an accident or fall off a roof, I should last another 20 years or more. As long as I am able to take care of my goats, I'll be sittin' in here with the stumps."

THE OLD SKINFLINT

A 68-FOOT OBELISK rising out of fields of tomatoes and bell peppers on a huge farm in Tuttle, a Central California hamlet, is a mystery to hundreds of motorists who pass it every day. The granite shaft stands on a massive concrete base containing 13 steps on each of four sides. Carved in the side of the obelisk are two decorative scrolls and the inscription: "George Hicks Fancher, Born New York State February 9, 1828. Died in California March 30, 1900." Who was Fancher? Is he buried under the obelisk? Why is a monument out there in the middle of the tomatoes and bell peppers? To get the answers to these questions and more, motorists on their way to and from Yosemite National Park on California 140 often turn to Janice Brooklin, who runs Jan's Market, a country store across the highway, and has lived in Tuttle (population 20) east of Merced all of her life. Her mother, Jennie Earl, who died in 1987 at age 99 knew Fancher.

This is what Janice Brooklin had to say about the mystery monument: "Mr. Fancher was a wealthy banker and farmer who owned all the land for miles around. Mom told us that when Mr. Fancher died all kinds of stuff he valued as part of his life was buried with him under his monument, like the limbs of fruit trees, books and his favorite furniture."

Catherine Julien, historian and director of the Merced County Courthouse Museum, maintains a file of old newspaper clippings reporting Fancher's death and the 10-year court battle over the $25,000 he left for "proper interment of my remains in a suitable monument." "George Hicks Fancher was not a big spender during his lifetime," noted Julien. "He had a reputation of being a skinflint who scrounged away his money and spent little on himself. The obelisk is his monument to himself."

Fancher had come to California from upstate New York in 1850 to prospect for gold. He was a gold miner for six years, farmed in Stockton for 13 years, then moved to Merced in 1869, where he amassed a fortune as a farmer and banker. Never married, Fancher left an estate valued at $608,000 when he died at age 72. Except for the money for his memorial, he left it all to 17 heirs—brothers, sisters, nephews and nieces.

After Fancher's death, a local school teacher, Robert Gracey, filed suit to stop erection of the monument and calling for using the $25,000 instead to build a public library in Merced. The teacher saw a library as a more fitting tribute to the pioneer. But Fancher's heirs said no—the money had to be used to build the monument he requested.

It took 10 years and two trips to the appellate courts before the heirs were finally granted permission to build the obelisk. When completed in 1911, Fancher's fanciful legacy was reportedly the largest tomb for an individual in California. Fancher established a $1,000 trust in his will, the earnings of which were to be used for care and maintenance of the monument. The remaining descendants of Fancher's brothers and sisters have no interest in maintaining it, so the task of administering the trust fund has fallen to an attorney in San Jose, Robert Loehr, who took over the job from an attorney friend who died. Loehr would just as soon do without the honor. He would like to present the trust to an individual or group in Merced County to take care of the tomb. So far he has no takers.

"The earnings from the $1,000 trust fund are only enough to pay property taxes for the acre on which the monument stands," explained the attorney. "A historical society in Merced County or some similar group would be ideal to take it over. But I've had no takers. Everyone is concerned about liability and maintenance. There is no insurance. The trust is so small it cannot afford it. The whole matter is a bit bizarre," he admitted.

Historian Julien said Merced County Courthouse Museum would be pleased to be caretakers of the monument. But concerns about the cost and liability prevent that. "It's wonderful. I love it. I only wish we could do it," sighed Julien. "The monument is a big mystery to most people. We get calls all the time asking what it means," mused the historian. "It would be nice if there was a plaque on it explaining who Fancher was and that he left a big chunk of money to build the monument to himself."

HUMAN MOLE

AN ITALIAN IMMIGRANT spent 40 years living a mole-like existence beneath Fresno. With pick and shovel, Baldasare Forestiere created a 10-acre subterranean maze of curving passageways, rooms, courtyards, patios and grottos beneath the surface of his property.

"During his lifetime he was ridiculed and called the Human Mole," recalled Baldasare's nephew, Ricardo Forestiere, a Fresno schoolteacher. "His family tried to get him to stop his digging. And when he died they wanted no part of his caverns." The family, Ricardo said, wanted to destroy the tunnels and more than 100 underground rooms that had been created. "Uncle Baldasare and his underground diggings were an embarrassment to them," he explained.

Forestiere, who died in 1946 at the age of 67, left no will. But he left a fortune in real estate, including more than 1,000 choice acres of rich California farmland. "My father was the closest relative to Uncle Baldasare," related Ricardo. "My father did not understand his brother's obsession, but he admired his work. He agreed to accept the caverns as his share of the estate. The other relatives gladly let my father have the 10 acres and Uncle Baldasare's diggings."

Forestiere migrated to America from Messina, Sicily, in 1902 when he was 23. He worked in the subways and tunnels of New York before moving to Fresno. He began building his own tunnels in 1906. First he dug living quarters, then a room where he made wine and a vault where he aged cheese and cured meats. He built a chapel, then grottos, then a whole series of tunnels and rooms. One room is a gigantic auditorium, 100 feet long, 50 feet wide with a 25-foot ceiling.

In the ceiling of his rooms he dug skylights out of the hard bedrock for ventilation. He fashioned glass lids to keep out the rain. Forestiere's graceful symmetric arches and curved passageways were reinforced with tons of bricks, built in three levels at some places and as deep as 25 feet. He planted orange, tangerine, grapefruit, lemon and lime trees in his underground courtyards. The trees flourish to this day, producing fruit each season, their branches reaching to the surface out of deep holes.

"I remember when I was much younger and Uncle Baldasare was still alive, my father would worry about him after not seeing him for several days," Forestiere's nephew recalled. "Dad and I would go into my uncle's underground maze and start looking for him. It was easy to get lost. We would look with a lantern. Father would holler out his name—'Balde! Balde!' 'Hey, over here!' Uncle Baldasare would shout back. And we would find him busy at work late at night."

For five years after Forestiere died, his estate was in litigation and the underground diggings were unattended. "There were many stories all over Fresno that my uncle had buried a fortune in money somewhere in the tunnels or in one of the rooms," said Ricardo. "To this day people claim they have it on good authority my uncle buried anywhere from $100,000 to $500,000 in cash somewhere down here underground."

CHAPTER NINETEEN

*Statue of Eiler Larsen, Laguna Beach's
beloved town greeter.*

TOWN CHARACTERS

THE GREETER

FOR MORE THAN A QUARTER OF A CENTURY Eiler Larsen, a native of Denmark, was Laguna Beach's official greeter. The bearded six footer would wave his cane and shout greetings to every passing vehicle driving the busy coastal highway through the quaint, picture-postcard beach community. "Hello-O-O o-o-o! How AR-R-R-r-r you?" he yelled, his eyes flashing as he pointed his cane at each car. Nearly everyone waved back. Many women would blow kisses at the old man in a red coat.

We did a story on Eiler Larsen when he was 77. He was one of the most photographed and painted persons in the nation. Millions waved and shouted back at him in the 1940s, 1950s and 1960s. When he failed to appear at his usual corners in town, hundreds driving through Laguna Beach would stop to inquire about him. "Is the greeter sick?

Did he die?" they would ask. Once he was missing for several weeks, recovering from a lung ailment. "I happen to have a tremendous voice," said Eiler. "It's from shouting too much."

Eiler Larsen was to Laguna Beach what Bernard Baruch was to Central Park. Though he wasn't a philosopher sought by Presidents, he was a friendly character standing on the sidewalk in the heart of the art colony. People sought him out. Today there are several statues and many paintings in stores and prominent places in Laguna Beach honoring the memory of the greeter.

One year the people of Laguna Beach contributed nickels, dimes and dollars for an eight-week trip for Eiler to his hometown, Aarhus, Denmark, which he hadn't seen in 54 years. Eiler was one of the featured attractions of Copenhagen's 800th anniversary. He shared a platform with Denmark's then Prime Minister Jens Otto Krag.

When Eiler Larsen was hungry he would walk into any Laguna Beach restaurant and eat heartily. There was never a tab. He had a rent-free room at the plush Hotel Laguna. "Eiler is Mr. Laguna Beach," explained Bob Nielsen, owner of the hotel, like Eiler, a Dane by birth. "He has no money and at the same time no need for money. There is a committee in the community that looks after Eiler. He is loved by Lagunans."

"His whole purpose in life is to greet people, to bring a little joy into their lives," noted Nielsen. "I am always ready for adventure," Eiler said. "Every day is an adventure to me. I see many old friends and meet new ones. I have a God given gift that few men have ever had. I am The Greeter! When I was 19 I decided I wanted to get far away, as far away as I could get from my home in Denmark. I signed a contract to roam the Siberian countryside buying butter for a Danish company. For three years I lived and worked 24 hours from the Manchurian border."

Then he returned home for military service in the Danish army. After that he took a ship to South America, hiring on as a gymnastic instructor in Chile. He shipped out to America, joining the U.S. Army and fought in Germany in World War I, where an exploding shell injured his leg. He enrolled at Gustavus Adolphus College in St. Peter, Minnesota. "I am an educated man, well read, up to date on happenings here, there and everywhere," said Eiler.

He worked as a bank messenger on Wall Street, but his wanderlust led him out of the city to the Appalachian Trail and a 2,000-mile trek from Maine to Georgia with a dog named Happy. He tried being a greeter in the nation's capital, in San Francisco, and in Palm Springs but was run out of each place. He picked fruit up and down the San Joaquin Valley, became a gardener in Laguna Beach and in 1942 began waving to passing motorists from lawns and flower patches. "I settled in Laguna because it reminds me of Denmark," he said.

After a few months of shouting: "Haloo-oo-oo," "Delighted to see you," "Are you alive?" "Do you speak English?" in his booming, building-shaking voice, a group of townspeople wanted him removed from the sidewalks as a nuisance. But Eiler continued to shout and wave. In 1959 at a jammed-packed session of City Council, Mayor Jesse Riddle demanded Eiler be silenced. A poll by the local paper spared the Greeter. It showed 88% of the people wanted Eiler to stay. On a special day set aside to honor Eiler Larsen in Laguna Beach in 1967 when he was 77, Mayor William Martin named him official greeter as long as he lived. The Marine Band from El Toro saluted the bearded, red-coated Dane at the town's tribute to its beloved Greeter.

STREET SWEEPER

GEORGE (STREET SWEEPER) McPHERSON had been sweeping the streets of Guerneville, the Russian River village, day-in and day-out, for 16 years, "for the enjoyment"—without ever having asked for compensation. McPherson was 84 when we met him in Guerneville. Three years earlier town leaders decided their street sweeper ought to be paid something—at least to show the community's appreciation. And ever since McPherson had been receiving $70 a year from village general funds for keeping the town spotless. That figures out to about 19 cents a day. Street Sweeper McPherson was spending five to six hours a day, seven days a week on the job.

"I'm repenting for my sins," said McPherson with a laugh. "I really raised hell when I was young." Then he added with a twinkle in his eyes: "Supposin' you look at it this way. Anything that helps humanity is on God's side. Guerneville has been good to me. I don't see why I can't be good to the town." Guerneville, population 2,200, is in the heart of Sonoma County's redwood country.

McPherson was born in San Francisco, lived there until he was 52. "The political rot of San Francisco brought me up here," the old street sweeper said, explaining: "One day I got fed up with the filthy streets in my neighborhood. I proceeded to sweep up the dirt and debris. What the hell do you think I got? Thanks? Not on your life. A half dozen cops. Somebody called the police, said some crackpot was burnin' up the neighborhood. I wasn't burnin' it up. I was cleanin' it up. Burnin' the neighborhood trash in a vacant lot. That did it. If that's what San Francisco wants, I thought to myself, then to hell with San Francisco. I came up here."

McPherson, a lifelong machinist and painter, moved 70 miles north to the little town of Guerneville. He voluntarily started sweeping streets and sidewalks in Guerneville much to the surprise and delight of townspeople. In addition to the $70 a year for keeping the village clean, he also received his monthly Social Security check. "I'm what you would call an individualist," the old man said, as he rested an arm on his beat up pickup truck after tossing in a dustpan full of debris. "Don't belong to any organizations of any kind whatsoever—political, religious, union or educational. I don't belong to nothin'. I stick on the Bible from Genesis to Revelations." McPherson had been married twice.

"Both wives left me," said the street sweeper. "I blame the damn politicians. The whole scene for years has been one of the politicians milking the five appetites—stomach, greed, sex, religion, pride. Politicians are turning all of us into cows to be milked for their benefit. Look what they're doin' with sex. In 1920 they gave women the vote. Hell, you know what's happened since. Politicians should read Genesis 3:16. The part where God told woman her place in life." The old street sweeper quoted Genesis 3:16: "To the woman He said: Your desire shall be for your husband. And he shall rule over you."

A Highway Patrol car passed by. Two officers honked and yelled: "Hi, George." "They always salute me," said McPherson. "Everybody honks and waves. Oh, the people in this town are good. Look at this truck. Harry Leras, owner of Harry's Garage gave it to me. Whenever it needs fixin', Harry takes care of it, no charge to me. Women give me special fixin's. Bake me pies and cakes. There are many good women in the world, especially the ones that know their place," he winked.

The street sweeper brushed dirt from his glasses on his grimy trousers. "Damn dirty job," he allowed. "No sense for a man working in dirt every day to bathe—but I do once every week or so. You wouldn't think an educated person would sweep streets. But never judge a book by its cover. I went all through university—correspondence courses.

Mostly studied personal magnetism. Hell, I went into everything. General education they called it. Never did get a sheepskin. My house burned up a few weeks ago," he went on. "Guerneville people took up a collection to buy me a new mobile home. How about that? Do you think anything like that would have happened if I'd stayed in Frisco. Hell no! I'd been tossed in the clink years ago for tryin' to help humanity."

THE TOWN COMMUNIST

I T WAS NOT BECAUSE THOMAS JEFFERSON SCRIBNER, 82, was an avowed Communist that his statue graced the Santa Cruz city park. The plaque on the statue showing a wizened old man wearing a derby and playing a musical saw simply said, "Sawplayer."

There is no mention of Scribner being a revolutionary. "It should identify me as a Communist. Everyone in town knows my politics," insisted the old man. The year was 1981. The Soviet Union was still going full blast.

Everyone in Santa Cruz knew Scribner as the character in the derby who for 20 years had played the musical saw in the city mall supporting himself with donations dropped into his tin cup by passers-by. "I believe we should overthrow this clique of imperialist bandits who now run the works before they get us all blown to kingdom come in a war," proclaimed Scribner in his latest flyer. "Most people in town are fond of old Tom," said Neal Coonerty, 35, bookstore owner. "They close their eyes to the fact that he is a card-carrying Communist. Maybe it's because of his age. It might be a different story if he were younger. He is less threatening now."

"Aw, hell," allowed Scribner. "Most folks regard me as a harmless old crackpot, a bothersome old bastard. They don't take me serious. But I am serious. There's no escaping communism. The whole world will be Communist in time. I've been a left-winger all my life. When I was 15 I joined the Wobblies (the Industrial Workers of the World). I joined the Communist Party in 1928. Joe Stalin was my hero then and still is today."

Despite his age, Scribner did have his detractors. Many were unhappy about the statue put up in 1978. "We get complaints from people wondering how a Communist rates a statue in the city park right across from the town clock," said deputy police chief, Keith Duel.

"I don't like it at all. I'm embarrassed about it. That statue is there by accident," claimed Mayor Joseph J. Ghio, 42, an iris hybridizer by profession. The mayor contended the city arts commission ramrodded the statue through the City Council as part of a package deal calling for various art projects. "Once the statue was up it was too late. The fundamental issue has been is the statue a work of art? Are we going to censor art?"

Scribner worked in logging camps most of his life and was a Communist organizer. "I've been beat up, jailed and run out of town. I've had more fun," he chuckled. Some said he ought to be deported. "Where the hell would they deport me? I was born in Michigan."

His business card identified him as "sawplayer, revolutionary, lumberjack emeritus, writer, publisher, editor, veteran, union organizer, columnist, sex symbol and statue." "I added sex symbol because I posed nude for a 1982 calendar," said the old Red. A picket sign in his hotel room warned: "Stop U.S. Intervention Everywhere."

Stanley Ragsdale, age 10, (with cap) in front seat of Model T used to bus kids 52 miles each way across the desert to school. (Photo courtesy S. Ragsdale).

FIVE HAMLETS

TURN-BACK-THE-CLOCK TOWN

IN MANY WAYS DESERT CENTER, a wide spot in the middle of nowhere, is still in the 1930s. The Desert Center Café has its same old repainted Great Depression-days sign, copied from an Albers flapjack flour package. It's a silhouette of a burro, an old prospector sitting on a stump holding a frying pan over an open fire with an old-fashioned coffeepot next to the blaze, with the desert and twin peaks in the background.

The café looks the same as pictures taken of it in 1932, a wrap-around counter with swivel seats, plain dining tables and chairs, a fireplace, a wall full of photos taken in Desert Center in the 1920s and 1930s. An original 1934 Desert Center calendar hangs on a wall with this message: "Main Street 100 miles long. God knows you need us. Free room and board every day that the sun doesn't shine at Desert

Center." A faded 1932 Ford flyer tacked to another wall shows photographs and prices of that year's new line of cars including a standard coupe ($490), a sport coupe ($535) and a station wagon ($600).

Next to the café is a lineup of no-longer-used, 1930s-dust-covered gas pumps in front of the old, no-longer-used Desert Center Gas Station & Garage. This place is a page out of the past. That's the way Stanley Ragsdale wants to keep it. "People blame me for retarding progress. My question is, what's progress?" said the red-faced, silver-haired, 75-year-old owner of downtown Desert Center.

Signs proclaim "Population 120" at the Interstate 10 turnoffs to Desert Center, 60 miles of open desert and mountains east of Indio, 50 miles of the same west of Blythe. The turnoffs lead to the café, a general store, an old-fashioned hot-dog and hamburger stand, a modern gas station all owned and operated by Ragsdale, who also owns the local post office. A two-mile stretch of land straddling the interstate belongs to Ragsdale.

Ragsdale's property is half a mile wide. "People have been telling me for years that if I build a motel, a bigger and better restaurant, a couple of fast-food places, Desert Center will boom. They say I'm sitting on top of a gold mine with all that interstate traffic constantly whooshing by," he related. Ragsdale sat in his 1930s office under a bumper sticker that read: "Desert Center. Where God Rested."

On a wall hung a photo of seven boys and girls piled into a 1919 Model T touring car with running boards and a crank hanging down under the radiator. "I'm the one in the front seat with the cap," he said. "That was the Desert Center school bus in 1925. My brother drove us 52 miles each way to Thermal and back across the desert. We were never late or missed a day."

His mother and father founded Desert Center in 1921, where two ruts passing through served as a road. His father opened a garage that first year. When cars met, one had to pull off to a side to let the other pass. Frequently his father, "Desert Steve" Ragsdale, had to pull vehicles out of sand. The road was finally paved in 1930 and became U.S. 60 and, years later, Interstate 10. "Mama opened the restaurant in 1922. Desert Center Café has never missed a day of being open in all that time. Since 1928 it has been open around the clock," noted Ragsdale.

He never leaves town. "I never go anywhere. Why should I? I love the desert. I know this country like the back of my hand. No one

CHARLES HILLINGER

knows it better than me. The last time I was in L.A. was 20 years ago, Vegas, 30 years ago, Phoenix, five years ago. I need to be here to run the businesses." His face is red with skin cancer. "The ultraviolet from the hot sun gets me," he said. "People ask me how I stand it out here in the 100-to-120 temperatures in the summer. I tell them I enjoy the heat. "If they're from the Midwest or East I ask them how do you stand it back there in that awful cold, the blizzards, the tornadoes, the floods and all the rest of what you get."

BACKWARD VILLAGE

To THE FEW FAMILIES LIVING IN THE HAMLET OF RADEC nestled in the Agua Tibia (Lukewarm Water) Mountains, being backward is the town's claim to fame. "Even the name of this place is backward," said David Welch, a town father. "We wanted to be Cedar, California, but we're Radec." The name came years ago when this quiet village 100 miles southeast of Los Angeles in Riverside County was given a post office. Townspeople at the time gathered to decide on a suitable name. "Up until we got the post office," explained Vivian McGaugh, "we were nameless. When someone asked where do you live? People from here would always say, 15 miles up the road from Temecula."

At the town meeting called to give the hamlet a name, everybody agreed on Cedar. No one remembers exactly why because there aren't any cedar trees for miles around. The Post Office Department, however, turned down the name as there already was a Cedar, California. "We couldn't think of anything else we'd rather be called, so we spelled Cedar backwards and we've been Radec ever since," said Mrs. A.E.Bergman. People called her by her initials "A.E." instead of her first name. There was so little business at the post office that after a couple of years it was discontinued.

A controversy has raged ever since the town was named and it is heard regularly in Radec's two business establishments, Bartons and Coffers Corner, saloons across the road from each other. "I call it Ray-deck," insisted Vivian McGaugh. "It's Rah-deck," said Irene Barton Welch, proprietor of Barton's General Store and Saloon. Six other Radecans in the tavern joined in the friendly dispute, which all agree never will be resolved. Asked to name some of the outstanding features of Radec, Irene Welch with a quizzical look on her face, thought for a while, then replied: "You got me stumped. I can't think of a thing." Her husband mentioned the ranches in Radec Valley, but remarked: "To be truthful about it, farming up here isn't much. A celebrity owned one of the ranches years ago, Frank Morgan, the actor. But he's dead. Fact is there's more people in the Radec Cemetery than alive in Radec and there ain't many buried here either."

"Who stops in this town?" Welch was asked. "You did," said Welch, adding sadly: "To tell the truth you're the first one in quite a spell. We hadn't seen an outsider for days. Radec isn't much. No sidewalks. No streetlights. At night the place is so dark those goin' through don't even know they've been here. But there's no smog. There's a lot of quiet. Our TV reception up here in the hills is good."

Because there were no "city limit" signs approaching town, Clinton Davidson posted six huge RADEC signs strung from clothes lines around his old frame house. "I want people passing through to know they've been to the most backward town in America," he declared.

HAUNTED HAMLET

EVERY HALLOWEEN, as well as other times, someone hears the ghost of Rebecca Dorrington rattling around the 1853 hotel in the Mother Lode hamlet named after her.

Tiny Dorrington is in Ebbetts Pass in the High Sierra. Villagers believe the reason Rebecca Dorrington's ghost causes a stir from time to time has something to do with the way she met her end. Some claim she ventured out of the hotel on a blustery winter night making her way through deep snowdrifts to fetch something in a barn. They say she never made it back—that she froze to death. "I've always heard Rebecca was massacred by Indians," maintained Bobbie Lawler. "Old-timers tell me she fell down a flight of stairs in the hotel and bled to death," allowed Carl Sorenson. "I do believe Rebecca actually died from pneumonia sometime late in the 1860s or early 1870s," said Mrs. Leonard Anderson.

Rebecca's ghost is supposed to be responsible for all sorts of mischief at the Dorrington Hotel. Doors are supposed to fly open and bang shut, lights flash on and off, and old furniture in the attic, according to some of the stories, is constantly being shifted about by Rebecca's ghost.

The hotel was built by John Gardner, a homesteader, in 1853.

Gardner was a native of Scotland. After living in the Mother Lode country for several years, he went back to Scotland to claim Rebecca Dorrington as his bride. They made their home in the hotel. Ed Wilson, whose late wife, Rebecca Gardner Wilson, was a great-granddaughter of Rebecca Dorrington, debunks all the stories about the ghost. "A bunch of damn fools, drunks and historians made up all that poppycock," he insists. But he is unable to clarify the circumstances surrounding her death. "We never knew how she died," Wilson conceded.

One of those who doubts stories about Rebecca's ghost is Mrs. Dan Jordan. "Oh, they're always talking about seeing her figure in the window, hearing her ghost creeping around the attic," said Mrs. Jordan who has lived in the area 50 years. "Some years ago a woman managing the hotel came running over to my place. She said Rebecca's ghost was in the hotel. She wanted me to come along to see if we could see the ghost. We didn't see anything, of course, but there was a handprint on a kitchen table. The woman insisted it was Rebecca's handprint. It looked like the paw print of a large squirrel to me, but I couldn't convince her. People believe what they want to believe." Leonard Anderson, who had owned the hotel 13 years, said when there's nothing else to talk about villagers "use Rebecca's ghost to spice up the conversation."

"That ancient sugar pine hotel is so old it squeaks like 40 people walking around in it half the time," he related. "I know it's spooky and I've heard some weird noises over the years. But I'd hate to have anybody think I believe in ghosts." The Dorrington Hotel has but 10 rooms, a tiny restaurant and a bar. For years there was a sign in the restaurant that read: "Coffee 15 cents an hour." That was a long time ago when 15 cents would be more like 75 cents today. Room rates then were $4.50 one night, $3 if you stayed more than one night, $2 a night if you stayed at least a week. When people say they see the ghost of Rebecca Dorrington staring out one of the windows in the hotel, they say she's wearing a calico dress. They always say she's wearing a calico dress.

HALLELUJAH!

HAROLD STOY stepped away from the bar momentarily to answer the phone. "Hello. This is Hallelujah No. 1," declared Stoy. "She's not here. You've got the wrong number. You want Hallelujah No. 4."

Stoy returned to the bar and addressed himself to the minister waiting to talk to him. The minister said a town with a name like Hallelujah "ought to have a church not a bar." "It's just a name, reverend," allowed Stoy. "It goes way back in history. We're not using the Lord's name in vain or anything like that." Happens all the time, Stoy remarked after the minister left. "Shakes them up a bit."

This, the only Hallelujah in America as far as Stoy knows, is a dozen ranches and a gas station-bar-restaurant-motel 23 miles northwest of Reno on U.S. Highway 395. Hallelujah boasts one of the longest—and one of the bumpiest—landing strips in the country—the old Feather River Highway abandoned in 1954. "It's listed on all the sectionals (airplane maps)," said Stoy. His father opened a tiny gas station and café here in 1932. "Fliers are always touching down here. Guess they think it's the promised land," he laughed, "or headquarters for a religious sect. We've been calling it the Hallelujah International Airport ever since a bunch of Mexicans flew in here a few years ago."

Stoy has been owner-operator of the Hallelujah International Airport, Hallelujah Gas Station, Hallelujah Restaurant, Hallelujah Bar and Hallelujah Motel ever since his father, Orville, retired and moved to Truth or Consequences, N.M. He explained that the community has no religious significance. "James P. Beckwourth, the black pioneer they named the mountain pass behind us after, came through here with a party in 1852. When Beckwourth discovered that the 5,218-foot pass was one of the easiest to cross, one of the lowest in the Sierra Nevada, someone shouted: 'Hallelujah!'" It's been Hallelujah ever since.

Stoy and his wife, Doris, had a four-place Cessna Skylane they parked in the Hallelujah International Airport hangar. "The name gets us in trouble all the time," said Stoy, reminiscing about a flight he made to Wichita Falls when his son, Eugene, was stationed in the Air Force there. "I phoned my flight plans at Denver about 5 in the morning. Told the party at the other end of the line I was flying from Hallelujah to Kickapoo, the name of the airport at Wichita Falls. The fella replied: 'Go back to bed and sober up. It's a little early for this sort of thing.'"

Every day people passing through Hallelujah on the Mexico to Canada highway stop only to be disappointed. They want to mail letters or postcards from Hallelujah. But the mail sent from the tiny town carries the postmark, Doyle, a small town 20 miles north of here.

"People are always after me to put in a post office," said Stoy. "But

CHARLES HILLINGER

I'm kept so busy running the place and apologizing to preachers because there's a bar but no church in Hallelujah that I haven't gotten around to it. We're on all the road maps but not in the Postal Guide. One of these days I'll fill out the proper forms and we'll get a post office and our own postmark." "Hallelujah!" shouted the half dozen Hallelujahans in the Hallelujah Bar when Stoy made his promise.

CALLAHAN'S EMPORIUM

For hundreds of miners, mountaineers and escapists in California's rugged northwest corner, the hamlet of Callahan, population 50, is known as "the city." It's as close to civilization as many of the mountain people get all year. Focal point of activity for these residents of California's "Ozark country" is a two-story, stone structure built in the 1870s. It was a hotel until 1936 when it was converted into one of the most unusual backwoods general merchandise houses in the West, the Emporium. It's at the hub of a series of single-lane dirt roads fanning out in a 50-mile radius to remote settlements and isolated, generally primitive dwellings.

"It's got everything. That's why it's called the Emporium," noted Jesse James, a snaggle-toothed local miner as he sipped a beer in the Emporium's 1870s bar. And, indeed, it seems that it has. Tables and shelves on wooden floors are askew and warped with age and jammed with many items out of the past—but which are still useful to mountain people. Modern conveniences had not yet made it to wilderness settlements of Siskiyou and Trinity counties served by the store. Hanging from the walls were galvanized washtubs, backwoods families use for bathing as well as laundry—washboards, too.

Stove pipes for wood cook stoves. Bottle caps for home-brewed beer. Kerosene lanterns. Suspenders. Horseshoes and horseshoe nails. "We're told we carry the largest stock of boots in the West," said Charley Thompson, the Emporium's proprietor. Piles of work pants have been in the store 20 years or longer. The prices keep going up on the pants as time marches on. "Never worry about inventory," declared Thompson. "Sooner or later it all moves. Some of it just takes longer than others."

The store carries food, school supplies, women's purses, gloves, long underwear, party dresses, heavy jackets, suits and lingerie. The Emporium is open 8 a.m. to midnight, seven days a week. "This is the only town some of these people see all year," said Thompson. "This is as close as they get to civilization. Some get this far only once or twice a year. Some come in once a month. Some as often as once a week." Thompson tends bar in the Emporium's hoary saloon filled with relics from before the turn of the century when Callahan was a gold camp for Irish and Chinese miners.

Some of the liquor has been on the shelves for over 50 years. "Two will never be opened, never be sold," said Thompson, explaining: "During World Wear II, 122 of our boys went off to fight for this country. When each one left, a bottle was placed on a special shelf with his name. When the men returned home after it was all over they claimed their bottles. These two bottles—this Lord Calvert still wrapped in its original paper now faded with age, and this Harwood's—were never picked up. They belonged to two mountain men killed in the war."

CHARLES HILLINGER

CHAPTER TWENTY-ONE

Charlie Spurlock and his "perpetual motion wheel."

OBSESSIONS

CHARLIE SPURLOCK'S PERPETUAL MOTION WHEEL

IT LOOKS LIKE A FERRIS WHEEL WITHOUT SEATS. It's Charlie Spurlock's "perpetual motion wheel," a towering landmark in Planada, a small San Joaquin Valley farm center. Spurlock, who was 75 when we stopped by to see his magical wheel, had worked on and off for 37 years in his spare time trying to get the wheel to spin without stopping. "It's all a matter of getting it perfectly counterbalanced. I think I've been close, but close doesn't count," sighed Spurlock as he turned the wheel.

The retired home builder and lumberyard owner hadn't given up, but he wasn't spending much time with his dream at the time of our visit. He had been in poor health. "Oh, I get out here and tinker with it now and then. Spin it. Check the weights. I still think somebody will come up with a perpetual motion device. I would like to be that person," he explained. He's convinced someone will figure out how to do it. "It tells about just such a wheel in the Bible. Ezekiel in his prophesies said there would appear a perpetual motion wheel on Earth." Although many would dispute Spurlock's interpretation of Ezekiel 1:15-23, he had no doubts.

Doris Spurlock, Charlie's wife of 51 years, just shakes her head in bewilderment: "He has spent at least $20,000 on it. In the beginning, two men helped him with it. He has tried all kinds of different ideas, trying to get it to work. He will never take it down. He will never sell this piece of property the wheel stands on."

"If I ever get this to work," Spurlock allowed, "people from all over the world will come to Planada to see it. Man, I could put motion in cars and everything else with no noise, with nothing to drive it." He said he kept on all these years, "because I have faith. I've been laughed at but many great inventors were laughed at before they succeeded. I may be a fool, but fools can do wonders."

"I have grown up watching Charlie work on that wheel," said Lois Halstead, clerk in the Planada Post Office. "I was 4 years old when he first started. People may say a lot of things about Charlie Spurlock, but one thing everybody has to agree is the truth, is that he certainly has been persistent." Jack Richards, 77, a retired garage owner who sits in his living room and looks out at Charlie Spurlock's wheel, said half the people in town have always thought it would work and half thought it wouldn't.

"Charlie's a smart guy, a good engineer. He has a lot of confidence," said Richards. "He poured a lot of time and money into the wheel. I have always had a hunch that maybe he was onto something big, that maybe someday it would spin and just keep spinning on its own."

GEORGE HAYNES' PERPETUAL MOTION MACHINE

EVER SINCE HE WAS 10, George Philander Haynes had been trying to invent a perpetual motion machine. When I encountered him he was 77, and still trying. "Oh, I know everyone thinks it's crazy, but I'm still not convinced it's impossible," insisted Haynes as he demonstrated what he called his leverage control machine.

Haynes had been working on his invention—a series of cranks

mounted on a shaft, with balancing bars and counterweights in tension springs—at his Downey home 30 years by the time I interviewed him. "Once I can get the cranks on the shaft to rotate, I've got it made," Haynes beamed. Then he glumly admitted that he hadn't been able to achieve a complete rotation. "I get within 15 or 20 degrees of full rotation," he said. "It just seems I'm so damn close. I can't put it down. The potential is there. I know it..."

All through history, inventors have tried to come up with a perpetual motion machine—without success. As the Encyclopedia Americana says, "No self-contained purely mechanical piece of apparatus designed to run forever has ever achieved its inventor's aim, for the energy used to start it is consumed in overcoming friction while the machine is running." Yet, the George Philander Hayneses keep trying.

One Hughesville, Pa., inventor, announced that he had solved the problem with God's help. He never gave any details, nor did God. And no one ever saw his invention, so far as is known. A Phoenix inventor said he had created a perpetual motion machine—a closed cylinder filled with water. But it didn't work. A federal judge ordered four Portland, Ore., men to stop selling stock on their perpetual motion machine. Two men from Rockford, Ill., were killed in an explosion when their perpetual motion machine blew up. We already wrote about Charlie Spurlock's perpetual motion wheel. And, so it goes.

"When I was 10, my step dad had a blacksmith shop," Haynes explained. "That's when I first started trying to figure it out. I put weights on an old bicycle wheel trying to get it in perfect balance so the wheel would spin without stopping. I worked in the woods running a steam engine in a lumbering operation. I watched that engine work, trying to figure out how..." Haynes said that since he retired from carpentry 14 years earlier, he had spent all his spare time working on his leverage control machine. "We'd be eating with sticks, if somebody didn't try out different things years ago," he insisted.

Haynes has one patent for an invention, a farm implement he devised more then a half century ago. "This thing has such a terrible grip on George," Mrs. Haynes sighed. "When he thinks about it, he grinds his teeth. He's always grinding his teeth."

"We've got to come up with better energy sources, " Haynes said. "If we don't, it will be back to the old team of mules before you know it. You've got to stick with something like this. My friends all begin scratching their heads when I talk about my machine."

Haynes visited the McDonnell Douglas plant to see if an engineer would come see his invention. "I explained I had invented a machine that could possibly solve the energy crisis," Haynes said. An engineer checked out the old man's invention and told him it just wasn't in the cards. "I'm trying to come up with something worthwhile I can give to mankind," Haynes said. "I can't give up now. I really think there is a possibility, despite all the scientific evidence to the contrary."

THEY NEVER MISS A TRAIN

JERRY DRAPEAU, tall, spindly and wearing a Southern Pacific cap, arrived on his bicycle at the Ventura railroad platform as he did seven mornings a week to await the arrival of Amtrak's No. 774 from Santa Barbara. Minutes later the wailing whistle of the passenger train was heard, the ringing gates at the railroad crossing came down and the red, white and blue engine rolled around the bend into sight.

"Right on the button, 8:26," said Drapeau, checking his pocket watch. "Engine 289. Engineer Mike Fleischman should be in the cab at the controls." Drapeau, 62, was armed and ready with pen and notebook to record the engine number, the numbers and description of every car as he did for every daylight freight and passenger train going through Ventura. He didn't work for Amtrak or Southern Pacific. "I'm a railroad nut," explained the part-time courier for a local legal firm. "I do this for my own personal pleasure. I'm like an addict. I can't quit. For me there's something electrifying about trains."

Drapeau and a fellow railroad buff, Don Sease, 64, carefully kept and preserved records of every train—including passenger and freight cars, engines and cabooses—that has passed through Ventura since 1961. Both were lifelong bachelors. The two men knew all the engineers and conductors on a first-name basis. They called Drapeau the Ventura Yardmaster and dubbed Sease the Ventura Trainmaster.

Drapeau and Sease recorded descriptions of cargo, the number of passengers carried and any problems they observed on the passing train. The engineers shouted out the number of passengers to them. If everything appeared in order they flashed high signs to conductors indicating all is well. If there was a problem of any kind they get on the phone immediately and reported it to the SP or Amtrak. For 35 years

Drapeau had been keeping track of all the daylight trains and Sease recorded every train going through the city day and night. "Southern Pacific and Amtrak know who we are and what we're doing, but in all these years the railroad has never once asked us to look up information in *our* records about any of their trains," Drapeau said. "They know we'll gladly help them out if they ever need to dig into our archives."

Sease and Drapeau each had about 500 notebooks with information on more than 100,000 trains traveling north and south along the coast through Ventura. Drapeau's entries were done with a flourish in calligraphy. "We plan to leave our notebooks to the Ventura County Museum when we die," Drapeau said. "We cover for each other if one of us is sick or out of town. It's in our blood. Some people are religious fanatics. We're railroad fanatics," allowed Drapeau. "Don is worse than I am. He never leaves home. He doesn't want to miss a train. He lives next to the railroad tracks and records the passing trains from his front porch." From time to time Drapeau embarked on long excursions—by rail, of course. He has ridden trains throughout the United States, Canada and Mexico. Every Sunday he rode a train from Ventura to Santa Barbara and back, visiting with railroad crews on layovers in Santa Barbara.

When Amtrak No. 774 pulled into Ventura one day when we were with Drapeau, engineer Mike Fleischman leaned out of the cab and shouted over the noise of the engine: "How's everything, Ventura Yardmaster?" "No complaints, Mike! How's it with you?" yelled back Drapeau.

Sease, a disabled Korean War veteran was shy. He said he didn't want to be interviewed, that his friend, Jerry Drapeau, would do the talking for both of them. Sease comes from a long line of railroaders. His father worked for the railroad 53 years as a railway postal clerk. When he checked trains at night he used a powerful flashlight to record cars and engines. Every afternoon the two men met to compare notes, to talk about trains going through that day and to reminisce about trains that passed through Ventura, weeks, months or even years ago. Both men watched and rode trains as a hobby before they began keeping records of the trains that travel through Ventura. "You can't imagine what it was like here during World War II—troop trains, wartime freight. It was a busy place," recalled Drapeau, who plays the organ in his free time for residents of the Townhouse Apartments where he lives. Engineer Fleischman on Amtrak's No. 774 Santa

Barbara to San Diego run said he met many rail fans in his long career as a railroader, "but the Ventura Trainmaster and the Ventura Yardmaster are in a world of their own. I never heard of anyone else keeping track of trains passing through a town like they do."

ISKY CANNOT PASS UP A BARGAIN

ED (ISKY) ISKENDERIAN is a self-made millionaire with an obsession about bargains. "My problem," said Isky, "is that I cannot pass up a good buy." When we caught up with Isky he had paid about $300,000 for tons of machinery and tools that couldn't be replaced for less than $5 million. But the machinery gathered dust in a half-dozen huge warehouses and two acres of back lots. Iskenderian is one of the best-known names in car racing circles here and abroad. When we met him he was the largest manufacturer of racing car camshafts in the world. For many years his firm had a monopoly in the field.

Headquarters for Ed Iskenderian Racing Cams was an ultra-modern, block-long factory in Gardena. It was his fifth and newest plant. The factories he vacated were filled with Isky's bargains. Two of the four buildings in his latest facility were jammed with machinery he bought at auctions. An enormous lot behind his factory was crammed with equipment he couldn't resist buying although none of the items had an immediate value to him.

"I pay 2 to 5 cents on the dollar for the machinery I buy at auctions," Isky explained. "You see, I know the value of machinery. When I see specialty equipment no one has any use for, no one bids for, I just can't resist." But what are you going to do with all this stuff? Isky was asked. "I enjoy it all," he said. "I spend hours each week tearing a machine apart, putting another together, just looking at what I've got.

"Some I rebuild or plan to rebuild. You buy for the future. You never know when there might be some use for it. Oh, in the long run I suppose it's a waste. I probably shouldn't be buying all this stuff. But I just can't pass it up." He pays thousands of dollars each year in Los Angeles County personal property taxes for his collection of clutter.

There's probably not another millionaire's office quite like Isky's. It's a jumble of small automotive parts, gauges and equipment purchased at the most recent auctions, of the latest line of cam shafts he's perfecting, of records and personal items. "You should see my home," said Isky.

"Spotless! My wife is a fanatic about keeping everything in order. She has a hard fast rule about letting me bring any of my junk in the house."

Iskenderian's parents were immigrant Armenians of meager means. "When I graduated from Dorsey High School and before I spent three years in the Army Air Corps during World War II, I had a helluva time finding work," Isky said. "I stood in line at Lockheed in 1940 trying to get a 50-cent-an-hour job. I know what it's like to be without.

"When I started my business I scrounged parts to build my first camshaft grinder. I think that's probably why I got started buying this machinery. You know how it is when you're a mechanic and you need a part or a tool right in the middle of working on something. You get frustrated. Well," laughed Isky as he chomped on a cigar, "I'm never going to run out of a tool or a part again as long as I live."

In the yard behind his huge factory are all his old family automobiles, nearly all Cadillacs, and campers and trailers covered with dust, loaded with tools and parts. His friends kid him about driving the only one-passenger car on the road. The rest of the car he drives is always jammed with bargains. "One of these days I hope to clean out my old cars parked in back," he said. "I know I'll find a lot of good stuff I forgot about." His most expensive piece of equipment picked up at an auction is a 50-foot-long machine once used to fabricate airplane wings. "It cost the government $250,000 to build," said Isky. "What a bargain. I paid only $5,000. I've got it pickled in heavy oil to preserve it.

"Look at this!" shouted Isky as he climbed over odds and ends piled 15-feet high. "A huge drilling machine. Cost $15,000 originally. I got it for only $800. How could I turn down a buy like that? Look at everything out here. All bargains!" exclaimed Isky.

ANTIQUES TO HIM, JUNK TO THE BLM

"HOW ARE YOU DOING?" the bearded 74-year-old man was asked. "Mildewin'," said Alvin Coe. "Ever since this big mess with BLM (Bureau of Land Management), I've been goin' downhill. Lost 40 pounds. Hair turned white. Damn bureaucrats are wreckin' this country. Look here! Look what those lame brains posted all over my place." He pointed to signs posted on several pine trees: "NO DUMPING"

Beneath the acres of trees were tons of junk—old cars, stoves, refrigerators, radios, mattresses, furniture, tires, toys, television sets, pots, pans, tools, bed springs, toilets, tubs. Coe's wife of 20 years, Hazel, 42, walked over. "Alvin's a dreamer, or a schemer or whatever you want to call him," declared Mrs. Coe. "He just doesn't like to see anything wasted. Those Bureau of Land Management guys call him a scrounger. He's not a scrounger. He's a saver."

When we visited with the pack rat he had been collecting odds and ends for 36 years on his mining claims at the southwest end of Lake Isabella 50 miles east of Bakersfield. For months the Bureau of Land Management had been trying to get him to clean up the property. The BLM claimed collecting junk isn't mining.

Coe said he had thousands of discarded items scattered over 350 acres of mountain meadows and steep slopes. "I've got five mining claims, a mill site, and homestead land up here," he insisted. "Been settin' this stuff all over these hills 36 years now. And nothin' ever been said until somebody at BLM got a bug up his butt and started all this hoopla about cleanin' up the countryside.

"All of a sudden I'm illegal. They say I'm not a legitimate miner— that I'm a junk collector. Hell, I got holes poked all over the place provin' up my annual assessment work," he sighed. "And who's to say any of this stuff is junk? Yesterday's junk is today's antiques! What you're lookin' at is thousands of dollars worth of antiques."

Alvin Bryan Coe—"They call me ABC or Alco for short"—hopped onto the seat of a 1910 Little Giant truck. "You call this junk?" he bellowed. "This is a museum piece, son. Savvy? I can get $500 for it today. Imagine what it will be worth in 20 years.

"You heard the story about the Englishman who bought a vase from a Chinese fellow. Gave the man two sacks of rice for the vase. The Englishman brought the vase back to England. He sold it for $240,000. Who knows what gems I have among my collection here," he said.

As recreational land became more and more a premium in the Lake Isabella area, BLM officials began to take inventory of property managed by the federal agency. The federal government granted Coe permission to remain on a few acres so long as he lived. When BLM began removing Coe's "antiques," a California Rural Legal Assistance attorney representing Coe obtained a court injunction to stop the bureau's cleanup project.

When we visited Alco the matter had yet to be resolved. But the "junk" or "antiques" collector, however Alvin Coe strikes your fancy, was busy operating heavy equipment moving his "treasures" from his 350 acres of mountain meadows and steep slopes to 10 acres in and around his house. "I'm stacking the stuff as close as I can to the house in case those damn bureaucrats get their way," he sighed dejectedly.

CHAPTER TWENTY-TWO

The Great Razooly and a few of his fantastic creations.

A COUPLE OF WEIRD ARTISTS

THE GREAT RAZOOLY

EVERY DAY IS HALLOWEEN at the Great Razooly's Cavern deep in a redwood forest in California's North Coast. Razooly is a wizard at sculpting gargoyles, unicorns, dragons, centaurs, Cyclops, griffins, flying horses and a wild assortment of other mythical beasts often associated with All Hallow's Eve. "I create things not around anymore," Razooly explained.

The pixie-like sculptor was 26 when I interviewed him for this story in 1981. He lived in a castle he built 75 miles from Eureka, the nearest town of any size. His nearest neighbors were 10 miles away. His cavernous studio is crammed with his sculptured creatures and stalagmite-like columns of brilliantly colored leftover castings of clay used in their production.

The Great Razooly's name is really Tom Hrynkiewicz. "That's Polish for hare-in-the-cabbage," the sculptor said. "But I changed my name to The Great Razooly. It's easier to remember than Hrynkiewicz." He signs his checks The Great Razooly. That name is in the phone book. His wife is Denise Razooly; his 5-year-old daughter, Tonde Razooly.

"Denise's parents didn't want her to marry a sculptor," related The Great Razooly. "It had something to do with their religion. So I kidnapped her. That's how I became Razooly." He said he took his name from Ahmed Ibn-Muhammed Raisuli, a Moroccan kidnapper, who became a cause celebre during Teddy Roosevelt's administration. "All is forgiven now," Razooly said. "Denise's folks and I have become the best of friends."

Tonde was born in the castle she has lived in all her life—among the gargoyles, dragons and scores of other monsters. When asked what it was like living with such creations, the 5-year-old replied: "I really like them. They've always been here. They're my friends. It's just like they're real only they can't move or say anything."

Razooly's creations were sold in Disneyland and in magic and occult shops throughout the West. Because he sculpts monsters, he is invited to the elementary school at nearby Blocksburg, population 30, each Halloween. There The Great Razooly reads the same spooky story every year to the student body, Edgar Allen Poe's "Telltale Heart." Razooly is the pride of Blocksburg. He was named the tiny town's citizen of the year.

He gets weird letters. "People attribute magical powers to the gargoyles," Razooly said as he displayed some of the correspondence. "It isn't the clay. I just don't know," Razooly mused. One man wrote and said he was unable to get rid of a hum in his stereo. "Then I bought one of your gargoyles and, suddenly, the hum disappeared. One woman credited one of his gargoyles with ridding her house of poltergeists (spirits that throw things). A doctor told of how he keeps his gargoyle under his piano. "Only the gargoyle's feet show," the doctor wrote. "People are in for a shock when they bend over and look under the piano and come eyeball to eyeball with a gargoyle."

Fast forward to the year 2000. The Great Razooly's home and studio are still in his "Forgotten Castle" deep in the redwood forest where he continues to create gargoyles and other mythical beasts. An arch gateway, much like the entrance to a cemetery, marks the entrance to the castle. Two gargoyles and a four-foot-tall wizard guard the gateway to the castle.

5000 GIANT TEETH STANDING ON END IN THE DESERT

IT LOOKED LIKE A MINIATURE STONEHENGE. Or like 5,000 giant sharks' teeth standing upright in the middle of remote 7¹/₂-mile-long, 2¹/₂-mile-wide Silver Dry Lake 10 miles north of Baker. Whatever it was, it had the 600 residents of Baker baffled and buzzing. "We have a real mystery on our hands," reported Brian Booher, a U.S. Bureau of Land Management desert ranger.

"At first we thought the 5,000 tooth-shaped objects were cast from a mold. But on closer observation they look like each one has been formed individually by hand. There are impressions of fingers on some of them. Some are three-sided. Some are four-sided. They vary from 7 to 13 inches in length." The strange objects appeared to be made of clay and talc. "It's weird, I'll tell you," said Maggie B. Ware, 48, a waitress at Pike's Watering Hole in Baker. Maggie calls herself "the oldest and slowest waitress in the Mojave Desert and the biggest gossip."

"Nobody in town knows what it's all about," confided Maggie as she jotted down a dinner order. One of the diners kept feeding quarters into the jukebox to play over and over country singer Billy Swan's "Let Me Help. Let Me Help." "Maybe we ought to get Billy Swan out here to help," sighed Maggie B. Ware.

An old prospector, who had been staying in a camper on Silver Dry Lake 10 miles north of Baker, was the first to spot the mysterious objects. The old man drove into Baker and told townspeople: "There was one helluva explosion over the dry lake bed around midnight." The prospector believed a UFO blew apart and all the pieces from the spaceship landed standing on end. Some of the townspeople believe the odd-shaped objects did, indeed, come from outer space.

"One person I talked to is convinced it's a directional sign for airplanes bringing marijuana in from Mexico," said Arne Jacobson, 40, who runs the Royal Hawaiian Motel. Others believe a movie studio may have left them on the dry lake bed, but no one can recall anyone making a movie there.

The 5,000 giant "teeth" are scattered half a mile long and a block wide on Silver Dry Lake. "We thought maybe the kids in high school (Baker had 71 high school students at the time) stood them on end. Kids here don't have a lot to do," said San Bernardino County Dep. Sheriff Ron Mahoney. But the high school students deny knowing anything about the objects.

"Why should anyone make the mysterious figures in the first place," mused desert ranger Booher. "And if they were a bad run of molded objects instead of hand cast and were brought out here to dump, that wouldn't make much sense either. "Why come this far?" Baker is 200 miles northeast of Los Angeles.

At first it was thought the "sharks' teeth" had something to do with a commercial Peter Fonda filmed recently for a Japanese TV company on Silver Dry Lake. Burt Arne Jacobson squashed that theory. "Fonda and that bunch stayed at my motel," explained Jacobson. "They filmed a sequence with a sailboat on the dry lake. If they used those strange objects I would have known about it."

Whatever the strange objects are the people of Baker will be talking about them for years. Nearly everyone in town has at least one of the "sharks' teeth" standing upright on a mantle in his or her home.

Solution to the mystery that had puzzled the people of Baker for weeks came swiftly. The day my story appeared in the *Los Angeles Times* someone from the Cal State L.A. art department called the paper to say Donn Jones did it. It was a one-man art show by the Alhambra artist.

Jones, 31, formed the 7-to-13 inch figures from 10 tons of clay and talc. "It took me two months to scrounge up the scrap clay and mix it with talc," said Jones who had red hair and a foot-long full red beard. "Another four months to mold each figure individually." The figures, the artist explained, represented candle flames. He called his half-mile by 200-yard creation "Symphony One—Opus One." "I am very fond of music," Jones said. "Since this was my entry into the art world, I called it 'Opus One.' And since it was such a large undertaking, I called it 'Symphony One' as well."

The unusual artwork was set up in the middle of the desert dry lake. It was created by Jones to fulfill a requirement for his master's degree in art at California State University, Los Angeles. "I spent several days looking for an appropriate site," Jones continued. "I thought of placing the pieces on a beach or in a mountain meadow. Then I decided the show should be presented in the hottest place I could find to tie in with the flame-shaped objects." Jones headed for Death Valley.

"I spotted the dry lake at the base of a barren mountain. I knew it had to be the place for my art show." He returned to Los Angeles and spread the word around the campus to students and faculty that everyone was invited to see his work of art in the desert anytime during a three-day period.

"I rented two trucks. Six friends helped me load the more than 5,000 clay candle flames," the artist said. "Then the seven of us went out to the dry lake. We worked from sunup to sunset, standing each figure on its base. I was trying to create a feeling of a primitive emotional Stonehenge." Jones took along cold drinks, shrimp, squid and other canned delicacies for those who showed up to see his art show. He and his friends camped out next to the massive work of art for three days and three nights. "But only one person showed up to see my work," sighed the artist. "That was all right. I fulfilled the requirement for my master's degree. I really didn't expect many people to turn out. It was a long way to the dry lake and anyway it was in the midst of final exams."

"Symphony One – Opus One" was designed to be harmless to the environment. "Ecology was an important concept of the work," said Jones. "That's why I created the candle flames of unfired clay. I expected the pieces to weather out and blow or wash away in a short time. He fully expected his creation to disintegrate before being discovered by anyone, Silver Lake being so far out from populated areas. "I didn't tell anyone in Baker abut it," Jones said, "because I didn't think there really was any reason to. I don't know anyone in Baker."

Jones' art show went unnoticed for two months but his clay candle flames were not extinguished by desert winds or rain. Then the old prospector ran across the strange objects. He drove his camper into Baker the next day to report his findings, that he was convinced a UFO blew apart and all the pieces from the spaceship landed standing on end. The Alhambra artist said he is working on still another work of art—equally mysterious and even bigger than his first effort. But he said it was too early to talk about it.

CHARLES HILLINGER

CHAPTER TWENTY-THREE

Martha Linden, 86, crocheting in her café at Harvard Hill in the Mojave Desert.

FOUR SPECIAL WOMEN

MARTHA'S CAFÉ

F OR YEARS, MARTHA'S CAFÉ IN HARVARD HILL had a wide swath of the Mojave Desert almost all to itself. The café was 25 miles east of Barstow on what was California 91, once the main Los Angeles-to-Las Vegas road. It was a popular stop for motorists. Then in 1962, Interstate 15 was opened. California 91 was virtually abandoned. Whole stretches of it just disappeared.

"The new freeway robbed me of my highway trade," sighed 86-year-old Martha Linden, when I visited with her at the café in 1992. She was 5 foot 2, weighed 185. Even though only a handful of motorists traveled the old road the 30 years since it was replaced by Interstate 15, Martha Linden never closed her café.

Martha's Café was open seven days a week, Thanksgiving, Christmas and all the other holidays. If a dozen customers were served it was a busy day. Many days no one showed up at all. It was the same funky old 1950s eatery with the same old pool table, same jukebox playing 1950s records, same nine orange leather counter chairs, now patched, stuffing oozing, and two booths in a corner. And that World War II pinball machine—it hadn't worked in years. "I can't get anyone to come out this far to fix it," lamented Martha.

For breakfast she serves ham and eggs and bacon and eggs. The rest of the day, hamburgers, cheeseburgers and chili burgers. That was it. "Best hamburgers anywhere in the desert," insisted Dennis Casebier, a longtime patron of the café and chairman of Friends of the Mojave Road, a 900-member, conservation-minded recreational vehicle organization. "Anytime I'm in the area, I stop. Martha's always here."

For years, Martha recalled, her business had boomed. "Then overnight the roof fell in when the Interstate opened. "Everybody figured I'd thrown in the towel. My place was paid for. I decided I'm staying come hell or high water. It's been a struggle. But I ain't broke yet. Sure, I'm stubborn. But no one can call me a quitter," she allowed. "Forty years ago I escaped L.A., the rat race and all that traffic. I came out here a widow with six kids, bought five acres of raw desert. I built my café with my own hands and with the help of two teen-age sons. We poured the cement, pounded the nails, put up the walls, the ceiling, the roof, the whole works."

She once owned a Mohawk gas station along with the café. But when the old highway was abandoned and gas sales plummeted, the pumps were removed. To make ends meet, Martha crocheted and sold afghans, baby blankets and sweaters, doll clothes and pot holders. She strung beads and made ceramics. Until she remarried 17 years earlier, she lived in a rock house on her property. When she married her husband Mel, they moved into a trailer next to the café. She had 25 grandchildren, 33 great-grandchildren and five great-great-grandchildren.

"I enjoy the peace and quiet and visiting with the few people who find this out-of-the-way place and pop in for a bite to eat," she mused. "Biggest excitement around here is when one of my eight cats chases off a sidewinder or lizard."

CHARLES HILLINGER

MILLIONAIRE FRY COOK

SHE WAS A MILLIONAIRE WORKING 12 HOURS A DAY, seven days a week without pay as a cook in a cowboy saloon. "I work to live. I've got to do something. Sitting at home looking at the four walls would drive me nuts," said Ethel (Granny) Baker, a 77-year-old widow. "Sure, I can afford to travel all over the world. But I don't like to travel. I haven't even been to town in six months. I could watch the boob tube, but TV doesn't help your eyes."

Granny Baker lived on a ranch a couple of miles from the bar tucked away in a remote high mountain valley in Central California. Granny had been working there without wages for 10 years. "No sense payin' me. The government would get it all anyway. I can't afford to get paid," she explained. When the bar was sold a year earlier Granny went with the deal "as chief cook and bottle washer." When her three sons, 22 grandchildren and 22 great-grandchildren visited her, they didn't go to her big, rambling ranch house, they headed straight for the saloon.

"That ol' gal can out-bank-account everybody in this county. There's nothin' she can't afford to do, but she enjoys cookin' for the local cowhands," said C.W. (Sonny) Ball, a bar regular. "And she's the best cook in the county," chimed in rancher Chuck McCoy, an endorsement echoed by others in the saloon. She not only cooked at the bar, she also kept the peace with a baseball bat. "When anybody uses foul language, starts a fight or gets out of line, I start swingin'," allowed Granny as she grabbed her baseball bat and demonstrated. "They know I wouldn't hesitate to knock 'em over the head. The threat always works."

Granny said she started cooking in the bar when she no longer could run the ranch by herself. "The ranch got too much for me. I was up at 3 every morning, spending the entire day on horseback workin' the cows. I would do the whole works—feed 'em, doctor 'em, brand 'em, round 'em up..." She owned several ranches, all operated by her three sons. And from her main spread she pointed out, "All the mountains you see on both sides and the valley in between are mine."

"Ma is a highly respected lady in these parts," noted her second-oldest son, Tuffy, 57. "Cooking is what she likes to do. It keeps her young in spirit, young in heart. We think it's great." "She's a pistol," allowed her youngest son, Don, 50. "The other day I was making a bank run and needed her to sign a $150,000 check. I found her in the kitchen at the bar. 'Son,' she told me, 'You know better not to bother me at noon when all the boys are in for lunch. I ain't got time. Come back later...'"

"This is a damn site better than bein' in a rest home," sighed Granny.

SQUIRREL GULCH ELLY

"AMERICA'S GOIN' TO HELL FOR SURE. I'm being held prisoner in Trinity County," snorted hardrock miner Squirrel Gulch Elly, 84, a spinster who spent 50 years working her mining claims in Squirrel Gulch in the Trinity Alps of Northern California and was "fightin' mad." The year was 1978.

On the back of her driver's license the Department of Motor Vehicles printed the following restrictions: "Limited to operating a motor vehicle within the boundaries of Trinity County only." Many drivers have restrictions printed on their driver licenses, for example those not entitled to drive unless they wear corrective lenses, small people whose licenses required them to sit on a cushion to see above the wheel, others limited to driving only from sunrise to sunset because of vision deficiencies.

But Ellen Kadas, the feisty old miner known throughout sparsely populated Trinity County as Squirrel Gulch Elly was the only Californian confined to driving in just one of the state's 58 counties.

"Miss Kadas flunked her driver's test five times in the last couple of years," explained Donald Bell, 57, manager of the one-man DMV office in Weaverville, seat of Trinity County, population 9,000. "But she lives way up in the hills all by herself and she needs a car to get around. The closest place for her to shop for groceries is in Weaverville, 50 miles down the mountain from her mining claims. Her doctor is in Weaverville. She conducts business pertaining to her mining in the county seat. She picks up her mail at the small post office at Trinity Center, 18 miles from her home.

"I respect Miss Kadas," Bell continued. "She's a sharp old gal. And I'm certain she has no trouble getting around on the roads in our rural county. There are no main highways or traffic congestion here. So, I gave her the whole county to drive in—but restricted her from driving outside it. You see, I don't think it's safe for Miss Kadas or for the other drivers on the road if she drives on Interstate 5 or through downtown Redding in the next county."

"Hogwash," complained Squirrel Gulch Elly. "If I'm capable of drivin' these narrow, windy mountain roads in the Trinity Alps, it seems to me I should be good enough to drive everywhere else in this state. My God, what's happening to America?"

TOO MUCH LIKE FAMILY

ONE THING FOR SURE, Lucy Higgins would never take the three trained steers she inherited to the stockyards. "I just can't," she said. "They're too much like family. Could you turn your kids out into the streets?" The 65-year-old widow living on a small ranch in the old Mother Lode mining town of Fair Play had been "baby-sitting" a trio of 1½-ton animals three years. She worked as a housekeeper to keep them in hay.

Steers are normally raised by cattlemen for sale at the marketplace when the animals are yearlings. Not Lucy's. Freckles, Charley and Bulgy were going on 10 years, not months. "They're in their prime," she said. "Anyway they're much too old and fat to be made into steaks."

It wasn't Lucy's idea to have trained oxen for pets. "That was Nate's brainstorm," she explained. "My husband ran cattle at our place. For something different to do, when Nate was 70, he started training three newborn calves. People for miles around would come to our place just to see the steers. By the time the animals were a couple of years old he had them doing all kinds of tricks. He rode them like he would a horse. He'd rope other cattle from his steer. I'd stretch out on the ground and he'd have those monsters jump over me. I never had any fear because they were putty in Nate's hands."

Rodeos and fairs tried to get Higgins to form his own act and exhibit the huge beasts. "The California State Fair offered him $2,000 to show them for 10 days, but he couldn't see it. He trained them for pleasure, not profit," said the widow.

Higgins had a colorful career. He was one of California's last stagecoach drivers and drove wagon trains over the High Sierra. He operated the last horse-drawn steamers used by the Oakland Fire Department. Higgins was 78 when he died, 2½ years before our visit with his widow. "It was a shame how he worried about those pet steers," said Mrs. Higgins. "He didn't want them destroyed. Yet, he didn't think I could care for them properly."

Higgins sold his cattle except his three pets to meet medical and other expenses before his death. He and his wife had 170 acres. To make ends meet since her husband died, Mrs. Higgins sold 90 acres of the ranch. For several months she had been riding the huge beasts just as her husband did, putting them through their old tricks. She trotted and cantered astride the oxen, rode forward and backwards between poles. The animals knelt and bowed to Lucy's command.

"My friends think I'm tetched," said the widow. "They keep telling me to get rid of the steers and not be tied down. For awhile after Nate died, I just made sure Freckles, Bulgy and Charley had enough food and were healthy. They'd follow me all over the place right at my heels like three puppy dogs every time I'd make a move. Well, I'd talk to 'em. Give 'em a hug. I'd pet 'em. Pretty soon I was up on their backs riding them like horses, just like Nate did."

In 1970 Lucy rode in the annual Fiddletown Parade astride Freckles. After that she put the steers through their tricks at a few local horse shows. "Everybody tells me they never heard of a woman with a trained steer act," said Lucy. "I'm fit to be tied right now. I don't know if I should continue working as a housekeeper to keep the steers in hay. Or quit cleaning houses and try my luck with my own act in rodeos and county fairs. Nate wouldn't like the idea of me using his pets to earn a living," mused the widow. "But he would like it even less if I took the steers to the stockyards."

CHAPTER TWENTY-FOUR

Soaring Jenkins looks for signs of fire from her mountaintop post.

FIVE FASCINATING WOMEN

SOARING JENKINS

HER NAME IS SOARING JENKINS. She lived alone in a 13-by-13 foot glass house on top of remote Cone Peak, a mile-high mountain reached by a tortuous two-mile, almost-straight-up twisting trail. She had no electricity or indoor plumbing. Once a week the 115-pound, 5-foot, 7-inch mountain woman carried food and supplies up the steep, rocky footpath. Once a month mules delivered extra-heavy items like 20-gallon cartons of water to Soaring Jenkins' lair.

The 37-year-old woman spent several hours a day singing and playing Irish and Welsh songs on a harp as she sat on top of Cone Peak, one of the sheerest mountains in the West. The mountain spills into the Pacific Ocean midway between Big Sur and San Simeon. Between songs Soaring Jenkins scoured the skies in all directions looking for puffs of smoke. A U.S. Forest Service lookout on Cone Peak for five years, she was one of a vanishing breed.

In the early 1950s the Forest Service had 5,060 manned fire lookout towers across America, 3,470 of them erected by the Civilian Conservation Corps in the 1930s. When I visited the summit of Cone Peak in 1989 there were fewer than 600, fewer than 100 fire lookout towers in California. Satellites, aerial surveillance, computerized maps of lightning strikes, commercial and private pilots flying over the mountains, people with civilian band radios driving on far more mountainous roads than in the past are all able to spot fires as quick as the fire lookouts except in extremely isolated areas like Cone Peak.

"I live in a 360-degree world. I see the curve in the sky. I feel the curve of the Earth up here. I can see Mt. Whitney on a clear day, see 88 miles out to sea. I'm always the last one to see the sun set around here," related Soaring Jenkins. Her bed is four feet off the ground at window level so she can see at night. "If there are lightning strikes, I wake up with them. On a full moon I wake up squinting from the brightness," she added. She told how she recited an Indian prayer when the sun awakened her each new day. "Beauty's before me. Beauty's behind me. Beauty's all around me. Beauty's above me. Beauty's below me. Beauty's inside me." Were you given the name Soaring at birth, I asked. "Oh, no. I always hated my first name. I won't tell you what it was," she replied with a winsome grin.

She spotted and reported whiffs of smoke, mostly from lightning strikes from time to time during the seven months she lived on the mountain each year. She also had a big house in Big Sur where she lived when she wasn't on the mountain. She directed firefighters by radio to fires. She had a CB and occasionally had calls from people reporting a car over the cliff on California Highway 1 or a fishing boat in distress radioing for help. She relayed the calls to the Los Padres National Forest dispatcher.

"It was a baptism of fire my first month here. There was a huge fire all through these mountains. I relayed information over the radio to fire fighting crews. I couldn't see the fire approaching for the dense smoke," she recalled. "The lead plane of an air attack crew radioed that a helicopter better fly to Cone Peak right away or it would be too late to get me out. The fire was closing in. I was sitting on the floor operating the radios. I couldn't see out the window. I was on the floor where it was cooler. I was having a tough time breathing because of the smoke." A helicopter flew her to safety. The forest on Cone Peak was charred.

She later received a certificate of commendation for her heroic work during the fire and a $150 award. "They flew me back here five days later. Everything was black. Luckily my tower was not burned. She said she looked in every direction about every five to 10 minutes. "When I read a book, I turn a page and look. When I play the harp, I keep looking around. The first week on the job I was a nervous wreck. I looked every minute. You have to learn to pace yourself. You can't be too hyper about it." Although the trail leading to her mountaintop was reached by a seldom-traveled 13-mile one-lane winding mountainous road, the last five miles dirt, a few hikers manage to find their way to Cone Peak. "A guy from Italy was here yesterday. Being here is being both alone and being social. Being alone helps you sort out things deep inside," she related.

"Being social means being friendly with strangers who hike up. Sometimes I go for days alone. Some weekends as many as a dozen people will hike up here, mostly men, 93% of them real nice, 6% jerks and 1% weirdos who can be dangerous. Still the odds are better than in the city. The trail is a killer. Many who try are wiped out before they're halfway up. I have yet to see anyone arrive who is not dripping wet." It took an hour-and-a-half to walk up the steep, rocky, two-mile trail to the top of Cone Peak each week loaded down with a backpack full of necessities weighing at least 50 pounds. She was off the mountain two days a week. She was paid for a 40-hour week although she looked through her binoculars from sunup to sundown searching for smoke.

Her pay at the time of our visit was $6.75 an hour, "high in job satisfaction, low in wages," as she described it. Her one-room home was combination kitchen, bedroom and living room. It had a propane refrigerator, stove, heater and lights. The propane was flown in once a year on a helicopter. Twice a day she radioed weather information. She slept with the radio going all night. She was tuned in only to those calls that affected her. "I spent a year studying Zen meditation. Even when I'm sleeping I'm always present and know what's going on and respond immediately to calls for me." She was never really alone, of course.

Swallowtail and monarch butterflies and hummingbirds shared the top of the mountain. On the trail she encountered deer, quail, doves, chipmunks, squirrels. "One night I was sitting watching the sunset and felt something nibbling on my shoe. Eeek! It was a wood rat. What a horrible feeling. Once I killed a rattlesnake at the tower," said Soaring

Jenkins, describing the local wildlife. She was a vegetarian, drank juices, ate a lot of potatoes, sweet potatoes, salads and other vegetables. She was a teacher before she became a Forest Service lookout. "Living here has made me a better person," she mused. "Come fall, it's time to go down the mountain to my home in Big Sur, and I'm ready to leave. By then it's cold and blustery up here. Every spring I can hardly wait to return. I plan to be on the lookout on Cone Peak until I'm at least 87."

"HELP YOURSELF BABY"

THE COW BELL CLANGED as the door swung open at California's only fully automated saloon. "Who is it?" squeaked a voice from within the back room. "It's me, Mother Scott—Dorothy," shouted Dorothy Myers. "OK, baby. Help yourself," responded the saloon keeper from her bed at the rear. Mrs. Myers took a can of beer from the refrigerator in the empty barroom. The cash register was open and she tossed a quarter and a nickel into the till from her bar stool before she drank her beer. When we stopped by her watering hole, Mother Scott (Mary Susan Scott, 88) had been a Maricopa institution 59 years, ever since she arrived with her husband in the tiny oil town 115 miles northwest of Los Angeles.

During the early years, Mother Scott ran a boarding house in the nearby Elkhorn Hills and later she operated cafés and bars along Maricopa's main street. She had been operating her saloon, "Mother Scott's" for 20 years when we first met her.

Her husband, Lee, an oil worker, died 35 years earlier. The couple's only daughter had died. They had no grandchildren. Arthritis had slowed down Maricopa's "institution" and although she was bedridden most of the time she managed to keep the bar operating. "It's the arthritis in my spine and hips, baby," Mother Scott explained. "Got to where I can't sit up. So I lie in bed most of the day."

The saloon was operated on the honor system and residents of Maricopa (population 800)—including most of the merchants, police, even the local PTA and a Catholic priest—kept a watchful eye on Mother Scott's customers to keep the operation honest. "It's the only automated bar in America, so far as I know," laughed Mother Scott. "So far as I know nobody's ever taken anything. I've never missed a nickel. I open the doors in the morning and keep them open to 8 or 9 at night—even later, baby, if anybody cares to hang around." The cow bell let her know when a customer arrived. "We think the world of her," said Mrs. Myers. "We sweep and mop out the place. When the beer runs low in the refrigerator, we go down to the basement and load up the box."

Mother Scott noted: "It's the only income I've got. It pays my taxes. Feeds me. Pays the doctor bills and buys my medicine, baby." Mother Scott called everybody "baby"—even the Rev. Ignatius Loughran, pastor of St. Mary's Catholic Church in Taft, who stopped by from time to time to visit with his parishioner who no longer could make it to Mass regularly. "It's just a habit," said Mother Scott explaining why she called everybody "baby". "You see I'm a southern gal, born in Cullman County, Alabama. All southern people have phrases they use. Some say darlin', others sweetie pie."

Mother Scott sold beer, soda pop and V-8 juice in her bar. She started selling V-8 juice because Mrs. Myers usually drank it as a beer chaser. Many of Mother Scott's customers adopted Mrs. Myers habit of drinking vegetable juice with their beer. "It's an old Egyptian custom," said Mrs. Myers. "I lived in Egypt eight years."

Mother Scott's "baby sister," Victoria Austin, 85, dropped by almost every day. "I never touch liquor," allowed Mrs. Austin, "but if anybody offers to buy me a can of beer, I take it. Just to help my sis out."

GUARDIAN OF A STRANGE TUNNEL

FOR 11 YEARS a retired Navy nurse had lived in a shack perched on a remote ledge of a barren desert mountain. She was the guardian of a strange tunnel. "Somebody's got to take care of the tunnel," said Tonie Seger, a 56-year-old widow. "My sister keeps telling me: 'Why don't you sell that place and get back to civilization.'" Her response to her sister's plea: "Where's civilization? My family won't come around here. But I enjoy my lonesome life. Why should I care what others think," she mused. The widow's vigil was the entrance to "Burro" Schmidt's Tunnel. The tunnel was nine miles from the nearest highway by a dirt mining road into the El Paso Mountains.

Tonie's place, for the few who find it, is 20 miles west of the old mining town of Randsburg on the Mojave Desert, near the upper slopes of mile-high Black Mountain. It's a wonder Tonie ever found it. "The man upstairs directed me," she said. "My husband was dying. The doctor said

MECHANICS' INSTITUTE LIBRARY
57 Post Street
San Francisco, CA 94104
(415) 393-0101

the high desert was the best place for his health. We bid on 800 acres of raw desert, sight unseen, at the probate court in Bakersfield. This is it. The price was $5,000." The Segers were living in Huntington Park at the time.

"We gave up a beautiful home, a beautiful car, for a tired old truck and this damn place," Tonie continued. In less than a year her husband was dead. But the retired Navy nurse stayed on. "We never heard of Burro Schmidt before coming up. He was something else." William Henry Schmidt was 29 when he came to Black Mountain. He prospected all over the El Paso Range, locating 24 claims. He said he found rich veins of copper, silver and gold.

"But the logical shipping point was on the other side—the south side—of the mountain," Tonie said, picking up the story. "So, he started digging his tunnel for transporting his ore. He dug for 38 years without the aid of mechanical devices. Just a pick. A shovel. A hand drill. A minimum of blasting powder. A maximum of effort.

"They called him Burro Schmidt because he was all alone out here digging the horizontal hole with the help of his two burros. You walk through his half-mile long tunnel and it takes you only 17 minutes. I walk through at least a couple of times each day. You're walking through half of one man's lifetime."

Before Schmidt finished, Civilian Conservation Corps crews had pushed a road through to his campsite and to Last Chance Canyon. "Hell, that didn't slow old Burro Schmidt none," Tonie said. "He was German and he was a New Englander. He was double stubborn. He went right on working until he saw daylight at the other end."

Legend has it Schmidt struck a glory hole, that he had a bathtub full of gold in a room off his tunnel. "Oldtimers swear to it," Tonie said. "Many told me they've been in the room, that Schmidt sealed the room before he died. He was a loner. Close mouthed. When he died they found $2,700 in cash and $1,400 in gold in his cabin." Tonie Seger had poked around in the tunnel for years trying to find the sealed room. The tunnel is 5 feet wide and 7 feet high, through solid granite. There's no shoring.

A rail track leads from one end to the other. Schmidt's ore car is still here. So is the old prospector's cabin, rusted tools, pots and pans, cook stove, iron bed, lanterns, harnesses and collars for his burros. Nailed to the ceiling of the shack are copies of *Collier's, Life, Saturday Evening Post* and *Liberty Magazine* from the early 1930s, pictures of Shirley Temple and other celebrities of that era and scores of Aunt Jemima pancake mix boxes. Insulation from the heat and cold.

Somehow people found Tonie's place. And when they came she let them walk through the tunnel, even led them as they carried lanterns and flashlights. "Some gives a dollar to go through. Some gives a quarter. Some a dime and some nothin'," Tonie said. "I'll grant you, I'm not gettin' rich." Over the Memorial Day weekend a few days before we visited Burro Schmidt's tunnel the donations amounted to $41.33, the best weekend of the year. Toni kept track in a record book.

$35-A-MONTH LIBRARIAN

THE SHARP-EYED 89-YEAR-OLD SHEEPRANCH LIBRARIAN leaned on the century-old board fence and repeated the stranger's question: "When's the library open? From 5 or 6 in the morning until at least 10 at night—whenever I'm awake. Seven days a week." Antoinette Guidici (Jude-a-see), 4 feet tall and at the most 80 pounds, wasn't kidding. The library was open when she was up and around and whenever she was home—which was almost always. Yet the position only paid her $35 a month.

Sheepranch Library was part of the California County Free Library system. It had been ever since Antoinette Guidici took the job 32 years earlier. Sheepranch, population 60, is a Mother Lode hamlet 85 miles southeast of Sacramento. It's a tiny town way back in the hills, reached by a winding two-lane country road few ever drive. Those who lived here at the time of our visit in 1972 were mostly retired miners and their wives, and ranchers who run sheep in surrounding mountains.

"You'll never believe how I got the job," the little librarian said. "I was walking up the street one day when this car loaded with books drove into town. It was Roxie Hill who had just been appointed first librarian for Calaveras County. She said she was looking for somebody to set up a Sheepranch branch. I told her I'd gladly do it."

For years Mrs. Guidici ran a boarding house for Sheepranch gold miners. But the miners had all left by 1940, the year her husband—an ex-miner died. That was also the year the boarding house dining room became Sheepranch's library.

Antoinette Guidici continued to live in the other rooms of the weather-beaten, century-old clapboard house. She usually sat on an old bench or a tree stump outside the library door when she wasn't inside checking out books. Or when she wasn't cutting firewood, or hauling water, or laundering her clothes on a washboard, or chopping ice on the porch if it was winter.

Frances Hunt, Calaveras County Librarian at the time, swore by her. "She's simply amazing," Mrs. Hunt said. "So alert, such a wonderful sense of humor, such an asset to the community. Ever since Antoinette was appointed librarian the job called for her to open the library only one day a week. That's why the pay is so little. But her books are her babies. She mothers them. She checks out 80 to 100 books a month. Maybe that doesn't sound like many. But it's really phenomenal for so few people living in that remote little place.

"Antoinette has insisted from the beginning she keep the library open seven days a week. She always says, 'Without my books, what would I do?'" The wallpaper in the old house was faded and worn; spider webs hung from the ceiling. The floor was made of old 1-by-5s with a quarter-inch open space between boards. The library was lighted with two pull-chain bare bulbs. She gave up using library cards years ago. "Why bother? I know everybody. I just stamp a return date inside the cover," she explained. "The books always come back and almost always on time."

The little librarian had 1,800 titles of recent vintage for circulation. She received a new batch from the central library each month. "If you want a book Antoinette doesn't have," Mary Scott said, "you just give her a request and she gets it for you. I mean you get the book in no time at all." The library was the love of her life—that and her four children, grandchildren and great-grandchildren. "I'm here all the time. I have nothing else to do. I might as well keep the library open," explained the little old librarian of the leftover gold-mining town.

MAD ROSE

WHEN SENIOR CITIZENS, fraternal organizations, Masons and others in the San Francisco Bay Area planned trips to Nevada to gamble, they often called on a Catholic nun for help. Sister Madeleine Rose Ashton didn't pray for them. She told them how to place their bets. One of the most popular professors at Holy Name College in Oakland, Sister Madeleine Rose—or "Mad Rose" as her students called her—was a math and probability expert.

She earned her doctorate in math at Stanford University. She had been a nun 50 years when we met her. Holy Name College loaned her out on the local speaking circuit as part of the school's policy to share its resources with the community. Her speech was entitled: "How to Gamble—If You Must." She suggested, "Know the game. Know the odds. Know money management.

"The best game to play is craps," said Sister Madeleine Rose. "The house advantage is only 51% to the players 49%. In craps there are only a certain number of good bets. Play the pass line and take full odds. Or play come or don't come. Don't play the field. It's a bad bet. No one-roll bet is ever a good bet." As for the game with the poorest chances of winning, she points to keno. "It's the worst game for gamblers, and slot machines aren't much better," she said.

"The standard three-reel slot machine with 20 symbols on each reel has 8,000 possibilities. There are 984 winning combinations and 7,016 losing combinations, giving players a 12.3% chance to win and the house an 87.7% winning opportunity." Is it a sin to gamble? "No, I don't believe so," the nun replied. "Life is a gamble. We gamble on investments. I think gambling is neutral in the sinning category. Of course it's wrong if you're gambling your grocery money. But gambling is old as the hills. Dice were found in the pyramids. The Great Wall of China and Columbia University were built with lottery money." Sister Madeleine Rose was all for a state lottery for California when it was first proposed.

"I think it's a great idea, if the proceeds are to go to education as planned. Nobody is forced to bet in a state lottery. It makes the winners happy." Mad Rose said she isn't a gambling nun. "Math and probability are my bag. That's the reason for my interest. I got started giving the gambling lectures when a chief of police of one of the towns near college talked to me about probability. The chief's Kiwanis Club was planning a trip to Reno and he asked me if I would talk to the club about gambling odds. After the speech the club wanted to take me along on the trip to Reno and pay my way. I turned down the offer. "I don't go to Nevada and gamble because I don't have that kind of money," Sister Madeleine Rose said. "Anyway, I'd rather watch the Oakland As. I'm a baseball nut."

CHAPTER TWENTY-FIVE

Sid Smith (left) and Charles Hillinger with plaque commemorating "scarlet women."
(Photo by Ray Graham).

THE OLDEST PROFESSION

PLAQUE FOR SCARLET WOMEN

"I T'S A TOUCHY MATTER," said Verne Farewell, chief of police of Jackson, looking at the heart-shaped plaque. "I'm not quite sure how the PTA will react to this." "This is our history," replied Pete Cassinelli, mayor of the little city (pop. 2,100) in the Mother Lode. "We live with it. It's nothing to be ashamed of." So, Chief Farewell dutifully blocked off traffic so that townspeople—most of them, to be precise, townsmen—could dedicated a plaque to one of the oldest professions known in Jackson. Or, for that matter, anywhere.

In the 49er days the community was well known for two things: a large pile of empty whiskey bottles in the center of town (miners and travelers always dumped them there, giving the town the Gold-Rush name of Botilleas); and, on the periphery of this monument, one of the early California's most flourishing colonies of bordellos.

The bottles were cleaned up some time in the past century. The bordellos took longer. Until 1952, in fact. When they were put out of business, state agents said they were the last permanently established, known and locally tolerated houses of prostitution in all of California. It was to commemorate this history that the Valentine's Day plaque was dedicated with mock solemnity.

Said Larry Cenotto, field deputy to Assemblyman Eugene Chappie: "We cast not stones, but a plaque to mark their toil." Said Duff Chapman, a stock broker, in the dedicatory address: "For over 100 years the region surrounding this spot supported a full and enlightened economy based on the world's oldest profession, and its related business, gambling. But new ideals have washed away the grandeur of an established immorality as old as time itself." Said Hildy Barham, operator of an antique shop: "Why not? After all, that's what this town was famous for. It's about time these women got the recognition due them. Miners, Chinese, everybody else has plaques and monuments—but not these women, who played a major role in the old mining days."

The plaque was set in a downtown sidewalk not far from three large frame houses rich in history but poor in upkeep. The plaque reads: "World's oldest profession flourished 50 yards east of this plaque for many years, until this most perfect example of free enterprise was padlocked by unsympathetic politicians."

As the local Irish band (drums and baritone sax) played temperance selections, the brief ceremony was concluded—and civic leaders began to plan their next betterment project for the county seat of Amador County. Jackson, it seemed, had another home industry—perhaps inspired by that monumental heap of empties—that flourished long after the Gold Rush ended. "Next," said dentist Allan Robello, "we need a plaque to commemorate bootlegging in the city."

SALLY STANFORD

WHEN SALLY STANFORD was a member of the Sausalito City Council, the picturesque San Francisco Bay town just north of the Golden Gate Bridge, she was never invited to join the local woman's club. "They probably think my past would wipe out their future," Sally said. She ran one of San Francisco's best-known brothels for 20 years. Her house was a mansion on one of the city's highest hills, two blocks from the fashionable Fairmont and Mark Hopkins hotels. It was frequented by some of the biggest spenders on the Pacific Coast. But Sally Stanford went straight once she retired from the world's oldest profession. She was now operating a fashionable restaurant, the Valhalla, on Sausalito's waterfront.

Sally Stanford was 70 when we caught up with her. She believed she was the only former madam in the nation holding political office. "It wasn't easy," she said. "I ran for a City Council seat seven times before I finally won." What's a former madam doing in City Hall? "You wouldn't believe the rip-off people in this town have been getting from city fathers," she maintained. "The damn master planners pushing everybody around. The high handiness. The corruption. Talk about Watergate..." A problem getting a permit to remodel her kitchen "pushed me into politics," she explained.

"For three years and eight months I fought for the permit. Finally I hired the right guy and got the permit. But he insisted I redo my parking lot as well for an outrageous price. I told him to go to hell. Then and there I set my guns on City Hall." It took her 14 years, but she finally made it. "Some of the citizens objected to an ex-madam sitting on City Council deciding what's good for their children," Sally admitted.

But through the years she had become one of the leading citizens of the community, sponsoring Little League Baseball teams, supplying the high school band with instruments, championing pay raises for police. She became a City Hall fixture before she was elected, speaking out on all issues at council meetings. The mayor, Robin Sweeny, 47, a nurse, was a member of the council when Sally Stanford ran for office. "Mrs. Sweeny said she would resign if I was elected," Sally said. "But she didn't. And by virtue of me, she's the mayor. I cast the deciding vote when it came time to elect a new mayor." Mayor Sweeny said she has had " a very tenuous relationship with THAT woman the past two years in City Hall." The mayor always refers to Miss Stanford as "THAT woman."

Sally Stanford lived a busy life. She was a bootlegger and ran a speakeasy in Ventura County during the 1920s. There were the years during the 30s and 40s as a madam—years for which she said she had no regrets. "I have no apologies for something I always considered a community service," she allowed.

She has been married a half dozen times, once to socially prominent

CHARLES HILLINGER

Robert L. Gump, member of one of San Francisco's most influential mercantile families. Her restaurant was one of the most popular spots in the Bay Area, accommodating 250 guests at one sitting. The restaurant furnishings were lush Victorian—luxurious red carpeting, Tiffany lamps, gilded mirrors originally in the Mark Hopkins Hotel, fine paintings, fresh flowers everywhere. The maitre d's dressed in a black gown with plunging neckline.

A red light glowed around the clock in an upstairs window. Highly polished brass bedsteads retired from service were the grillwork between the bar and main dining room. The motif was obvious. But Sally Stanford's house was strictly a restaurant, nothing more. She ran the Valhalla from a 19th-Century dental chair at one end of the bar. There she sat and welcomed all guests. She wore expensive, custom-made gowns, and was bejeweled with fancy necklaces and earrings.

She dressed as elegantly at City Hall. At a council meeting the chamber was packed as critical issues were being debated. During one vote, all four council members sounded their "ayes," then it was Sally Stanford's turn: "Absolutely not!" she thundered.

CHAPTER TWENTY-SIX

Wayne "Mr. Lighthouse" Wheeler, founder-president of The Lighthouse Society.

MR. LIGHTHOUSE, MOON LEE, REDHEADS & RUBELIANS

MR. LIGHTHOUSE

There is no structure as altruistic as a lighthouse. Its only purpose is to serve humanity. —GEORGE BERNARD SHAW

ON FEB. 4, 1989 WAYNE WHEELER officially launched the start of the Bicentennial of the Lighthouse by cutting the ribbon and delivering the keynote address at the rededication of the 1846 Key West, Fla., Lighthouse. Wheeler, known to lighthouse aficionados from coast to coast and around the world as Mr. Lighthouse, knows more about the quaint sentinels that guide ships into safe harbor than anyone alive. The bearded, blue-eyed San

Franciscan is founder-president of the 11,000-member nonprofit historical and educational U.S. Lighthouse Society, sponsor of the year-long salute to the lighthouse.

Lighthouse Society members are people who deeply care about the restoration and preservation of America's lighthouses and lightships. "There is a wave of lighthouse restoration projects going on all along America's coasts and the shores of the Great Lakes," Wheeler explained. "At Key West, for example, $250,000 was raised in fund drives to restore the lighthouse declared excess to the Coast Guard's needs in 1969." Wheeler was busy all through the 200th year of lighthouses, attending a number of lighthouse rededication's at bicentennial celebrations. Many of the ceremonies were held on July 4th and Aug. 7, the day set aside by the U.S. Senate as National Lighthouse Day.

It was on Aug. 7, 1789, that President George Washington signed the Lighthouse Act, the first public-works act of the new nation, transferring 12 lighthouses to the federal government. Newport, Rhode Island was the site of the 200th birthday party for lighthouses in 1989. The Newport Navy Band performed. There was a big parade saluting lighthouses. There were photographic and historical exhibits of lighthouses, workshops and lectures pertaining to the history of lighthouses, old lighthouse keepers swapping stories.

"Mr. Lighthouse" was there, of course. Legendary lighthouse keeper Ida Lewis' name was recalled time and time again. Ida Lewis died of a stroke at the Lime Rock Lighthouse in Rhode Island in 1911 after tending the light for more than 50 years. She saved 18 lives and became a national hero, with her picture appearing on the cover of *Harper's Weekly* in July 1869.

In 1910 there were 800 lighthouses in operation in the United States, manned by 1,659 civilian keepers from the U.S. Lighthouse Service. It was the heyday of the colorful structures, which the Senate resolution described as symbolizing "safety, security, heroism, duty and faithfulness." In 1939 the Coast Guard assumed responsibility for lighthouses. Now all but one—in Boston—of the existing 600 lighthouses have been automated. Many have been replaced, in the words of Wheeler, "by rotating zero beacons stuck up on ungainly poles." So much for lighthouses. Now, for "Mr. Lighthouse."

Wayne Wheeler, a native of Buffalo, N.Y., was a Coast Guard officer from 1963 to 1975, and the civilian assistant chief to navigation aids for the Coast Guard in San Francisco from 1976 to 1987. "I started the U.S. Lighthouse Society in 1984 in the dining room of my San Francisco home," Wheeler recalled. "For three years I worked 40 hours a week for the Coast Guard, 30 hours a week for the Lighthouse Society. The society got so big I had to quit the Coast Guard prior to retirement," explained Wheeler, a self-proclaimed "lighthouse nut." In 1979, he put together a slide show on the history of lighthouses, beginning with the 45-story Pharos at Alexandria, Egypt, constructed in 280 BC and one of the Seven Wonders of the World. During his presentation he recites lighthouse poetry, sings sea chanteys and delights audiences with legends and lores of lighthouses. "Mr. Lighthouse" has been on the lecture circuit with his one-man lighthouse show ever since.

"I quickly learned there are people all over America, who, like me, are crazy about lighthouses, even people in landlocked places like North Dakota. I decided there ought to be an organization for lighthouse nuts like myself." Lighthouse Society members live in all 50 states and 20 foreign nations. During the lighthouse bicentennial year, the U.S. Lighthouse Society's vice president was Walter Fanning, who was 80 at the time. He was born in a lighthouse. Among the members was Connie Small, then 87, an ex-lighthouse keeper's wife who wrote the book "Lighthouse Keeper's Wife."

Members of the organization receive the Keeper's Log, a quarterly edited by "Mr. Lighthouse," filled with features, photographs, sketches and historic accounts about lighthouses and those who staffed them. Each issue of the Log carries stories about famous lighthouses, like America's first lighthouse, Little Brewster's Island, erected in 1716 in Boston and blown up by the British in 1786, about famous keepers like George Worthylake, America's first keeper, drowned two years after the Boston Lighthouse on Little Brewster Island was erected, a fate remembered over the years by scores of keepers in storms and in rescue attempts.

In its archives the Lighthouse Society headquarters at 244 Kearny Street, San Francisco has more than 1,000 books and 12,000 photographs of lighthouses. The Lighthouse Society sponsors photography contests and works tirelessly for the preservation and restoration of lighthouses throughout America.

"Mr. Lighthouse," who turned 60 in 1999, leads society members each year on tours to lighthouses in the far corners of the world, to countries like Russia, Greece, Portugal, New Zealand, Ireland, Norway, up and

CHARLES HILLINGER

down the Pacific, Atlantic and Great Lakes. The society owns the 128-foot lightship Relief in San Francisco Bay, one of the last of the Coast Guard relics that served as a floating lighthouse, and its members adopted a Coast Guard light station to care for. All this and much more because of "Mr. Lighthouse's" fascination and obsession with lighthouses.

MOON LEE

FOR YEARS MOON LIM LEE worried about Won-lim Miao—the Temple Amongst the Forest Beneath the Clouds—on the Russian River in Weaverville. Then Lee was struck with the idea—"Why not give it to the people of California." That's how Won-lim Miao became a historic monument. Won-lim Miao, oldest Chinese temple in America in continuous use, is the most perfect example of a Taoist village temple outside China.

For Lee and his wife, Dorothy, the arrangement has worked out splendidly. "As long as we live we will be able to worship in the temple as we have since childhood," explained the third-generation Californian. "And when we die, we know the temple will be in good hands, cared for by the state, for all to appreciate as a memento to the part played by the Chinese in early-day California." Mr. and Mrs. Lee were the last descendants in Trinity County from a colony of 2,500 Chinese gold miners who once worked there.

"When the temple was built in 1874 to replace the original temple erected in 1852," related Lee, "this mountain village (northwest of Redding) had one of the biggest Chinatowns outside China. There was a huge Chinese business district here. There were two Chinese theaters featuring traveling troupes of actors directly from China." Chinese swarmed to Trinity River diggings in the early 1850s to make their fortune. "As quickly as they made as much as $1,000, they returned to China. That was enough to retire for life," said Lee. "The ones that didn't make it stayed on. My grandfather was one of those who failed."

Lee's grandfather's name appears among the list of founders in the temple. For 2,000 years Taoism has rivaled Confucianism in its influence on Chinese philosophy and life. The Taoists worship a multiplicity of gods, many of whom are depicted in elaborated gold leaf statues in the temple presented to the state by Lee. It is a spacious and colorful structure. Inside enormous entry doors are two, 12-foot high false doors or "spirit screens."

"We believe evil spirits go in a straight line and not around corners," explained Lee. "So it is always safe in the temple." There are three altars in the sanctuary on which rests the statues of the gods. In front of the altars is a wooden table on which the Lees since childhood had been placing fruit, bread and other food and wine offerings for heavenly spirits. Worship, Taoist fashion, is something carried on individually rather than in a congregation. For 30 years the Lees had been the sole worshipers in the temple, except when visitors who practice the religion passed through Weaverville.

"Chinese Taoists have come here from throughout the world. For the reputation of the temple is widespread among Taoists," noted Lee. He can remember as a boy that nearly 1,000 Chinese still lived in Weaverville, an out-of-the-way hamlet. The Chinese who lived here in the early 1900s left, moving to Sacramento, San Francisco and other parts of the state. By the 1920s few were left. By the 1930s there was only a handful. Lee stayed on operating a hardware store and serving as a Trinity County highway commissioner. Even the Lees' children moved away from Trinity County.

That is why he and his wife worried about the temple. For with no Chinese left he thought when he and his wife are no longer here, there would be no one around to look after Won-lim Miao. The Division of Beaches and Parks accepted the temple in 1961 and opened it for daily public visitation, except for brief moments when Lee and his wife enter to pray.

REDHEADS

THERE ARE AN ESTIMATED 12 MILLION REDHEADS in the United States. One of them is Laguna Hills piano player Steve Douglas who decided that it was time redheads united to promote their identity. "There's a society for everything else," said Douglas, who organized Redheads International in 1982. "There might as well be one for redheads."

Douglas quit his job in a band, sold his $4,000 baby grand, his $5,000 synthesizer and $6,000 worth of recording equipment in order to launch his club. He ordered redhead bumper stickers and membership cards along with T-shirts bearing the Redheads International logo.

He rented a cubbyhole office in Laguna Hills in Orange County. He ran ads in Rolling Stone magazine and in local and national newspapers. Within nine months more than 1,000 redheads paid $10 each to join and several chapters of the club were formed.

The walls of Douglas' headquarters were covered with photos of bricktop members as well as of such famous redheads as Little Orphan Annie, Red Buttons and Lucille Ball. On the bulletin board was a Dear Abby column letter from a 32-year-old man who complained that he couldn't find a girl because of the "terrible curse of being a redhead. Was there a club for redheads he could join?" Abby didn't know of any. Douglas fired off a letter to Dear Abby denying that it was a curse to be a redhead and told her about Redheads International. In the letter Douglas asked: "Did you know George Washington and Thomas Jefferson were redheads? Or Nero, Napoleon, Henry VIII, Winston Churchill, Sarah Bernhardt and Mark Twain?"

Douglas said he got the idea for the club when he saw a television show in which two UC Berkeley coeds told of being "put down" because they were redheads. "All redhead kids take insults and ribbing because of the color of their hair," he sighed. He decided it was time to unite "to show we're proud to be redheads."

WHAT IS A RUBELIAN?

WHAT IS A RUBELIAN? It's the mad, mad, wonderful world of Michael Rubel who failed as a farmer and was building a castle in a reservoir. When Rubel (roo-bell, accent on the bell) was about 7, he started building marvelous forts out of scrap lumber and junk. We visited the castle when he was 34.

"Every now and then the city dispatched huge trucks, cranes and cables to pull my forts down, declaring them a menace," recalled Rubel, a portly, 6-foot-2-inch mustached man. Author-publisher Harry Austin Deuel Jr., wrote a book about the boy's forts, entitled "Castles by Mike."

Rubel's father, the late Henry Scott Rubel, was pastor of an Episcopal Church, an orange grower and gag writer. He gave Joe Penner his famous line, "Wanna buy a duck?" Rubel's mother, Mrs. Dorothy Rubel, had been a chorus girl. The Rubels' property in the San Gabriel Mountain foothills adjoined the 1,400-acre citrus ranch of

Albert Bourne, president of Singer Sewing Machine Co. "Mr. Bourne had this big concrete reservoir for irrigating his oranges and a super old citrus packing house," said Rubel. "I was his buddy as a little kid. I kept telling him when I grew up I wanted to buy the reservoir and packing house."

When Rubel was 20, Bourne gave the packing house, reservoir and the 2½ acres of which it stands to the Rev. Rubel's church with the provision the church sell the property to the youth. By this time, young Rubel was ready to settle down.

"I had been traveling all over the world trying to find myself," he explained. He had hitchhiked through Europe, Asia and Africa, worked as a jackeroo (cowboy) in Australia and as a purser on a Spanish ship. The captain of the ship, an old Dutch seafarer, had taken a liking to young Rubel. "He hired me on as a paint chipper. In time I became the purser. We sailed through the Mediterranean, the Suez Canal, to the East Indies, Japan and Australia. After a couple of years, I returned to California to figure out what I should do with the reservoir and packing house. Five years ago, many, many years after I had sailed with the captain, I was informed he had died and left me a bunch of money.

"The captain was my salvation. Now, I can spend my life building the castle with the money he left me." Before Rubel got the inheritance, he tried growing cucumbers and eggplants hydroponically (with water instead of soil) in the half acre reservoir.

"It was a complete fiasco. As a farmer I proved to be a total washout," said Rubel. So, now he was concentrating on his castle, except for the two hours he worked each weekday driving a school bus in the afternoon, delivering mountain children to their homes on a 110-mile run. Rubel was building his castle strictly for fun. "But I work hard at it," he quickly added. Up at 5 in the morning. Mixing cement all day.

"The castle really has no function, no purpose. It's all a big wild dream, just as the forts were when I was a kid." Rubel was constructing the castle with tons of rocks, piles of bottles, discarded pipes, old telephone poles and railroad ties, with bedsprings, coat hangers and just plain junk. Friends dropped by and helped. Several segments of the castle were completed. There was a tree house in the branches of a 400-year-old live oak complete with a swimming pool (an old 12-foot-deep, 10-foot-in-diameter oil tank.) There was a house built of old bottles, a potter's shop, a house made of railroad ties and a house made of orange crates. At the time of our visit, Rubel was living principally in the Tin Palace, the old sheet-metal packing house.

The Tin Palace was 158 feet long and 42 feet wide. There were 7,536 square feet of floor space. Rubel lived in nine mammoth rooms in the old packing house. A sign at the entrance proclaimed: "Thou shall maintain thy airspeed lest the Earth shall rise up and smite you." The Tin Palace was richly furnished, filled with fine paintings, with a grand piano and rich tapestries. It had two elevators, one to the subterranean kitchen, the other down to an enormous wine cellar. In the center of the Tin Palace was a 1928 Chevrolet truck. Rubel's bed was mounted on the flatbed of the truck.

He had no TV. But there were several 1920 and 1930 radios. He had a cast-iron bathtub shipped around the Horn in 1872 and a century-old working pull toilet with the water box near the ceiling. Outside the Tin Palace was the ladies rest room (Rubel was a bachelor)—a modernized outhouse with carpeting on the walls and ceiling "to make it feminine."

Rubel had two giant natural gas engines formerly used to pump irrigation water. He used a 7-ton engine to turn his barbecue spit, a 14-ton engine to fill his tiny birdbath. He had a fleet of 14 cars, vintage '20s and early '30s, his favorite a 1932 Ford. His towering 1909 windmill next to the Tin Palace operated his washing machine. The Tin Palace, tree house, orange-crate house, fancy outhouse, railroad-tie house, castle segments in the reservoir, the windmill, his cars and all the rest were aptly called by those who know him "the Rubelian." As was Rubel's life-style.

"My mother wanted me to be an attorney," he related. "But after flunking out of my first semester of college, I came to a conclusion it would be sheer nonsense for me to try to make a success of my life. I would rather build a castle. It keeps me off the streets. Everybody has to have something wrong with them."

CHAPTER TWENTY-SEVEN

Warmly Ormly Gumfudgen playing his bazooka.

MORE FROM THE LIGHT SIDE

WARMLY ORMLY

ORMLY GUMFUDGIN collects semantic oddities he calls "profundums" like: "Nobody goes there anymore; it's too crowded." Gumfudgin utters philosophical sayings such as: "He who laughs, lasts." "The darker the light, the darker the dark." When I first met Gumfudgin in 1975 he was a columnist for the *Sunland-Tujunga Record-Ledger*, writing weekly under the heading "Warmly Ormly." His name popped up frequently over the years in Southern California newspaper columns. He published Society for the Preservation and Encouragement of Barbershop Quartet Singing in America publications. He was Southern California correspondent for the *Wretched Mess News*.

Warmly Ormly raises giant bonsai trees. He plays an electrically amplified kazoo. He drives a 1927 Model T depot hack. He is a member of a barbershop quartet called the Neighbor Hoods. He is the Chief Keeper of the Great Seal of the L.A. Pod of the Chili Appreciation Society International. Gumfudgin wears many hats. He claims it has taken him only 20 years to rise from obscurity to oblivion. He has a one-in-the-world scrutari collection. "I am a scrutabilist," O.G. explains. "A collector of inspection slips. You know they come with new shirts, shorts, coats, dresses, pants. Nobody collects them. But I do."

Gumfudgin is a spindly 6 feet 3 inches and weighs 175 pounds. A Missouri Meerschaum corncob pipe constantly dangles from his mouth. His mustache is a la Wyatt Earp and Cantinflas. He has a flowing beard. He hardly ever sits down. He even stands when he types. Ormly Gumfudgin isn't his real name. He really is Stan Locke, for 20 years head of Jet Propulsion Laboratory's recreation club when I first interviewed him. He edited the JPL house organ called *The Thing*. But many people know him only as Ormly Gumfudgin.

"I needed a nom de plume for writing," explains O.G. "I wanted something to spread happiness." He happened to be reading a turn-of-the-century book about the Old West and spotted a poem by Frank Gumfudgin. "I never have been able to track down Gumfudgin. But I do believe he was a real person," said Warmly Ormly. "Gumfudgin is a genuine family name. Some years ago an outfit making plaques contacted me to see if I would buy one of their Gumfudgin offerings. It was cheap. The plaque company knew of at least 50 Gumfudgin families in America." O.G. has his own "Plead of Allergence" which goes as follows: "Facing L.A. place right hand over left lung. I plead allergence to the city of L.A. and to the cloud of smog under which it stands. One big mass of air pollution with eye irritation and lung congestion for all (Cough)."

Then there is the gospel according to Gumfudgin: "And a loud voice was heard over the land, and it saith unto Noah as he was building the ark, 'Noah, when are you going to get your ship together?'" Ormly manufactures a boat repair kit—five different size corks. Then there's Ormly's Magic Oil. The legend on the bottle notes: "Supposed to be good for rheumatism and arthritis but hell, beggin' your pardon, I can't tell if it works or not so why don't you try it and let me know. Satisfaction NOT guaranteed. Also recommended for attacks of Painintheass."

"I'm the world's only bazooka player," declared 77-year-old Warmly Ormly in the year 2000, quickly explaining: "because I have the world's only bazooka." He learned the bazooka from Bob Burns, the radio and movie star who invented it. "The bazooka is a long horn with a low, mournful sound between a low trumpet and tuba, it sounds like a dying calf in a hailstorm," allowed Warmly Ormly whose motto is: "Anything worth doing is worth doing."

LAUGHING IN THE LIBRARY

PEOPLE ARE FOREVER BURSTING INTO FITS OF LAUGHTER on the third floor of the San Francisco Public Library and no one shushes them. The laughter spills over from the Nat Schmulowitz Collection of Wit and Humor. Comedians from across the nation visit SCOWAH, the acronym for the collection, jotting down one liners and funny stories or reading material into tape recorders.

When the late attorney Nat Schmulowitz was not busy with his clients he was traveling the world in search of books of humor. As a result of his half-century odyssey through the bookshops of Europe, Asia, Africa, North and South America, the San Francisco Library has what is considered a most remarkable collection of books and magazines on wit and humor.

The Schmulowitz Collection includes more than 17,000 volumes written in 35 languages spanning four centuries, plus a huge collection of magazines and other materials. "With a name like Schmulowitz, he had to have a keen sense of humor," said Johanna Goldschmid, curator of the special collections of the library.

Schmulowitz achieved national attention in 1921 with his successful defense of comedian Roscoe (Fatty) Arbuckle in one of the most sensational murder trials of the 1920s. The attorney was a member of the library commission of San Francisco for seven years and served as president in 1944. On April 1, 1947, the beginning of National Laugh Week, Schmulowitz donated his collection to the library. He died in 1966 at the age of 77. The shelves of SCOWAH are filled with books of humor of every type—humor in the Bible, sports humor, ethnic humor, political humor, etc.

There are stacks of humor magazines such as *Judge* and *National Lampoon*, two rows of Joe Miller Joke Books dating back to the original, published in London in 1743, and copies of "Poggio the Florentyn" written in Latin in the 14th-Century. "Poggio Bracciolini was the father of wit and humor," Johanna Goldschmid explained. "He was a monk who jotted down ribald jokes."

What was humor like in the 14th Century? Here is a sample of Poggio's: "A man who had just purchased an expensive gown for his wife figured out every time he lay with her it cost him at least a ducat. Hearing his complaint, his wife replied, 'It is your fault. Why don't you lie with me more often so that each time it will cost you but a penny.'" And the early Joe Miller story entitled "Reason for Weeping: A gentleman taking an apartment told the landlady, 'I assure you Madame I have never left a lodging but my landlady shed tears.' She answered, 'I hope it was not, sir, that you went away without paying.'"

Schmulowitz never married. He lived with his sister, Kay, a spinster. Kay Schmulowitz who outlived her brother by many years, provided the collection with subscriptions to foreign humor magazines. The magazines included *Krokodil* (Russia), *Szpilki* (Poland), *Candido* (Italy), *Blagues* (French), *Urzica* (Rumania), *Fabula* (Germany), *Ludas Matyi* (Hungary), *Nebelspalter* (Switzerland) and *Pourquoi Pas* (French).

"Humor," Kay Schmulowitz told the author, "is what keeps sanity in the world. It is a very important part of daily living."

JOKE PROFESSOR

ALAN DUNDES, professor of folklore at the University of California, Berkeley, had a room full of jokes. There were absent-minded professor jokes, good news/bad news, knock-knocks, windup dolls and shaggy dog stories, Martian and moron jokes, Little Audreys, Confucius say, elephant jokes, Tom Swifties, ethnic jokes and jokes from Afghanistan to Zambia. He had file cabinets spilling over with myths, tales, riddles, games, customs, pranks, graffiti, latrinalia, limericks, parodies, proverbs, puns, rites of passage, yells, blessing, dances, gestures and obscenities. There were supernatural, cadaver and nose-picking stories, toasts, taunts, evil eyes, will-o'-the-wisp, witchcraft and weather stories.

"It's just endless," the professor said. "Pick a country. Take Iran, for example. Here are hundreds of folk songs, dances, legends, lores, jokes, superstitions from Iran," he said as he opened his Iran files. During the interview someone sneezed. Dundes whirled around to the opposite wall and opened a drawer full of sneezing stories. "Dites. You know dites?" he asked. "Dites are definitions." He pulled an envelope full of dites from his files and recited definitions like: "Snowing: An old lady shaking her pillows. Raining: God's tears. Thunder: God moving potato wagons."

From his knock-knock collection, Dundes read: "Knock. Knock. Who's there? UCLA. UCLA who? When there's no smog UCLA." He had a list and descriptions of thousands of games played around the world including the traditional American favorites "Kick the can," "Mother, may I?" and "Ring around the rosie." His jump-rope rhymes included old standbys like "Charles Chaplin went to France," "Grace, Grace, dressed in lace," "I love coffee, I love tea," "I was born in a frying pan," "A sailor wen to sea" and "Pickle, pickle." There were Tom Swifties, also known as Wellerisms, such as: "Doctor, I think your knife slipped," said Tom halfheartedly." There are transpositions of sounds called spoonerisms, like, "Let me sew you to your sheet" for "Let me show you to your seat."

There are drawers full of proverbs, such as "It's always darkest before the dawn" and "lightning never strikes twice"; of weather lore, like, "Ring around the moon," "Mackerel skies and mares' tails"; of tongue twisters, "A skunk sat on a stump," and taunts, "Fatty, fatty, two-by-four, can't get through the kitchen door."

Dundes has collected thousands of superstitions, like the traditional Chinese parents' warnings to their children about rattling chopsticks against their bowls. Beggars in China would always rattle their chopsticks against their bowls to attract the attention of passersby. The superstition goes that if you rattle your chopsticks, you, too, will end up a beggar.

At the time we met Dundes he had written nine books and more than 100 scientific papers about his material including his contribution to the Kroeber Anthropological Society papers entitled, "Here I Sit—A Study of American Latrinalia." The Berkeley professor coined the word latrinalia to describe writings on bathroom walls. His paper on the poetry of the smallest rooms includes references about the influence of television in the latrines: "Smile, you're on candid camera." "Content of latrinalia commentaries varies," Dundes notes. "Some are unexpectedly intellectual: 'God is dead.' Nietzsche. 'Nietzsche is dead.' God." Dundes

CHARLES HILLINGER

said anthropologist Allen Walker Read spent several weeks compiling everything he saw written on restroom walls in an extensive trip across America. Read at the time attributed the practice "to the well known human yearning to leave a record of one's presence."

A prime source of the professor's material was from students who were required to turn in at least 50 items per semester for his archives. "I have an average of 250 students a semester; that totals on the order of 25,000 items a year," Dundes said. "All of these subjects are important ingredients of our culture and cultures throughout the world. We analyze the historic and social significance of the material."

CHAPTER TWENTY-EIGHT

John Kenny hanging rubber snakes on wall of his house
to scare off woodpeckers who've filled it with holes.

BIRDS OF A FEATHER

TOWN UNDER ATTACK BY WOODPECKERS

JOHN KENNY leaned out the second-floor window of his mountain home in Wrightwood, a mile-high mountain village, 75 miles northeast of Los Angeles. He nailed a 6-foot long rubber snake to the cedar shingle siding. The snake was hammered onto the siding near three owl decoys and strips of shiny metal. Kenny's house looks like a sieve. Nearly every shingle on the south side of his cabin is drilled with holes.

"It's the damn woodpeckers," swore Kenny. "And, this is the worst year in the 48 years my wife's family has had this weekend and vacation cabin in Wrightwood. We keep trying different tactics all the time to try to scare away the woodpeckers. Someone said use owl decoys. That hasn't worked. Somebody said try metal strips. No luck there. The latest suggestion is rubber snakes. If I saw a rattlesnake this long I know it would scare the hell out of me."

Redheaded acorn woodpeckers begin hammering away on the house at daybreak. "My wife, Mae, and I come up here for rest and relaxation. We look forward to sleeping in late. At 6 in the morning the woodpeckers sound like jackhammers pecking away at the side of the house," sighed the frustrated homeowner.

Woodpeckers, perched on branches in nearby pine trees, watched seemingly with great interest as Kenny nailed the rubber snake to the side of his house. No bird attacked the house for several hours. Eventually one brave woodpecker took a chance. Soon several wood-peckers were banging holes on the side of the house, ignoring the owls, the metal stripping and the fierce-looking rubber snake. Cabins and homes in many Southern California mountain communities with stands of oak trees come under attack especially in years of abundant acorn crops. Woodpeckers drill holes in sides of wooden homes and then shove acorns into the holes as they prepare for the winter ahead.

"The birds stash the acorns into the holes and feast on insect larvae that develop on the acorns during winter and spring," explained Kent Smith, Department of Fish and Game coordinator for non-game birds. "Once the acorns are gone from the oak trees the woodpeckers stop drilling holes in houses, utility poles and trees."

So, how does one prevent woodpeckers from drilling holes in a house? In a book published by the University of Nebraska regarding prevention and control of wildlife damage, the following suggestions are offered: "Nail mothballs, long strips of foil, metal sheeting, owl or snake decoys to the house. Cover the house under attack with a fishnet. Make noises like clap-ping hands, firing a toy cap pistol or banging on garbage can lids. Hang beef suet from nearby trees to draw the woodpeckers away from the house."

A sticky bird repellent that discourages woodpeckers without harm-ing them also is recommended, but it also discolors paint, stain and natural wood siding. In Wrightwood, homeowners have tried all these suggestions and many more but to no avail. "Nothing works but shoot-ing them, but you can't shoot them because woodpeckers are protect-ed," sighed Ted Goossen, a long time resident. "Woodpeckers not only have torn up my house, they riddled my apple tree. Someone said put tar on the apple tree. I did. They ate right through the tar."

Treena Anderson, owner of Wrightwood Lumber, said she had an inflated owl on her house. It doesn't work. Les Rowland, manager of

Mountain Hardware, has a duck whirligig on his place. The duck's wings move and the duck squeaks when the wind blows. "That seems to work if the wind is blowing," said Rowland.

BIRD DIALECT EXPERT

LUIS BAPTISTA warbled the nine different dialects of the white-crowned sparrow sung by San Francisco Bay Area birds. Bird watchers listened in awe. They had come from all over the West to Golden Gate Park to a bird symposium sponsored by the California Academy of Sciences. "Birds have dialects in their songs, as humans do in their speech," explained the bird dialect expert between whistles, trills and buzzes.

While other ornithologists band birds, Baptista listened to the birds' songs to tell what part of the state or country they come from—or even what part of town. "Some birds are bilingual. Some are trilingual," said the dialect expert.

Behind the General Pershing statue in the park, he pointed out a group of white-crowned sparrows from Seattle, another from Coos Bay, Oregon, that had flown in recently to winter in California. "They have dialects different from the San Francisco Bay Area birds," he said. Near the statue were two white-crowned sparrows from Oakland and some hometowners from the city by the bay. Although the birds were identical, each group sang a different song, Baptista explained. "It gets crazy. Along the shores of Lake Merced in Oakland, the white-crowned sparrows sing one song. Across the street they sing another."

Males often mate with females singing a different tune. Songs are not inherited or inherent. Young learn from adults. Baptista had lab birds raised from young that "babble like human babies" and don't learn to sing unless instructed by an adult while the bird is young. The ornithologist told of placing a young white-crowned sparrow in a cage facing a cage with a strawberry finch from Thailand. There were other white-crowned sparrows in the room that could be heard singing. "But the sparrow looked at the finch all the time. The sparrow grew up singing in Siamese," Baptista said.

Arcane bits of bird lore abounded at the weekend meeting. Robert Bowman, who had visited the Galapagos Islands 20 times during a 30-year period to study finches, talked about bizarre feeding habits of the birds. "There are 14 species of finch in the archipelago," noted Bowman as he showed movies and slides. "One species I nicknamed the vampire finch feeds on the blood of the big booby birds. The finch bite the boobies on the rump, causing the birds to bleed. The finch drinks the blood."

And paleontologist Kevin Padian offered his answer to the age-old question: Did birds learn to fly from the ground up or from trees down? "Birds evolved from small dinosaurs. It's believed the animals leaped into the air to catch insects. Through centuries, little by little they developed lift and found thrust for sustained flight," Padian postulated.

Bob Stewart of the Point Reyes Observatory, in a discussion on "Sex and the Breeding Bird," told how female spotted sandpipers lay eggs and let their mates do the incubating. "Then she goes off with another male, has another clutch, lets that male incubate those eggs, and goes off with still another male, and on and on," said Stewart.

The *piece de resistance* on the program was the king of America's 20 million bird watchers, Roger Tory Peterson of Old Lyme, Connecticut, who received a standing ovation. Peterson is the author-illustrator of the most successful and influential bird book of all times, "Peterson's Field Guide to Birds." It is the bible of bird watching, with more than 4 million copies since it was originally published.

A world expert on penguins, he showed slides of his 15 trips to the Antarctic, where he followed the footsteps of the big birds, photographing, painting and studying them. Among the 17 species he discussed were the jackass penguin (because it brays), the macaroni penguins (because of rakish plumes reminding British sailors of fashionable fops called macaronis), and Adelien penguins sitting on eggs up to their heads in snow.

THE OWL

IT WAS HALLOWEEN. Candles illuminated scores of ornamental owls in an old mansion high on a lonely hill hovering above Hollywood. Trick-or-treaters gulped and ran as the front door creaked open and the owner of the house appeared standing beneath a flying owl. The bird was a stuffed great horned owl suspended on a wire, one of hundreds of owls in the old building.

Owl Mansion was the home of an ornamental iron worker whose legal name had been The Owl for 15 years when I interviewed him at the Owl Mansion. The name appeared on his California driver's license, on his U.S. passport, on his bank account and checks. "It's the only name I have. My original name ceased to exist when I legally became The Owl," he explained. His obsession with owls began when he was 5 and living in Columbus, Ohio. He was on an outing with his parents and grandmother in a forest, became separated from them and then realized he was lost.

"At one point I saw a great horned owl in a tree. The owl flew away and I followed it. The owl would fly a short distance, stop and land in a tree, then take off. I ran through the woods after the owl and came upon my grandmother, mother and dad who were frantically trying to find me. For that reason alone, I think it is easy to understand why I changed my name to The Owl. I owe the birds a debt of gratitude." It was shortly after being lost in the forest that The Owl's Uncle Freddie gave him a blue glass owl to remember the incident. "I've been collecting owls ever since," he said.

He slept under sheets and blankets and on pillows embroidered with owls. He wore an owl watch, had an owl radio and an owl clock. He owned expensive Baccarat, Lalique, Cybis and Steuben porcelain and crystal carved owls. He had a dozen stuffed owls, hundreds of owl figurines, owl rings and owl pins. He had a library of books, magazines, scientific papers and other publications about owls.

"I like what owls stand for—quietness, wisdom," said The Owl. "For 8 years an owl named Owlfie lived with me in the Owl Mansion. I gave lectures about owls at elementary schools, high schools and colleges and would bring Owlfie along with me," related The Owl. He went on: "In recent years laws have been passed prohibiting ownership of owls because they are on the endangered species list. Today it is illegal to have an owl stuffed. But anyone owning stuffed owls predating enactment of the laws may still keep them."

PELICAN MAN

A wonderful bird is the pelican,
His bill will hold more than his belican,
He can take in his beak / Food enough for a week,
But I'm damned if I can see how the helican.
—"THE PELICAN" by DIXON LANIER MERRITT

ELLIS THOMPSON gave up teaching school to carve pelicans "The principal of my school said: 'That's dumb!' My parents, relatives and friends said: 'You're crazy!'" recalled the wood sculptor, who uses only his first name professionally. "My wife and kids said: 'Go for it!'

"It wasn't that I just cut the string without giving it much thought. I had the pelicans pretty well figured out," said Ellis. People really love those big funny looking birds." The huge shorebirds are so popular that the woodcarver had his entire family helping him keep up with demand. Ellis' life-size pelicans are sold in galleries and novelty shops on the West, East and Gulf coasts as well as in Canada, Hawaii, Australia and New Zealand. When we visited Ellis' shop his largest pelicans were 3 1/2 feet high and retailed for $500. The smallest were a foot tall including white-daubed pilings and sold for $24.

They came in various poses—beaks open, beaks closed, and all with generously sprayed posts. "I went through a period where I didn't paint the pilings. We call it the time when the pelicans were constipated. Sales plummeted. People wanted the poop," recalled Ellis. His creations are conversation pieces. "I hear couples argue," he said. "The boyfriend or husband will say, 'I want one of those pelicans.' The woman will reply, 'I wouldn't have one of those dirty birds in my house on a bet.' Some of the large pelicans find homes on rooftops and at the end of piers at lakefront homes."

When Ellis was teaching junior high shop in Loomis, a small town 25 miles north of Sacramento, he carved a variety of different animals and birds. "For a time I was heavy into whales—carving hump backs, sperm, fin backs and blue whales out of redwood. But redwood makes me sneeze. I was glad to make the switch to pine pelicans," he said. It was while on a trip to Morro Bay with his wife, Delores, that he got the pelican inspiration. "I had never seen so many of the big birds in all my life. Morro Bay was alive with them. It was a spiritual experience," remembered Ellis. "I did a number of sketches of the pelicans and went home and began carving. The bird sold well at craft shows and I knew I was onto something big. That's when I decided to quit teaching and devote all my time to pelicans."

To meet the demand, his two sons, Bill and Brian were also carving pelicans. Father and sons also carved seagulls perched on white-splashed pilings. Production was 80% pelican, 20% seagull. The woodcarver was driving a new Mercedes and lived on a five-acre country estate with his own private lake thanks to the pelican. And his ex-boss, relatives and friends are eating crow.

CHAPTER TWENTY-NINE

Tony "Mama" Vidovich, official weigher for the
fishermen's union at the San Pedro waterfront.

SCALES, SNAILS, CHIRPS, & WRIGGLES

MONSTER FISH

"I'VE BEEN FISHING ALL MY LIFE up and down the Pacific coast from Alaska to South America and have never seen or heard of fish this size," said Tony "Mama" Vidovich, 63, as he weighed the 1,009 pound Pacific blue fin tuna. "This tuna weighs nearly three times what I weigh," laughed "Mama," a giant of a man nearly six feet and tipping the scale at 330 pounds. "Mama," a San Pedro commercial fisherman since he was nine years old, was the official weigher for the local fisherman's union.

The San Pedro waterfront buzzed with excitement in November and December, 1989. Some 135 local fishermen on 15 boats caught 767 of the biggest Pacific blue fin tuna ever taken by commercial boats in waters off the Southern California coast—enormous 6-to-9-foot long fish that weighed from 300 pounds to the biggest of them all a 1,009 pound goliath weighed by "Mama" Vidovitch. Normally, Pacific blue fin tuna caught by the fishermen weighed 20 to 100 pounds.

"We have no idea why these fish are suddenly showing up or why they have grown so old and are so big," noted Bill Bayliff, senior biologist for the La Jolla based Inter-American Tropical Tuna Commission. "Age determines size, and it is obvious these are old, old fish—a bunch of senior citizens swimming together in schools." Ron Dotson, fishery biologist with the National Marine Fisheries Service, said, "Historically, we know of blue fin tuna caught in the 300-pound range in the 1930s and 1940s in the western Pacific, but nothing near the size of the monsters being landed now have ever been caught anywhere in the Pacific Ocean." Blue fin tuna spawn in the Pacific Ocean off Japan and migrate back and forth 6,000 miles in each direction from Japan to the coastal waters off Southern California, Mexico, and Central and South America.

All of the giant tuna were packed in ice upon being brought ashore and flown to Japan where they commanded a record $20 to $32 a pound at the Tsukjii Fish Market in Tokyo. Japanese connoisseurs eagerly paid as much as $10 a bite in restaurants for rare tuna such as this—the bigger and the older the fish, the better price it fetched.

The giant tuna were an incredible bonanza for the local fishermen. The fish pumped $3.5 million into Los Angeles' waterfront economy. On two nights nine fishermen aboard the weather-beaten, 52-year-old, 84-foot purse seiner Maria caught 131 of the giants weighing 41,290 pounds—an average of 315 pounds each. Each of the fishermen on the Maria received $37,648.56 for two nights work. "I made more money those two days than I made in any one of the 26 years I have been fishing aboard the Maria," said crew member Miguel Vuoso, 56. "My best previous year was $26,000. My poorest year was $3,000. If there are no fish, you don't make any money." First thing Vuoso did when he received his check was spend $850 for a new golf bag and a set of top-of-the-line clubs.

The monsters paid for fisherman John Dimeglio's trip to Italy, for Vince Piscopo's new Lincoln. Jose Magana used his windfall as a down payment on a new house. "The big fish are God's gift to San Pedro fishermen," said skipper Sal Russo, 59, skipper of the 66-foot Tooter. "I have been fishing 50 years here, ever since I came to America from Sicily. Nothing like this has ever happened." Each of the nine fishermen aboard the Tooter received $22,000 for catching the giants.

Fishing has been a mainstay in San Pedro since the turn of the 20th century. In 1903, the first tuna cannery in the United States was erected here. From then through the 1920s and 1930s, San Pedro's population swelled with immigrant families from Yugoslavia and Italy who moved here to fish. The fishermen and their families have been an integral part of the waterfront community. When Mary Star of the Sea Catholic Church was built in 1950, it was the fishermen and the cannery workers who provided most of the funding for the new church. "Our parish gets its name from the fishermen—the Virgin Mary guiding and protecting them when they are at sea," explained the pastor, Msgr. Patrick Gallagher.

The statue of Mary on top of the church on the hill overlooking the harbor is lit every night so the fishermen can see her when they enter or leave the harbor on their boats. Inside the church on the main altar is a large statue of Mary holding a fishing boat in her arms. The boat represents the local fishing fleet. "Our collections at Sunday Masses are much higher than usual," said Msgr. Gallagher. "We can thank those big fish for that."

THE GREAT CALIFORNIA SNAIL PROBLEM

IT WAS ANTOINE DELMAS who created the great California snail problem. But Delmas never knew his love for escargots would generate anguish in his adopted land. Delmas emigrated to San Jose from his native France in the 1850s. Accompanying him on the ship were his family and a sack of living snails, a favorite delicacy. Some of Delmas' snails later escaped. The billions of *helix aspersa*, or brown European snails, now crawling all over the Golden State's landscape are descendants of those brought here by the French emigrant.

For years snails have been the home gardener's No.1 pest in California. The spiral shelled mollusks cause millions of dollars of damage to citrus trees, farm crops, flowers, plants and lawns in the state each year. "If only Americans enjoyed eating snails a fraction as much as the French, we would not have the great snail problem," said Theodore W. Fisher, University of California, Riverside's in-house malacologist (snail expert). Fisher suggested, tongue in cheek, one solution would be to encourage thousands of Frenchmen to come to California on vacations and harvest the snails from the backyards.

"It is nothing for a Frenchman to sit down and eat a couple dozen snails at one meal," Fisher related. In France, he said, after a rain, men, women and children snap up every snail in sight. "There's a lot of protein on the hoof in the backyards of Californians," noted Fisher. "But few Americans relish the escargots." So, Californians spend a small fortune sprinkling their lawns and gardens with snail poisons trying to eradicate the snails.

Hoping to achieve biological control over the pesky mollusks, Fisher imported another species of European snails, much smaller than the brown garden variety, called *rumina decollata*. The *rumina decollata* feed on the *helix aspersa* but from all indications they are not plant-eaters. Thousands of the *decollatas* have been produced in laboratories at UC Riverside for release to feed on the backyard pests. "But it's a slow process. It would be much better if Californians developed a taste for escargots and started eating their backyard snails," sighed Fisher. Fisher is full of vital statistics about snails. Such as the fact that backyard snails have a life expectancy of two years.

The common garden snail is hermaphroditic yet mates with another snail once during a lifespan. The mating ritual lasts from four to 12 hours. Each snail produces roughly 300 eggs in a lifetime. Snails with dental problems really have a tough time. A backyard garden snail has 14,175 rasping teeth located on the tongue in 135 rows, with each row containing 105 teeth.

To encourage consumption of the backyard pests the University of California Cooperative Extension Service publishes a pamphlet entitled *Snails as Food*. "Edible brown snails considered a pest in California gardens are a tasty meat," the leaflet reports, cautioning: "Never eat snails until at least six weeks after poisons have been used for snail control. Snails must be purged of any off flavor or toxic materials from previously eaten foods."

To purge a snail it is suggested snails be placed in one half inch of damp cornmeal in the bottom of a container. "Let the snails purge themselves by eating cornmeal for at least 72 hours," the pamphlet continues. "Then plunge snails live into boiling water and simmer for 15 minutes. Pick snail meat from shells. Remove dark-colored gall.

Wash snail meat several times under cold running water. Boil empty shell for 30 minutes, using one-fourth teaspoon of baking soda per pint of water. Drain shells, wash them in cold running water." Escargots are served in the shell.

The snail belongs to the same family as the abalone, is low in calories, high in protein and rich in minerals. "Snails can be prepared zillions of different ways," Fisher explained, "in tomato sauce, in garlic butter, in cream sauce and in wine sauce to name but a few methods. But don't eat them plain," he cautioned. "It's like chewing on the rubber at the end of a pencil."

CRICKETS GALORE

YOU COULD HEAR KEN JENKINS' STORE A BLOCK AWAY—it never stopped chirping. Jenkins and his wife, Comoleta, were cricket breeders, selling more than two million of the singing bugs a year to fishermen, pet stores, universities and zoos. "I could sell 3 million crickets a week in summer to fishermen alone, but I haven't got my stock up that high yet," sighed Jenkins.

It should not have taken too long to build up his inventory. A female cricket lays about 300 eggs in her lifetime—usually 10 to 12 eggs a day for a month beginning when she is eight weeks old. Crickets have a life expectancy of four to eight months.

Jenkins was one of about 40 cricket breeders in America when we visited his Los Angeles cricket store. "As far as I know my wife and I are the only commercial cricket growers west of the Rockies," he declared. "The rest are all back East."

The cricket man got into the bug business by accident. A lifelong fresh water fisherman, Jenkins had always preferred live crickets for bait. "I caught my own crickets around the house and around the block as many fishermen do," explained Jenkins. "But I could never come up with enough." He decided to grow his own. He bought 1,000 crickets from an eastern breeder. "Comoleta and I went nuts for those crickets. We read all the literature. We wrote letters to entomologists. Pretty soon our garage was busting at the seams with crickets."

So, three years before we stopped by his shop, Jenkins, a carpenter by trade, put aside his hammers and nails. He and his wife opened the Golden West Cricket Mart at 12705 Venice Blvd. in the Mar Vista area of Los Angeles.

The couple got into the bug business shortly after legislation made it legal to raise the insects in California. "Crickets have a miserable reputation in the West," said Jenkins. "Crickets have been like locust at times. Wiped out whole crops in past years. Really got a bad name. But we raise only domesticated house crickets—you know the type, the friendly, on-the-hearth songsters, harmless little characters."

Crickets come in 2,000 different varieties—some good, some dreaded by the farmers. There are Chinese, Spanish, and Sicilian crickets; blue, green, gray and black crickets; sand, camel, ant, mole, pigmy, cave, broadfaced, mitred, besprinkled, black-horned, golden bell and snowy tree crickets.

The Sicilian is a shrill cricket that can be heard a mile away. The Golden Bell is a Japanese cricket so called because its notes are like the tinkling of soft golden bells. In the Far East a prized gift to all newlyweds is a cricket in a bamboo cage. Chinese and Japanese for centuries have caged singing crickets as other people do songbirds. Instead of cock fights, Chinese are big on cricket bouts. Fighting crickets have sold for as much as $500 in China. Most famous of all battling crickets "Gengis Khan of Canton" won fights with as much as $90,000 at stake. Imagine that kind of money for a couple of fighting bugs. But the Chinese rank among the biggest gamblers on earth.

Jenkins said about 10% of his crickets are sold as pets. "People keep six or eight. Only the males sing. Males rub their wings to attract the attention of female crickets. Crickets are among the great lovers of the insect world."

About 45% of the cricket man's crickets were sold for pet food. "Pet stores sell crickets by the thousands," noted Jenkins. "Crickets are choice food for reptiles, birds, monkeys, frogs, lizards, bats, tarantulas, scorpions and praying mantis. You'd be surprised the number of people that have praying mantis, scorpions, bats and tarantulas for pets." The balance were sold to sporting good stores in cricket containers for fishermen.

When we were in the cricket store crickets were retailing for anywhere from two to five cents each. "Zoos and universities are big customers. Zoos for animal food, schools for animal food and research," noted Jenkins. "We sell crickets to UCLA, USC, the Cal State campuses and many other universities and colleges. One school is using crickets for research in a big sound study program. Another uses crickets for hereditary research."

Comoleta and Ken Jenkins never cease to be fascinated by the troubadours of the bug world. "That saying about telling the temperature by counting a cricket's chirps for 15 seconds and adding 40 is true, you know" allowed the cricket lady. Mrs. Jenkins sits by the hour watching the insects through a magnifying glass. "Female crickets are fanatics about cleanliness," she noted. "While males flutter wings in song, females are cleansing their bodies cat fashion."

Hardly a week passed without someone calling the Golden West Cricket mart to report finding an albino cricket. "What happens," said Jenkins, "is crickets shed their skin once a week for the first seven weeks of their brief lives. They're snow white for 15 minutes. They then turn gray again." Such was life at the store that never stopped chirping.

THE BLOODWORM BUSINESS IS BOOMING

THEY HAD BEEN MARRIED 42 YEARS when we met them. They were nuts about each other. But they did argue. And they were together all the time—for 39 years running Harry's Bait & Tackle Shop in Playa del Rey. When not in the shop, chances are they were out fishing.

"My God, Harry, don't smile. You left your teeth at home," said Cora Edilson, 62, to her husband as the couple ran their fingers through a fresh shipment of bloodworms packed with seaweed. "You know I always forget my teeth. Why bring it up?" snapped Harry, 67, flashing a big toothless grin. The bloodworms were the hottest item in the shop, flown in from the seashore in Maine.

"Can't beat bloodworms for surf fishing," Harry insisted. "It's miracle bait. But you gotta be careful and not get stung. Cora's allergic to bloodworms. When the worms sting her we rush her to the hospital."

They were selling the worms for $3.50 a dozen, $1.80 a half dozen, 35 cents a worm. Fishermen cut them up for bait. The worms were a foot long. Some would buy only one. "We can hardly keep enough in stock," Cora noted. "We don't just sell them to fishermen. Universities buy them too. Universities study them for some kind of research."

Harry and Cora sold rods and reels, tackle, leaders, weights—all the necessary gear for fishing off the nearby rocks, the jetty or from boats. But they were selling more bait than anything. Anchovies, mussels, squid, peas. *Peas?* "For opaleyes," Harry explained. "Beautiful fish. A vegetarian. Loves peas. We sell a lot of peas."

What is it about fishing? Harry was asked. "The excitement of catching a big fish. You forget all your troubles fishing. You got problems. Go fishing. You don't have them. Go home. You got the problems again." Cora chimed in: "They come in here in dirty clothes. You never know. The person could be the greatest surgeon on earth. Rich and poor come in here to go fishing. You can't tell them apart."

Harry's wife limped. She had recently been shot through the right leg. With Harry's gun. "We had burglars at home. Harry bought a gun to be on the safe side. I put my scarf on the piano. Harry put the gun on the scarf. I wasn't aware he did. I pulled the scarf off the piano to put it on. The gun flew to the floor and went off. I was sure I was dying when I saw the blood. When the gun went off Harry had a heart attack."

Their son drove them both to the hospital. "Harry was turning purple," said Cora. "She should have passed out from the loss of blood but she didn't want to," said Harry. "She wanted to watch me die." Both of them, as well as their relationship, survived, and the bloodworm business continues to boom.

CHAPTER THIRTY

Students take milk cow to college in Cal Poly's unique dairy farm program.

CAMPUS CAPERS

STUDENTS TAKE COWS TO COLLEGE

EIGHTY FIVE MILKING COWS were brought to Cal Poly San Luis Obispo by students to live with them on campus. The cows were paying young dairy farmers' way through school. Cows on campus is but one of many unique programs at Cal Poly—a state college boasting the fifth largest agriculturally oriented student body in the nation and by far the largest in the state. Cal Poly students run large beef and dairy ranches on campus.

The school has its own slaughterhouse, a cannery, creamery, frozen food plant, commercial nursery and flower shop. Students also learn and earn by growing, harvesting and marketing broccoli, grapes, tomatoes, sugar beets, onions, bell peppers, squash, carrots, corn, hay and grain on 500 acres of cropland.

On campus are 1,000 head of beef, 350 swine, 350 sheep, 250 dairy cattle, 60 horses, 10,000 hens and 200 turkeys cared for by agriculture majors. Livestock and poultry are leased from the school by some students who keep books on the animals' care and maintenance costs, profit and loss. Students lease campus fruit trees for orchard management studies and earn money during harvest to pay part of their education.

It is a big campus, 5,169 acres in all, with 4,795 acres devoted to farm and ranch operations. Total student body at Cal Poly this particular year was 12,000—agriculture enrollees number 2,274, or one in six. No grades or credit are given for growing crops, running the ranch, caring for sheep, swine or poultry or milking the cows. It is strictly on a volunteer basis. But nearly 1,000 students were taking part in the highly successful enterprise programs.

As for the 17 students who brought their 85 milking cows to college with them, they live in special dorms close to the cows. "We have to live close," explained Larry Godinho, a junior from Ferndale. "We get up at 3 every morning, seven days a week to milk the cows. That takes about an hour. Then we crawl back into bed. But we milk again at 3 in the afternoon. We also feed, breed and do everything else that needs to be done to a cow."

Godinho brought eight cows to live with him on campus. One of Godinho's cows, Doyk, was a classic cow at Cal Poly. He purchased her from a graduating senior. "She's 13 years old," noted Godinho. "I'm the fifth student to own her. She's helped four other guys through school. Doyk's a sad looking beast," Godinho admitted. "Sure her udder droops almost to the ground. But I couldn't resist the buy, $300. She was about ready to have a calf when I bought her. The deal was if she didn't get up after having the calf, I'd get half my money back."

The cow not only got up, but because she had been such a productive animal and had been mated to a good sire, the young dairyman was able to sell the calf for $800. Godinho was averaging 10 gallons of milk a day from the old cow. Godinho's mother visited the campus, took one look at Doyk and solemnly declared: "Honey, you better get rid of that cow, before she falls over dead."

Cows begin to give milk at age 2 to 2 1/2, Students were paying an average of $550 for a mature animal. They could borrow money from the school to purchase more animals and pay back loans at a small rate of interest. Milk produced at the college dairy is sold by students through regular market channels, to the school cafeteria and also through the school's Produce Store. Butter, eggs, cheese and fresh fruit and vegetables all produced on campus are sold at the store. The store features canned and frozen goods bearing the Cal Poly label, a mustang, the school's official mascot.

BILLY GOAT DAVIS

THE LUCKIEST THING that ever happened to Leland (Billy Goat) Davis was when Columbia College jumped his mining claim back in 1966. Davis was 86 when I interviewed him on the Columbia College campus in 1981. "I really struck pay dirt the day they broke ground for that college on my claim," he said with a big grin. "The college built me a new home—rent free and tax free for as long as I live. The school pays all my utilities and gives me $100 a month to boot. It was one hell of a strike for me."

"Columbia College did jump Davis' claim. And it was the least the school could do," said Paul Becher, 59, dean of students. "That's why all the school teams are nicknamed 'Claim Jumpers.'" Davis lived in a weather-beaten, dilapidated mining shack with a dozen goats when the school took over. The old man didn't own the land where his claim was located. The federal government did. But as long as he actively worked his claim he was legally entitled to live on it. So, the school made a deal with him.

"His shack on the claim was where we wanted to put the college administration building," related Becher. "We built him a house a few hundred yards down the hill next to his garden. We had no intention of trying to evict him." Billy Goat Davis filed his claim on the present site of Columbia College in 1926.

"I worked a big quartz vein all through here. I called my claim "Big Enough" because the vein was 2½ feet wide," the miner recalled. "The mine kept my wife and our seven kids in groceries through the Great Depression." Then he mentioned how fate intervened when the college jumped his claim. "Ain't this somethin'. Here I am livin' in a center of higher education and I never went further than 6th grade in school."

Davis spent much of his time every day strolling around the campus chatting with students and faculty, and checking his claim. He raised his own vegetables on the school grounds and had his own grapevines.

CHARLES HILLINGER

"The faculty and kids thoroughly enjoy old Billy Goat Davis," said Pete Sullivan, the college athletic director. "He's full of life and tells marvelous stories about gold mining in these hills the last 65 years. He isn't considered a curiosity. He's part of the scenery."

CAMPUS BREWERY

T HE STUDENTS WERE SIPPING BEER in the classroom. Their professor beamed with obvious pride. "This week's batch was some of the best beer brewed all year," declared Professor Michael J. Lewis, congratulating the class. The University of California at Davis was the only college or university in the nation with a brewery on campus.

Within Cruess Hall, UCD's food science and technology building, the modern, stainless steel and glass brewery in miniature had fermentation and storage rooms, carbonation and finishing equipment. Its daily production was 5 gallons of beer. Many students on campus said they would give their eye teeth to sign up for Lewis' class. But only a few had the necessary credentials to qualify for the course on the science and technology of brewing beer.

"These are heads-up kids studying at the brewery," said Lewis, 40, who holds a Ph.D. in microbiology. He was associated with the British School of Malting and Brewing before coming to America. Prerequisites for the course included three years of chemistry, microbiology, physics, math and the goal of working for a brewery after getting a university degree.

Students whipped up batches of beer and ale, cooking the malt in lauter vessels, boiling the hops in kettles, getting a good brew going in the fermentation process and moving it on to the larger cellar where it ages and matures. "We brew a variety of beers. Many of the beers produced by students are as good as commercial beers found in the marketplace," Lewis said. Each student was involved in the making of at least five different brews during the lab course. Sometimes the student brewers give their beers fanciful names, like Elephant Ale, a very heavy brew, Ace of Spades, a dark beer and Tree Frog Ale, a top fermented beer. None of the beer was allowed to leave the classroom. No one except the students and Lewis was permitted to sample the campus brews. "Nobody has ever pinched a bottle of our beer as far as I know," the professor said. Almost all the students who have completed the course are now working for breweries in various parts of the country. "Brewing is a very ancient art that has become a science in the last 100 years. There are a great many things we still don't fully understand," the professor said.

"We take a lot of kidding from everybody on campus," said Greg Walter, 22, of Lafayette, one of the beer and brewing students. "They think we spend most of our time drinking the beer we're making in the lab. There's a lot more to it then that." Neither of the two women students in the class, Monica Osa, 22, of San Diego and Christi Landenberger, 22, of Sacramento enjoyed beer. "My husband likes beer, but I don't," Christi confided. "I just like to make it."

PREVENTION OF PROGRESS

A PLATEAU IN ANTARCTICA and two species of sea spiders have been named after him. As a marine biologist, Joel Hedgpeth was an acclaimed authority on estuaries and *pycnogonida* (sea spiders). And, for 40 years he had been founder-president of the Society for the Prevention of Progress. Hedgpeth, who sang in Welsh and Gaelic and played the Irish harp, was convinced that "man's doom is only decades away because the abuse of nature seems to be part of human cussedness. Four factors have had a disastrous effect upon the environment since the 1940s," he noted, "pesticides, antibiotics, detergents and atomic energy."

He explained that the purpose of his society is "to oppose, and if possible, prevent the further encroachment of material civilization on the natural environment because such exploitation violates the terms of the lease granted to mankind by nature." The SPP's publishing house, Clandestine Press, also published *Poems in Contempt of Progress* by Professor Jerome Tichenor. The poet-professor is identified as holding a doctorate from Piltdown University and possibly being the natural son of Ambrose Bierce, the American writer who disappeared in Mexico in 1913. Tichenor is Hedgpeth.

The following few lines are a sample of the professor's poignant poetry:

> *Garbage heaped at the cities' edge in piles,*
> *Freeways intertwined like snakes for miles.*
> *Fields cluttered with advertising signs,*

Ugly wastes piled from mills and mines.
If this were not enough, man now has power,
To blow his world apart within an hour..."

It was Hedgpeth who wrote the page-long report on *pycnogonida* in the Encyclopedia Britannica and edited the prestigious 1,296-page text *Treatise on Marine Ecology and Paleoecology.* He authored several books about marine biology and more than 100 scientific papers, the vast majority on sea spiders and estuaries.

A former professor of marine biology at the University of Texas, Stanford, Scripps Institution of Oceanography, UC Berkeley, Oregon State and the University of the Pacific, Hedgpeth was working out of his Santa Rosa home at the time of this interview. His garage was filled with jars of pickled sea spiders from all the oceans of the world.

VAMPIRE PROFESSOR

ENGLISH LIT 230. VAMPIRE IN WESTERN LITERATURE. Three units. That was the name of the class regularly taught by Professor Leonard Wolf at California State University, San Francisco. There was always a long waiting list of students eager to enroll in the course. It is believed to be the only class on the legends of vampires ever offered in any college. Wolf is an expert on the subject. He is the author of the book *A Dream of Dracula.*

"I'm not a vampire. I am a vampire scholar," laughed the bearded professor. He reached behind his desk and suddenly flashed a sinister beheading knife. He went to the back of his desk again, this time coming up with a 4-foot-long pointed stake—"to drive through the hearts of unwary vampires. They're props I use on the lecture circuit," Wolf explained. "I have to check them separately aboard airplanes. I don't dare do otherwise." His interest in the Dracula myth and vampire legends in general stems, he said, "from trying to figure out ways of making freshman English more interesting to students.

"The class was approved. It led to the book." Wolf confesses to a lifelong fascination with Dracula and vampires beginning at an early age in Transylvania. "I was born in Transylvania where Hungary, Czechoslovakia, Russia and Romania all come together in the Carpathians," he noted. "Where the Dracula myth was spawned." The Wolf family moved to Cleveland when Leonard was very young.

For a time he was a serious "head crushing" poet. *The New Yorker,* *Harpers* and *Atlantic Monthly* published his works. His first book was a book of poetry. Several books have been published in recent years about Dracula. "Dracula and the whole subject of vampires are in the midst of a renaissance," Wolf said. "Kids are eating a Dracula cereal called Count Chocula. There are Dracula puppets and Dracula dolls." The centennial of Bram Stoker's classic *Dracula* occurred in 1998.

"The idea of the vampire appears everywhere in literature. It is age-old," Wolf continued. "Centuries ago Chinese were writing about vampires sliding down chimneys. When anyone bleeds there is the folklore of vampires. The vampire bat is named after the mythical monster. During the 14th century plague, thousands upon thousands of people died. Two things happened: Some were buried too soon—buried alive. Some of the bodies did not corrupt. In the minds of superstitious people those conditions added to vampire lore.

"Those people cast aside and left for dead when in reality they were still alive were said to have been vampires kept alive by spreading the plague—by drinking the blood of others. The bodies that did not rot were in good shape, so the belief went, because of fresh supplies of blood." Wolf mentioned the more than 200 films based on the Count Dracula story. Dracula movies continue to be made. "Recently I saw a long line of kids waiting to get into a theater to see three blood drinking films. It scares the hell out of you," laughed the professor.

CHAPTER THIRTY-ONE

Barber Bill Davis cutting hair in California's oldest barbershop.
(Photo courtesy Calif. Dept of Parks & Recreation)

BARBERS

STATE'S OLDEST BARBER SHOP

FREE MUSICAL ENTERTAINMENT went along with a haircut in Columbia, the tiny 19th-Century gold rush town. Barber Bill Davis, 63, strummed a gutbucket—a nylon cord connected to a hoe handle attached to a washtub. His sidekick, Patrick Clarke, 80, played the banjo. After a customer was shorn, the duo played and sang old favorites like "Clementine", "Oh, You Beautiful Doll", "She's Only a Bird in a Gilded Cage", and "Has Anybody Seen My Gal?"

The music suited the mood of the place. The Columbia Barber Shop was the oldest in the state, in continuous operation since 1854. And during the 126 years since it was started until my visit there in 1980, there had only been three barbers. Bill Davis had been the barber 16 years.

"I've got only 50 years to go to tie the record of my predecessor. He barbered here 66 years," said Davis. Frank Dondero was the barber from 1898 until he dropped dead while cutting hair in the old barber shop in 1964 at the age of 94.

Charley Koch was the Columbia Barber Shop's first barber. He cut hair in the shop from 1854 until 1898. Koch not only cut hair and gave shaves, he pulled teeth and let blood to cure miners of their ailments. When miners stopped by the shop in the early days they would often take a bath in one of the two galvanized bathtubs in the back room. "Miners would leave their diggins' and come to town to spend their gold," said Davis. "They would hit the local saloons and the bawdy houses and swing by the barbershop for a shave, haircut and bath. Then they would head back to the hills."

The barbershop had changed little since 1854. A potbellied stove still heated the place in winter. The single barber's chair was hand carved with claw feet. Haircuts didn't cost much at the barber shop in 1980—$3.00. Balding customers got off cheaper—$2.50.

HYMNS AND PRAYERS COME WITH HAIRCUTS

"MANY OF OUR CUSTOMERS have accepted the Lord while getting their haircuts. We like that," said Cyrus Alvah Bennett, owner of Bennett's Barbershop in San Bernardino. When you had your haircut in Bennett's Barbershop in San Bernardino you not only had your locks trimmed but the barbers prayed for you as well. The barbers in the shop were both ordained ministers.

The Rev. Cyrus Bennett recalled a recent conversion in his shopping center tonsorial: "A middle-aged man and his wife came into the shop. We had never seen them before. The song 'Amazing Grace' was sung on a religious radio program we had on in the shop while they were here. The woman wept. I asked her if I could pray for her," said the barber-minister. "She told me of a dream she had where someone prayed for her and she accepted the Lord. I told her she could accept Him here and now." Bennett said the woman and her husband made confessions in the barbershop and "dedicated their lives to Jesus while they were both getting their hair cut."

The barbershop owner was a pastor with the Church of Gospel Ministry. His assistant, the Rev. Jerry Wiley, was a minister with the

Inland Christian Center Church. Throughout the day at their religiously oriented barber shop hymns and prayers were heard over gospel radio station KQLH.

Instead of Playboy Magazine and the Police Gazette, religious tracks and publications like Pentecostal Evangel and Worldwide Challenge were in magazine racks. Framed prayers hung from the walls. Customers often requested prayers while getting haircuts or asked the barbers to read favorite passages from the Bible. "We feel we have a unique and very important ministry here in the barbershop," said Wiley. "Many of our customers never darken the door of a church. We are able to bring the Lord to them as we cut their hair."

Most strangers to the shop found it all a bit unnerving. "Some come in and feel uncomfortable. But we feel it is good for them to be uncomfortable," said Bennett. One mother in the shop said it was a comfort to know her young boys could get their haircuts without having access to "dirty" magazines.

A local Catholic priest, a captain of the Salvation Army and several San Bernardino ministers had their haircuts in the unusual barbershop. The shop was not only for the pure in spirit but the pure in body as well. "NO SMOKING' signs hung from all four walls.

A regular customer once told the two ministers he suffered a heart attack and had to sell his business and move out of the area. "We prayed for him," said Wiley. "He owned a worm farm. Our prayers were heard. He sold his worm farm a couple of days after he got his haircut," Wiley related.

WILD WILLIE SLADE

EVER HAD AN ENGLISH BULLDOG LEAP TO YOUR LAP while you were getting a haircut? That was one of the hazards of being trimmed by Wild Willie Slade, the zany bushy-bearded barber of Newcastle, tiny Placer County Mother Lode community 30 miles northeast of Sacramento.

Cars throughout Northern California had bumper stickers supporting the barber's latest "projects." He campaigned to make Newcastle, population 318 and 5 miles west of the American River, a deep water seaport. To do this Folsom Dam needed to be relocated. "Newcastle needs a deep water port," explained Slade, displaying elaborate blueprints for his plan. He was for extending Bay Area Rapid Transit from San Francisco to Newcastle. Bumper stickers supporting this project call it Freeway Area Rapid Transit with the capital letters huge on the bumper stickers and the small letters very small.

Another of Slade's projects involved one of the most impressive historical monuments in the state dedicated at Ophir, suburb of Newcastle. Nearly 1,000 people attended the unveiling of the 8-foot-high, concrete and natural granite monument. Assemblyman Eugene A. Chappie served as master of ceremonies. "We are assembled here," Chappie began, "to remind us not to take ourselves and our infernal do-good activities too seriously." Ophir—named after the Biblical land—blossomed overnight in 1852 as a roaring gold mining camp. Today it is a forgotten relic of the past—a handful of homes, a few farms.

But Ophir has an historical monument. The inscription on it reads: "Ophir State Prison. Credo Quia Absurdum. This monument is near the reported site of the world famous Ophir Prison known by many, visited by few. A maximum security prison which was, in its heyday, a prototype of modern-day penal institutions second to none. First reported use June 31, 1802. Last reported use 1852. Monument dedicated in memory of the warden, his staff and the prisoners who were never acknowledged in the Old West."

For months before the unveiling hundreds of cars throughout Northern California sprouted bright yellow "SAVE OPHIR PRISON'" bumper stickers. Many supporters were not quite sure what the cause was all about. The bumper stickers showed up in such unlikely places as Nome, Alaska, and Bangor, Maine. The monument to the prison that never was is a brainstorm of Slade, started because of a dilapidated chair someone brought to his barber shop. "I strung wires across the chair," said Willie, "and put a sign on it—Antique electric chair from Ophir Prison. Everybody kept asking what's new up at old Ophir Prison. Then they began inventing some of the damnedest stories about the old days at Ophir. Next thing you know, we had a full blown campaign—bumper stickers, monument fund, the works."

When we visited Newcastle, cars for miles around had "Save Willie Slade" bumper stickers. The barber was not quite sure what that was all about. Willie, who shaves the top of his head, is the opposite of the image most barbers want to portray. His shop was cluttered with dozens of old car jacks, a barbed-wire collection, blown safes, gold

CHARLES HILLINGER

pans, old bottles and campaign buttons from every 20th-Century Presidential election. There were old license plates, World War I helmets, rusted guns, old spittoons, rusted coffee cans dug out of 19th-Century mining camps, hundreds of other items. Everything in the shop was brought there by customers. "I don't know why they do it. They still get clipped same price when I cut their hair, no exceptions," said Slade. Garret Noyen retired and virtually bald came to the shop once a week. Noyen said it was worth the price of the haircut to sit in the chair and listen to Wild Willie Slade talk.

Slade's business cards had his photo on one side and on the reverse, this note: "I am not one of the Smith Bros. Nor do I belong to an oddball religious cult. I just want to grow a beard and shave my head." It was easy to lose track of time in Slade's shop. During spring and summer when California is on daylight time, Slade's clock was on standard time plus 7 minutes "so I'm always sure to go home early." When the clocks were turned back in the fall, he pushed his ahead to daylight time plus seven minutes.

He made all appointments and lived strictly by his own time. And, as for Stonewall Jackson VII—Slade's husky English bulldog—he went with the territory, sitting on the customer's lap while the customer had his hair cut.

CUTS HAIR, TRAPS RACCOONS

BARBER ROSS BISBEE, 78, provided two services—he gave a good haircut at a decent price and trapped raccoons for nothing. He was Whittier's official raccoon trapper. He had been cutting hair since he was 17, trapping raccoons since he was 12.

Bisbee's Tip Top Barbershop was in his front yard. When we met him he had just raised the price of his haircuts the first time in 22 years—from $2.25 to $3. "I hated to do it. I thought about it for a long time," he sighed. "A lot of my customers are older fellows who have to watch their money. Before I raised the price I asked them if they would mind. I explained barber supplies and everything else had gone so high, I just had to do it."

His customers agreed to the hike, many telling Bisbee he should have upped the price a long time ago as most other shops charged two and three times what he did. He never charged anything for his raccoon-trapping services. "Raccoons are a real problem in some sections of Whittier," explained Dick Bundy as he was getting a haircut from Bisbee.

"Raccoons tear up lawns, eat goldfish in backyard ponds and get into attics," Bundy said. "Ross trapped 17 raccoons in my backyard alone. Raccoons have a feast on goldfish in my pond." What does he use for raccoon bait? "Well sir, it may sound queer," said Bisbee, "but I entice those old raccoons into my traps with chocolate doughnuts and Fig Newtons. My hound dog Katie loves it when I trap raccoons. I trap the raccoons and turn them loose in the San Gabriel Mountains. When I release the raccoons, Katie chases them up a tree. That's how Katie and I get our exercise, walking through the woods and chasing raccoons." The barber said he released the raccoons in the wild where he was certain there was plenty of food and water available and the animals would fare well.

CHAPTER THIRTY-TWO

Bill Groves outside his Abraham Lincoln Cabin Theater.

SHOW BUSINESS

LIFE AND TIMES OF OLD ABE

I N A TINY LOG CABIN at the end of a half-mile dirt road in Morongo Valley, Abraham Lincoln and his family were brought to life every Sunday afternoon through the magic of theater. When my wife, Arliene, and I attended a performance in 1993, Bill Groves had presented 15 original, hour-long plays about the 16th President over an eight year period week in and week out except in July and August when it was too hot in the Southern California desert town.

Groves was then 64, a tall, spindly actor, director and playwright who had a life long fascination with Old Abe. Groves wrote, directed, produced each of the plays and portrayed Lincoln in every one except the production we saw, *Mrs. Lincoln's Insanity Hearing* at the Groves Abraham Lincoln Cabin Theatre.

"I cannot believe this trial is taking place. But I'm sure it is because

I'm the presiding judge," said Groves as Judge Bailey in the opening scene of the play. Mary Todd Lincoln's trial opened in May, 1875, at the Cook County Courthouse, 10 years after the assassination of Abraham Lincoln. In bringing the insanity charges against his mother, Robert Lincoln shocked Chicago and the nation.

"The performances are all based on historic fact. Nothing is made up," Groves noted. "While one play is in production, we're working on the next one, and I'm busy researching and writing still another." Groves Abraham Lincoln Cabin Theatre was the smallest of the 50 theaters in the Palm Springs, Indio and High Desert region, seating only 32. The 1930s theater was the size of the tiny Kentucky log cabin where Lincoln was born. What unfolded was award-winning theater, with highly charged and emotional performances.

The previous year, the Lincoln players won top honors at the annual Desert Theatre League competition at the Annenberg Theater in Palm Springs. They were awarded best drama, best director, best actor, best actress, best supporting actor and best original writing for their performance of *The Man Who Won the Civil War*. Groves had been a member of the Screen Actors Guild for 32 years and was a member of the New York and West Coast Dramatists Guild.

He had appeared in episodes of "Knight Rider," "Quincy," "Bonanza," "Rawhide" and numerous other TV and film productions. He also portrayed Lincoln in productions in other theaters, at schools throughout the desert and at elementary schools in the Los Angeles Unified School District. His wife, Joy, a high school teacher, joined him as Mary Todd Lincoln.

"So far as I know, ours is the only theater in the United States exclusively doing Lincoln plays," said Graves. In *Mrs. Lincoln's Insanity Hearing*, nuclear medicine technologist Ken Guinn portrayed Dr. Danforth, who described Mrs. Lincoln's hallucinations, the strange voices she hears and the taps on the table she perceives as being from her late husband. "It is difficult to testify against such a fine First Lady who lost her entire family except one son and is ridiculed by society for her eccentric ways," said the doctor, who nonetheless concluded that "Mary Todd Lincoln is mentally incompetent and a fit subject for a mental institution"

Piano teacher Virginia Jaroch, as Mrs. Lincoln's housekeeper, Mrs. Harrington, calls the President's wife "crazy as a loon who needs to be looked after. To think she was once a First Lady of our country. It's a damn shame, a damn shame." Scott Bachman, a mail carrier, and a Lincoln player for four years, portrayed Robert Lincoln. He testifies that "my brother Taddy's death was just too much for my mother. Every night she wakes up terrified."

As Mrs. Lincoln, Joy Groves cries out: "You are no longer my son. I rue the day I gave birth to you. Your father would turn in his grave. You'll have to answer to him." The lights in the house dim as Bill Groves is heard saying: "On May 21, 1875, a jury of 12 men found Mary Todd Lincoln insane and she was sent to a mental institution."

Other Lincoln plays by Groves included *Lincoln vs. Booth, the Showdown, Mrs. Lincoln Died Today*, and the musicals *That Hellcat, Mrs. Lincoln,* and *A Musical Evening With Abe Lincoln.* After the performances, Bill and Joy Groves and the cast and production staff served apple cider and cookies and visited with the audience. Reservations were necessary and hard to come by. Even in downpours, with the road leading to the theater a sea of mud, all 32 folding chairs were taken.

THE WILD BUNCH

IT WAS LATE AFTERNOON and hot when Eva and the "Wild Bunch" stepped out into the barnyard at their home in Zamora for a jam session. Their audience of 200 cackling chickens came running from all directions of the Wild family farm in Yolo County about 30 miles northwest of Sacramento.

Listening to the Wilds' schmaltzy little musical group in the summer of 1983 was like spinning a record on an old Victrola in the 1920s. The family orchestra—two sisters, Eva, 72, and Margaret, 68, and three brothers, Fred, 70, Harold, 67, and Claude, 62—had been playing together 50 years. When not busy farming, they were practicing or playing gigs in Grange halls, town halls and at neighbors' homes.

"None of us ever married," said Fred. "Never even came close," added Claude. "Always had to play. Couldn't dance with anybody," chimed in Margaret. "Never had time to fall in love," lamented Eva. "We all pitch in and do the farm chores and in our free time we work on our music. That's our life," explained Harold, who played banjo and did a bit of crooning, with Fred on trumpet, Margaret on drums, Claude on fiddle and Eva at the piano. They lived in the century-old farmhouse where they were born. They all graduated from the one-room Zamora School as did their mother and father. Counting the Wild Bunch, Zamora had a population of 42. The old house had no television, but it did have wallpaper out of the 20s, old carpets, linoleum, tintypes and family portraits of more recent vintage (20s and 30s) draping the walls.

Their instruments were older than the musicians. Fred got his trumpet when he was 15 in 1928. It was secondhand then. Eva's drums were handed down from her father, who bought them in the early 1900s. Their mother died when Eva, the oldest, was 12. Their father was a one-man band and his brood just naturally took to playing musical instruments before enrolling in the one-room school.

Fred Sr. ran the Zamora General Store from 1912 to 1932. On the side he played for neighboring farmers. The Wild Family Orchestra continued that routine. "We play for birthdays, anniversaries, parties, harvests, plantings," said Eva. "Usually they pay us $100, sometimes as much as $200." Songs like "Little Old Rag Doll," "Rienzi Two-Step" and "Zig Zag Waltz" were popular hits in the homespun repertoire of the Wild Bunch.

CHAPTER THIRTY-THREE

Mountain that looks like profile of President John F. Kennedy lying in state.

JFK LYING IN STATE

E VER SINCE EDWARD BORZANSKY DISCOVERED THE FIGURE on the mountain in the Southern California desert it haunted him. Especially after the assassination. The figure is a striking likeness of President John F. Kennedy lying in state.

Jacqueline Kennedy sent a letter of thanks to Borzansky for a photograph of the profile on the mountain and for his efforts to have it set aside as a memorial. Robert Kennedy expressed the gratitude of the entire Kennedy family for letting them know of his discovery. "Plans were being set in motion for me to take Bobby Kennedy to see the mountain. Then he was gunned down like his brother," said Borzansky, a long time prospector who knew the California desert like the back of his hands.

"It was twilight when I first saw the mountain," recalled Borzansky. "I was alone in my jeep, following an abandoned trail. I drove through a dry wash, up over ridges, then down into this natural bowl and there it was. That mountain bothered me from the moment I caught sight of it." That was nine months *before* President Kennedy was assassinated.

Borzansky snapped a few pictures, then left the remote area, a desert range with no human habitation for miles. "I could not get that face on the mountain out of my mind," Borzansky said. "The pictures I took disturbed me the same way the mountain did. The President was so full of life at the time. I didn't want to think about it. I put the pictures away." Then the President was assassinated.

Jack P. Welch of the State Division of Beaches and Parks accompanied Borzansky to the mountain in 1966. "It's an amazing likeness," he wrote in his official report. He recommended that the mountain on federal land between Needles and Barstow be set aside as a memorial. It never happened. The uncanny likeness of President Kennedy lying in state is rarely seen because of its remote location.

CHAPTER THIRTY-FOUR

*Charles Hillinger and Austin Stirratt outside cabin
on trail to summit of Hundred Peakers mountain.*

HIKERS, DUST DEVIL & THE PRINCE

HUNDRED PEAKERS

NUCLEAR PHYSICIST AND BASSOONIST JOHN BACKUS, 76, hiked to the top of Garnet Mountain in San Diego County and became the first member of the Sierra Club to climb 270 mountains—six times. "Hooray for John, the mightiest mountain climber of them all," shouted Austin Stirratt.

Stirratt was one of the 17 Sierra Club "Hundred Peakers" accompanying Backus on his latest assault, the climb to Garnet Mountain's 5,680-foot summit 15 miles south of Julian. It was one of the shortest hikes of the 270 peaks on the "Hundred Peakers" list, only one-third mile from the road, cross-country and straight up over rocks, through snow-covered, icy slopes and dense manzanita thickets.

Earlier in the day Backus had hiked eight miles round trip to the summit of 5,054-foot Oakzanita Peak, leaving at 8 a.m. in 15-degree weather. That jaunt took him four hours. Then he drove 16 miles to scale the second mountain of the day, three miles round trip to 5,880-foot Garnet Peak, an hour's hike. (Garnet Peak and Garnet Mountain are two distinct places.) Garnet Mountain was the third peak Backus ascended on that chilly winter day. When he finally completed his sixth time around the 270-mountain loop—meaning he had climbed 1,620 peaks—he broke into a few lines of poetry from Alice in Wonderland:

> *Oh Oysters said the carpenter*
> *We've had a pleasant run,*
> *Shall we be going back again?*

As is custom with "Hundred Peakers," there was a champagne celebration. Austin Stirratt, 66, who climbed his 200th peak that day, pulled a bottle from his knapsack. Hiker Charlotte Bourne, 67, who completed the list, her 270th peak also being Garnet Mountain, provided the glass. And Backus quenched his thirst. "I would have brought along my bassoon and played a tune if I hadn't had a recent operation on my lip," apologized the mountain climbing professor who lived in Eagle Rock.

The Hundred Peak Section of the Sierra Club was the brainchild of the late Weldon Heald, a conservation writer, who compiled a list of 180 peaks in Southern California in 1945. A person could become a "Hundred Peaker" by climbing 100 of the 180 mountains on the list. The list has grown through the years to 270 mountains in eight Southern California counties including 11,499-foot Mount San Gorgonio. By the time John Backus completed the circuit six times, some 765 men and women had hiked to the top of 100 of the peaks; 240 had done 200 peaks; 123 had hiked to the top of all 270 of the mountains on the list. Only seven men and two women had gone around twice. Only three men had gone around more than three times. Backus, Dick Akawie, 68, a Santa Monica chemist and Frank Goodykoontz, 61, head of data processing for Hacienda-LaPuente School District. Goodykoontz had 24 mountains to go to complete the loop four times. Akawie was about 50 peaks behind Backus.

During World War II, Backus worked on the development of the atomic bomb at the University of California, Berkeley. He attributed his seven cancer operations over the previous 11 years to his exposure to radiation at the lab. But he didn't let cancer interfere with his hiking. He taught physics at USC, had written as many scientific papers on musical instruments as he had on physics. He had been an orchestra leader and played first bassoonist for years for the El Camino Community College and Pasadena Community orchestras. He also played the kettle drums and piano and produced clarinet reeds as a hobby.

"Climbing mountains is my exercise. I love the fresh air, looking at the magnificent scenery and getting out of the smog," said Backus with a twinkle in his eyes. "It keeps me young. But climbing mountains is also like hitting yourself with a hammer. It feels good when you stop. It's hard work," insisted the physicist.

In addition to doing the Hundred Peaker list six times, John Backus had climbed the highest points in all the western states, climbed the Sierra Club's 88 desert peaks and 101 High Sierra summits. At a potluck party on the slopes of Garnet Mountain after his record climb, Backus said he didn't think he would try to make the loop again. But he said the same thing after his earlier conquests.

"DUST DEVIL DAN"

T HEY CALLED HIM "DUST DEVIL DAN." He pursued spiraling pillars of dust and debris across the desert on foot, on the seat of a motorcycle, behind the wheel of an old truck. He spiraled upward riding towers of the whirling winds in sailplanes. Daniel E. Fitzjarrald earned his doctorate degree at UCLA studying desert dust devils. He was 29 when I first wrote about him.

"I have always been intrigued by the phenomena," explained the young meteorologist. "There has been very little research on the subject." Fitzjarrald sometimes stood in the center of the spinners clutching an anemometer to measure rotating wind speed. "I close my eyes, hold my breath and wait until all the dust flies by," he said. "Have you ever been sandblasted? That's the sensation." To see how far the whirling winds travel he tracked spinning columns of sand as far as 10 miles. The one that lasted longest danced across the desert for nearly an hour.

"Someone was supposed to have followed a dust devil for eight hours on the Great Salt Lake," said Fitzjarrald. "But most of them last only 5 to 10 minutes, then poop out." Some whirling columns of sand he studied were wisps only 6 inches across, others were violent whirlwinds—mini tornadoes—more than 100 feet in diameter. "Dust devils," he said, "March along at times at very slow speeds, at other times they move 20 to 25 m.p.h.

"It depends upon wind speed. But when the wind is too powerful, dust devils don't last. The wind tears them apart. There are two things needed to set a dust devil going," Fitzjarrald said. "First is something to make air rise, and second, something to make it take on a circular motion." He said heat makes air rise. Air that is hotter than the surrounding air will rise and lab experiments indicate rising plumes of air occur at random places on the desert floor. An analogy would be the way hot water rises in a pan of water that is sitting on the stove. "What makes the rising column of air start turning is a mere breath of air along the flat plain of the desert," Fitrzjarrald said. "It doesn't take much to start it turning, but once it starts, it whirls faster and the turns get tighter, the same principle that makes an ice skater whirl faster as he pulls his arms in closer to his body."

Fitzjarrald said what snuffs out dust devils is complicated. One factor probably is that the supply of heated air at ground level gives out, and the dust devil runs out of "fuel." Dust devils, he said, are unpredictable. "You can't look out across the desert and say one will spring up over there."

He photographed and studied nearly 1,000 dust devils of various sizes, shapes and speeds. He made motion pictures of them taken from the ground, from the air, from inside, as they spin toward and away from him. Some rise as high as 8,000 feet above the desert floor. "Dust devils play an important role in the scheme of things," he said, "transferring heat from the ground into the atmosphere." Some are pretty violent. Roof tops have been ripped off by the spinning columns, lawn furniture and kangaroo rats swooped off the ground into the air. For buzzards and vultures, dust devils are roller coasters in the sky. The big birds soar in the spiraling pillars.

Fitzjarrald believed his work may be of value in the continuing study of hurricanes and tornadoes—much larger versions of basically the same phenomena. He believed his knowledge may be of some help in understanding giant dust storms detected on Mars by the Mariner 9 probe.

He reproduced dust devils in a UCLA lab. He constructed a 3-foot-high test chamber in which a heated aluminum plate takes the place of the desert floor and 20 adjustable Plexiglas panels simulate the surrounding atmosphere. He used smoke and strong light to make the vortex visible, glass bead thermistors to measure temperatures and a laser to measure wind velocity.

In the United States dust devils are known by several other names, devils, sand devils, dust whirls, diablos, molinas de arina and sand mills. In India where the phenomenon is quite common over that nation's great plains the whirling winds are called bagoolas. "Dust Devil Dan" Fitzjarrald's favorite dust devil story is that of Mohammed's first battle. Mohammed, so the story goes, scooped up a handful of desert sand, hopped astride his horse, then rode off to battle leading a legion of his followers.

He is supposed to have hurled the sand into the air triggering a mighty dust devil. Mohammed reportedly rode across the desert beside the whirling pillar of sand. As his forces approached the enemy the dust devil spun violently into and blinding enemy horsemen enabling Mohammed to win the battle easily.

PRINCE OF PISGAH

"THE "PRINCE OF PISGAH" struck a guru-like pose—legs crossed, arms folded as he perched on the tiny platform high above his crater. "I know how Moses must have felt when he looked out at the Promised Land," the bearded "Prince" said. He gazed at miles and miles of emptiness—at the endless sand stretching in all directions, at black streams of long-cooled lava that once flowed from his volcano, at purple mountain ranges and at a cloudless azure sky.

Nowhere was there a sign of man or man's imprint. Moses was permitted by God, the Bible recalls in the last chapter of Deuteronomy, to see the Promised Land from the top of Mt. Pisgah near the Dead Sea.

Leonard Kopp's Pisgah (piz-guh) is a 200-foot-high inactive volcano rising from the floor of the Mojave Desert 175 miles northeast of Los Angeles, 35 miles southeast of Barstow. Kopp, was 35 when we interviewed him seated on a platform overlooking Pisgah Crater. He had a long-term lease on the volcano from the Santa Fe Railroad. He was mining volcanic cinders.

He was introduced by friends as the "Prince of Pisgah"—caliph of a Southern California crater. He hosted parties at the peak of Pisgah Crater. A week before we were there 400 of his friends showed up for a barbecue in the volcano's vent.

"My children get very defensive about Pisgah," the "Prince" said. "None of the other kids believe them when they say: 'My daddy has his own volcano out on the desert.' So, I'm forever driving a carload of boys and girls out to the volcano from schools attended by my son and three daughters." For many years the railroad used crushed cinders from Pisgah Crater for track ballast. The U.S. Bureau of Mines conducted elaborate tests on the composition of Pisgah as a prelude to man's flight to the moon. Basis of the study was that the volcano might be similar in makeup to the moon's surface. Hughes Aircraft Co. test-landed prototypes of moon vehicles in Pisgah Crater. Thousands of tons of Kopp's volcano were trucked to Disney Studios in Burbank to make a NASA moonscape training film.

TV commercials have been filmed on the volcano. Pisgah cinders have been used as exterior facing on numerous hotels and building in Southern California—places like Airport Marina, Newporter Inn, the Van Nuys courthouse. The "Prince of Pisgah" sold cinders for fireplaces, stepping stones, artificial firelongs, for landscaping and dozens of other uses.

Two vulcanologists, Bill and Russell Harter had been spending weekends for six years on Pisgah's 15-mile-long lava flows that stream out across the desert. "Pisgah is a classic volcano for study," explained Russell, who, with his brother, had been recording scientific data on the crater and lava flows.

They were attempting to learn why the lava acted as it did when spilling from the crater and the various processes that occurred in creating tunnels and tubes. They date the eruption that created the crater to as recent as Columbus' arrival in the Americas or as long as 8,000 years ago.

Hundreds of caves, tubes and tunnels honeycomb the lava flows. The longest cave discovered was 1,100 feet long. "I would feel rather badly if it ever erupted again," observed the "Prince of Pisgah" solemnly.

CHAPTER THIRTY-FIVE

Do-it-all editor Nettie Brown wearing Imperial Valley Weekly *sweatshirt. (Photo courtesy Imperial Co. Hist. Soc.).*

WRITERS OF THE WEST

NETTIE BROWN

"I'M LIVING IN A MANNER THAT BEFITS 1915," laughed Nettie Brown, seated in front of her worn-out typewriter with a couple of missing keys. The 68-year-old woman had been editor and publisher of the *Imperial Valley Weekly*, circulation, 550, for 31 years.

Nettie did it all. Sold the ads. Wrote the copy. Took the pictures. Laid out the pages. Until her shop burned down 14 years earlier, she set the type and ran the presses. When we visited with her the *Imperial Valley Weekly* was being printed by the *Holtville Tribune*. Her proudest accomplishment was raising seven sons and two daughters by publishing the paper. She was the breadwinner. Her husband was ill when they bought the newspaper for $1,000 down. He died five years later.

"I've always published the paper on time," she said with pride. "Not childbirth, earthquakes, floods, fire nor broken equipment has stayed us!" One of the days she layed out her newspaper she worked until 5 p.m. Then she hopped into her car, drove to the hospital and gave birth to a 9-pound son. The next morning she was back in the shop running the presses.

Her children grew up helping their mother getting the paper out. Now she was putting out the paper by herself with the assistance of a 13-year-old grandson, George. She had 17 grandchildren, one great-grandson. Her seven sons were printers scattered in print shops and newspapers throughout California. One daughter was a nurse, the other worked for IBM. Nettie Brown was much more than publisher of the tiny weekly that barely paid her bills. She was one of Imperial County's most visible and best-known characters. For years she was the *Los Angeles Times* stringer in the southeast corner of the state. Almost every issue of her newspaper contained her poetry. The county Board of Supervisors named her Poet Laureate of Imperial County.

And, she was godmother and historian of the Navy's precision aerobatics team, the Blue Angels, based in winter at the El Centro Naval Air Facility, where the pilots learned and practiced their maneuvers flying over the isolated desert. Every week 150 of her newspapers were mailed to every present and former pilot of the Blue Angels. Two books written by Nettie Brown about the supersonic jet pilots have been published.

"Nettie knows more about the Blue Angels than any of the Blue Angels," said Capt. Anthony Less, a former flight leader of the eight-pilot squad. The highest mountain in Imperial County, 4,500 feet, was officially named Blue Angels Mountain, thanks to Nettie Brown. Through her efforts, a road in the county is called Blue Angels Drive. She campaigned to get the post office to issue a Blue Angels stamp.

At least one full page of each issue (anywhere from four to 14 pages) of the *Imperial Valley Weekly* was devoted to Blue Angels news—where the team was flying, stories on individual members, letters from former Blue Angels. "Former Blue Angels keep in touch with one another through Nettie's paper," said Comdr. Dick Schram, director of community relations for the Navy's Office of Information, Washington, D.C. Schram was on the phone every week updating Nettie on the latest Blue Angel news. She also authored a book published during the Vietnam War: *Grandma Wore Combat Boots—A Hometown Editor's Visit to the Fighting Front in Vietnam*. Three of her sons served in Vietnam.

All seven have served stints in the Army. Brown published her paper out of her modest home surrounded by farmland south of El Centro. She lived in one of the hottest valleys in America, but said she could not afford air conditioning. And, in winter, she heated her home with firewood that she chopped.

"You don't make much money on a weekly with a circulation of 550. But I wouldn't trade my life with anyone," Nettie insisted. "I bet I'm the only woman in America who ever attended a $100-a-plate dinner for a President (Eisenhower in 1953) wearing a 99-cent dress." For fillers, pages of her newspapers contained her homespun philosophy, one-liners such as "Trouble with experts they know so damn much that ain't so."

THE WIDOW'S TEARS

IT WAS A WIDOW'S TEARS that kept Lee Perry from leaving Needles, a small desert town on the Arizona border. When we encountered him he had been there 28 years since the widow cried, recording local events in his weekly newspaper, the *Needles Desert Star*. Crime never made the front page. Anniversaries, births, birthdays, deaths, church bazaars, high school football games did. And that was the way folks in Needles liked it.

Perry was a Wisconsin linotype operator when he came to Needles to look at the *Desert Star*, up for sale at the time. "The town was too little, too isolated, too hot. And the paper too small. Eight pages and a circulation of 1,500," he recalled. "I told the owner, Myrt Williams, I couldn't see buying it. Then she started to cry. She hadn't been able to sell the sheet. She wouldn't let me out the door. So I bought it and seldom left Needles again." To residents of Needles, population 4,500, Perry had been affectionately known as "Mr. Publisher," "Mr. Editor" or "Mr. Perry" ever since. But it was the way he edited and published that won the respect of folks in Needles.

"Mr. Perry presents people as people," said Gail Hornady, owner of a Needles answering service. "He catches the spirit of the town every week. My family has lived here only five years and our pictures have been in the paper 26 times." Perry had everybody's picture in the paper as often as possible. "Pictures are sure circulation grabbers," said Perry. "All the friends and relatives want copies." The circulation had grown to 3,400 copies a week, attesting to Perry's philosophy. Founded in

1888 by Dr. James Booth as *Booth's Bazoo*, the paper had been renamed the *Needles Eye*, then the *Needles Nugget* and finally the *Desert Star*.

"Oh, it's fun, but you never make any money on a paper this size," confided Perry. "It's a hand-to-mouth existence. And you're a slave to the operation. For 12 years I did it all, now my son and daughter-in-law help. And we have two part-time workers." But he was still writing all the "important stuff," meaning three-fourths of the copy in the newspaper. He hardly ever left town. "When you run a weekly, you can't. You've got to keep your hand on the pulse," said Perry. He was last in Los Angeles 10 years earlier. He went to San Francisco once, for three days. He drove to the Grand Canyon and back one day years ago just to see what was there. That was the extent of his travels. "I'd probably still be in Wisconsin if that widow hadn't cried," mused Perry.

OF MAC AND MAGGIE

M AC AND MAGGIE MCSHAN called their five acres in Needles "The Rats Nest." Said Mac, "You could spend several weeks here and not begin to see it all." Their spread was crammed with an unbelievable hodgepodge of desert debris that the couple had been collecting for more than a half century. It was the home of a homespun, humorous and informative monthly magazine called *Footprints*, produced, printed and published by the McShans since 1973.

The masthead on the 34-page publication provided an inkling of what lies within. It proclaimed: "Wildflowers, rockhounding, archaeology, field trips, fishing, gardening, cooking, history, travel—Keep Smiling." About 1,200 desert lovers throughout the United States and overseas subscribed to Mac and Maggie's journal selling for $5 a year at the time we caught up with them. A lead story in a recent issue headlined "Cactus Strikes Back" told how a man fired several shotgun blasts at a 27-foot-high saguaro cactus. The cactus toppled and crushed the man to death. There were stories about creosote bushes, road runners, snakebites, woodpecker watching, burro roundups, boojum trees, petroglyphs, Indians, old mines and ranching.

"It is unbelievable what unfolds in front of your eyes out there," Mac McShan said. For 50 years Mac, then 68, and Maggie, 67, had been scouring the desert for "artifacts." Amid the cactus jungle on their five acres were 20,000 old bottles, piles of tin cans and rocks, a mishmash of junk, a dozen old buildings filled with rubble and a collection of cats. There was a boxcar in the McShan's backyard, "a dehydrator for fruits and vegetables," Mac explained. "I bought the boxcar for $31 and paid $300 to move it here."

Over the years, in the midst of it all, the McShans raised bees, bullfrogs and chickens. Mac and Maggie's main house was built of used bridge timbers and railroad ties and was crammed floor to ceiling with books, bottles, cow skulls and file cases filled with 200,000 mineral specimens. Maggie was a well-known writer of desert stories not only in *Footprints* but in newspapers and magazines as well. Scholars, historians, rockhounds, Bureau of Land Management officials, desert lovers in general beat a well-worn path to "The Rats Nest" to see this most unusual desert shrine and visit the couple who created it.

CHRONICLING THE WEST SINCE THE 1930s

PROSPECTOR CHARLIE BREYFOGLE was found nearly naked, without food or water, near death and babbling deliriously about discovering a golden ledge on a Death Valley peak. He was clutching a dirty bandana filled with chunks of gold. The year was 1864. For the next six years until his death, the prospector scoured the desert for the rich vein. Seven of Breyfogle's relatives continued to look for years afterward and were equally unsuccessful.

Frank (Shorty) Harris, the most famous of the Death Valley burro men, spent 50 years hunting for the lost Breyfogle mine until his death in 1934. Breyfogle was no fly-by-nighter, no run-of-the-mill desert rat. He was an educated man, Alameda County assessor and treasurer in the 1850s. "That bandana with the gold was the substance of a desert El Dorado that will haunt the imagination of adventurers, prospectors and sober mining men until doomsday," wrote Harold O. Weight in *Lost Mines of Death Valley*, a book in its seventh edition when we interviewed Weight and his wife, Lucille.

Men like Breyfogle and Harris might well have eluded history had it not been for writers like the Weights, a writing team that had chronicled the West since the 1930s. Lucille and Harold Weight had written half a dozen books and scores of magazine stories about lost mines and the early mining camps of the Old West. They spent years as associate editors of *Desert Magazine* and were regular contributors to numerous other magazines. For a period in the 1950s they published their own history magazine, the *Calico Print*. Beginning in the 1930s the team contracted as many men and women as they could find who played a role in the great mining booms at the turn of the century. They recorded their reminiscences, first in notebooks and after World War II on tape recorders.

All of their recorded sources from the mining camps of the 1880s, 1890s and the early 1900s are now dead. The Weights had several file cabinets filled with these histories in their home on the edge of Joshua Tree National Monument, where they had one of the finest private libraries in existence on the history of the Old West. When I visited they were working on a book about Rawhide, Nevada, a mining town that boomed from 1906 to 1910. Two of their principal sources for the book were the late Gumshoe Kid and the late Tonopah Kid, who were there when it happened. Howard Weight played a tape of Grover Kane, a Randsberg miner of the 1890s, who told how stealing was rampant in the old mining camp. "Hell, everybody was stealing ore, even the school kids were taking it out of the mines, hiding it in their lunch buckets," said the voice of the long-dead miner.

When I visited Lucille and Harold Weight in 1983 they hadn't lost any of their enthusiasm. They were as busy as ever, researching and writing in their rambling house, roaming the West in search of new story material to portray the life and times of the mining camps.

CHAPTER THIRTY-SIX

Gus Briegleb, 78, at the controls of his sailplane over the Mojave Desert.

HIGH FLYERS

HALF MAN, HALF BIRD

"THIS IS THE CLOSEST MAN CAN COME TO BEING A BIRD," shouted 78-year-old Gus Briegleb as he caught the whirling dust devil and soared skyward 500 feet per minute. Briegleb was piloting a two-place, slender-winged, silver with red trim Czechoslovakian Blanik—a sailplane without engine or propeller. A few minutes later, he maneuvered the glider into an "airwave" rolling off Mt. Baldy, enjoying the exhilaration of surfboarding in the sky. Fueled by the wind, his sleek sailplane soared silently in and out of thermals as he chased dust devils above the desert floor at El Mirage in San Bernardino County.

For 63 years, Briegleb had been catching thermals—rising columns of spinning hot air, miniature tornadoes, dust devils at ground level—

and riding wavelike air currents bouncing off mountains. He built his first glider in 1928 in the basement of St. Paul's Presbyterian Church in Los Angeles, where his father was pastor. It had been his passion ever since.

It was May 1991 when I spent 40 minutes surfboarding in the sky with this half man, half bird. Briegleb's sailplane was towed by a 300-foot rope attached to a Piper Pawnee flown by John Krey, 68, retired Lockheed engineer who bulldozed the glider airstrip at El Mirage, 90 miles northeast of Los Angeles three years earlier. The two planes rumbled across the desert in a cloud of dust until both were airborne. Briegleb released his towline 3,000 feet above the airstrip, made a run for a spinning column of hot air, then soared like an eagle.

"I've spent more than 7,000 hours flying gliders and have loved every minute. I can't get enough of it. I hope to keep doing this to my dying day," said the veteran pilot as the sailplane caught another whirling lift and headed toward the heavens. Briegleb reached heights of a mile or more on the flight before starting his slow, steady, sled-like descent back to the dirt strip at Krey Gliderport for a smooth touchdown.

Briegleb wasn't your run-of-the-mill weekend glider pilot. He was one of the oldest active glider pilots in America. At the National Soaring Museum in Elmira, N.Y., dedicated to the history of glider flying, an exhibit honoring Briegleb "for 63 years of contributions to the nation's soaring techniques" was one of three featured exhibits the year I flew with him. The other two exhibits marked the 100th anniversary of the first glider flight by Otto Lilenthal in Derwitz, Germany, and the 60th anniversary of the first national soaring contest in the United States held at Elmira.

Briegleb was one of the first glider pilots to be inducted into the U.S. Soaring Hall of Fame. He had been designing, building and flying gliders in Southern California since he assembled his first one in the church basement. Briegleb's highest flight in a glider was 23,900 feet out of El Mirage. The flight lasted $3^1/2$ hours. His longest flight was $6^1/2$ hours and 300 miles over Texas.

In 1934, Briegleb started *The Thermal*, a Southern California magazine for glider pilots. A plaque in his El Mirage home notes that he founded the California Soaring Association in 1936. At the Soaring Museum exhibit were models and photographs of a dozen Briegleb gliders, including his two-place BG8s and single-place BG6s flown by the U.S. Army Glider Corps in World War II. His build-your-own-glider kits, used around the world, were displayed as were photographs of his Sailplane Corp. of America hangar at El Mirage.

At age 78 he was still as active as ever with his favorite pastime— soaring like a bird. He flew for pleasure, gave lessons and as a commercial instructor conducted biennial flight tests for glider pilots. "I've known Gus since I was a little kid," said veteran glider pilot Vern Hutchinson, who was 65 at the time. "He taught me to fly gliders in 1947. He flew gliders with my mother and dad. Gus taught half the old-time glider pilots in Southern California how to fly and he's still at it, giving flying lessons to those who have just discovered the peaceful, solitude of flying without an engine, without a propeller. Gus Briegleb is half man, half bird."

HUMAN FLY

FREDDIE BEAVERS WAS A ONE-ARMED HUMAN FLY with a breathtaking job. He stood on an 8-inch platform perched atop 2 1/2 miles of cable that ran up and down the face of one of the steepest, most spectacular cliffs in the country. Beavers spent much of his time suspended nearly 1,000 feet above the canyon.

The 47-year-old grandfather was a cable and tower maintenance man on the Palm Springs Aerial Tramway—longest, double-reversible, single span in the world, and the highest tram in the United States. Beavers' "bench" the platform that was the traveling works for the tram ran along four cables high above the tramcar.

Most of the time as the tram and traveling works ascended or descended the craggy rocks and pinnacles, Beavers worked from the metal platform between two tool boxes, held by a safety rope fastened to the rig and his "iron-man's" belt. Often as the tram moved up the mountain 300 to 1,500 feet a minute at a 26 to 40-degree angle, Beavers unsnapped his safety belt to walk his "tightrope" to a better spot to work. Usually he gripped a grease gun, wrench or some other tool in his right hand, working without hanging on. "When I have to hang on," explained Beavers "my right arm grip is as good as that of any two-hand hold."

Beavers had been a cable man since his teens, building major dams and bridges. He lost his left arm on a dam project 23 years earlier. He signed on to be a tower and high wire man in building the $8 million tram and had been on the job five years, visually inspecting and servicing all moving parts, the towers and cables.

It surprised people riding the tram from the 2,643-foot Valley Station to the 8,516-foot Mountain Station on Mt. San Jacinto to look up and see Freddie Beavers riding the wires. One typical question to the tram operator was: "Say, there's a man up there on the wires above us. Wow! That's scary. Anything wrong with the car, with the cables?"

Beavers was an expert at changing flat tires in mid-air. "We have 360 rubber 8-inch tires over which the cables run in the five towers and on the traveling works of the two cars," he noted. "The tires go flat like car tires. I change them like changing a tire on the road." High winds stretched slack "rope" carriers out of line. Beavers adjusted the cables. "My ears are in tune with all the sounds as I travel the cables. I can spot problems by sight or sound." Scattered in the canyon below are metal objects that gleam in the sun as the tram moves slowly up the cliff. "Tools and hard hats dropped. Never go looking for them," Beavers said.

He said his ears "pop like popcorn every trip" from the rapid change in altitude. "It's like the four seasons each trip, from the desert to the snow going through summer, spring, fall and winter in 12 to 18 minutes. Right now it's usually in the 80s at the bottom and 10 to 30 degrees above zero on top."

Beavers made his runs in all kinds of weather. "Somebody's got to look at those carriers and towers. There are days when I ride the cables in rain, hail, sleet and snow. And, it's always slippery with all the grease up here. But when it rains and snows, I really have to watch my step." At times Beavers got off the traveling works to service a tower. The highest of the steel "toothpicks" jutting from the side of the cliff was 21 stories high. Then he climbed back to his perch above a passing tramcar. No roads lead to the five towers tacked to the cliff.

ONE-WINGED EAGLE

THEY CALLED HIM THE "ONE-WINGED EAGLE." It takes a lot of guts, steady nerves, split-second decisions and precision flying to be a crop duster. You fly by the seat of your pants, inches off the ground, dodging trees and irrigation stem pipes, ducking under wires in an open cockpit airplane.

Mike Jose was not only a crop duster. He was a one-armed crop duster. The World War II fighter pilot has logged more than 7,000 hours sowing seeds and fertilizing; spraying insecticides, herbicides and fungicides form single-place Stearman crop dusters. His right arm was severed at the shoulder—cut off by a propeller in an accident 25 years before we met him. He flew with his left arm, his legs and his knees.

"I use my teeth, ears, elbows—anything else that's handy," laughed "Big Mike," a 6-foot, 4-inch, 225-pound pilot. He was 52 when we flew with him. He was teaching other pilots basics of his hazardous profession. "Big Mike" was the sole instructor at Cal Ag Aero at Hanford Municipal Airport in Hanford, 30 miles south of Fresno. At the time the school was one of six crop dusting academies in America, one of eight in the world. Two were in Texas, one each in Colorado, Mississippi, Nevada, Cuba and Australia.

"Somebody's got to teach these guys how to fly without killing themselves," said Mike Jose, explaining why he took the teaching job. He was still spending several hours a day skimming the ground in his open cockpit planes in his role as flying instructor. Crop dusters were making good money. But the risk is always there. Many crop dusters have been killed in crashes over the years.

"We fly with closer tolerance than the Blue Angels," said "Big Mike." "Our wheels are one foot off the ground, one foot above the crops. We have to fly a straight line so seeds, fertilizers or spray are uniform. No skips or gaps. Timing is the key to everything."

Cal Ag Aero was established by 10 companies operating agricultural aircraft. "Big Mike" was asked if he would run the school. He wrote the only textbook on flying a crop duster ever published at the time. His students were paying $50 a copy for the book. Cost of the 13-week course, including the text and supplies was $3,000, a lot of money then. "It is a lot of money," said Dave Williams, 33, father of seven and one of four men then enrolled in the school. "But it's worth it. I've been an electrician, an ironworker, a warehouseman. This is the best way I can go. Crop dusters are well paid."

Three classes a year went through the school. "Big Mike" held enrollment to a maximum of 10 students, a minimum of four. Students included ex-military pilots, farmers, mailmen, aerospace engineers, school teachers, laborers, salesmen, iron workers. Sigurjon Sverrisson, 30, a crop duster in Iceland, flew to the United States just to go through the school. Students came from Canada, Syria, India, from all over the

United States. The Japanese government was sending 15 pilots for training. They learn everything about crop dusting, especially safety. "I tell them no sense looking like me—or even worse. Be careful," said "Big Mike." The school owned four Stearman crop dusters. Jose flew 35 hours with each student in a special two-place plane. Students were all licensed pilots before enrolling.

"I've been flying all my life," said Joe Patrick, a retired Air Force jet fighter pilot. "I did a lot of strafing and low-level flying over Vietnam. But crop dusting is different. And this one-armed character teaching us is a bear. He flies circles around any two-armed pilot I've ever met. It takes a pilot who's a little different to even consider this job. But a pilot with one arm flying these things? Well, it's hard to believe even when you see it."

Of the 55 men who had been enrolled in the school up to that time 85% were working as crop dusters, 5% washed out, the other 10% had second thoughts about the hazardous profession as a career. Pilots were paid 25% or more of the gross earnings of the plane. Fatalities for crop dusters were far greater years ago. Tighter laws were enacted to make the planes and conditions safer for flying.

Crop dusting is big business with 6,000 pilots flying ag planes when we flew with "Big Mike." But there was only one "one-winged" pilot licensed to fly by the FAA. That was Mike Jose, who, by the way, happened to be a FAA examiner in good standing himself. "Big Mike" came by instructing naturally. He instructed 2,500 Army Air Corps fighter pilots during World War II at Luke Field, Arizona.

But how did he manage the precision-type flying of an ag pilot with only one arm? He held the stick between his legs. "Those knobby points on the inside of my knees aren't just hinges," he laughed. "They're flight attachments." He squeezed the stick with his legs, moved it forward, backward, to the right and to the left controlling the ailerons and elevator.

He opened and shut the "dump" lever, worked the throttle, switches and knobs on the control board all with his left arm. He did all this while flying 100 mph inches off the ground, ducking under wires, dodging trees. He zoomed inches off the "deck" wearing a helmet, goggles and flight jacket in daily demonstrations to his students showing how to be a crop duster without getting killed. The one-winged eagle refused to be grounded.

CHARLES HILLINGER

FLYING SAUCER PILOT

"**D**on't laugh at flying saucers. You may be flying one soon," insisted Professor Paul Moller at the University of California, Davis. Moller was 29 and professor of aerodynamics when we interviewed him. He had designed, built and flown one flying saucer and was working on a second one. As far as the young professor knew at the time he was the inventor and owner of the only airship of its kind in the world.

He envisioned: "Housewives in flying saucers shuttling back and forth to supermarkets—secretaries, businessmen and women and workers commuting from home to office in the flying machines. If all goes well with the model I'm working on, flying saucers could become popular within a few years," he mused.

He believed "HOP-ACVs" may be an answer to traffic congestion in urban centers across the country. Moller explained that HOP-ACV is the letter designation for his vertical takeoff air cushion vehicle. "It should sell for something in the neighborhood of $3,000 to $4,000—about the same price as a medium-priced car. The flying saucer will cost about the same to operate as an automobile," said the professor. (The interview occurred in 1966. That was the first and last time I had ever seen a flying saucer.)

He described his flying machine as "very, very stable. It will be the easiest thing in the sky to fly." His flying saucer looked like a hamburger. It was 14 feet across, weighed about 300 pounds and stood four feet high. The interior was a maze of steel tubing with dual cut-down props flush with the top. The propellers were driven by two 72 h.p. engines. The exterior was aluminum sheeting and doped fabric. "My second saucer has four engines driving a single enclosed rotor. If one, two or even three of the engines quit, it can still be landed in a controlled manner," Moller said. This second saucer, the one he'd like to have mass produced, would be a two-seater. He was hoping to test flight it in a few months.

Moller flew his first saucer a dozen times, the first time only 6 inches off the ground, the other flights 3 feet in the air and for several hundred yards around the college airport. "I'm not a licensed pilot. That's why I haven't gone higher. However, I am convinced it performs as planned," he related. "The next one will be flown by a regular test pilot above 5,000 feet and for several miles over extended periods," he vowed.

He expected the craft normally would fly at 5,000 feet at 100 to 150 m.p.h. He expected his saucer to have military and commercial advantages over helicopters. And he predicted "it will be the ideal family flying machine. It will be safer than the helicopter for jungle warfare. Its hoverability is far superior. Where either rotor of a helicopter is hit, that's the end of it. Propellers are enclosed on my vehicle. One problem with helicopters is the relatively small amount of weight lift ability at low altitudes. No problem at all with my flying saucer."

Moller foresaw special air corridors established in urban areas to handle flying saucer travel in the future. "Microwave beams will facilitate traffic control for saucers shuttling all over the countryside," he said. "All a person will need to do is roll the family flying saucer out of the garage, turn on the ignition, zoom straight up and away."

CHAPTER THIRTY-SEVEN

First airplane ever constructed by prisoners. Unfortunately, the runway was too short.

TALES FROM THE SLAMMER

CONVICTS BUILD AIRPLANE

AN AIRPLANE, FULLY EQUIPPED AND READY TO FLY, was built by inmates at Deuel Vocational Institution, a California prison at Tracy. As far as authorities know, it was the first airplane ever put together in a prison anywhere. What bugged the 40 inmates who created the flying machine was they did not have a long enough runway. The yard they rolled the aircraft to was only 230 feet between soaring prison walls. They needed at least another 500 feet.

"We've thought of trying a giant rubber band," one inmate laughed. "We considered throwing together a ramp from the roof down to give us enough lift," said another. A third added: "Next time we get more practical—a helicopter."

The single-seat biplane was, obviously, not constructed as a means of escape. It was two years in the making. Wayne Kerr, whose idea it was to build the aircraft, planned to test it in a couple of weeks. "Every inmate in the place volunteered to take her up on the first flight," conceded Kerr, a Marine pilot for 20 years before becoming an instructor in the prison's airframe class. "I told the fellows who made the Shop Lifter Special—that's what we call her—that I would make a low pass over the yard so they could see how she performed," said Kerr. "Don't forget to fly slow Mr. Kerr and lower that rope," kidded one of the inmates.

The airplane was a measure of the success of Kerr's airframe course and a companion class in air engine mechanics conducted by Walden J. Thompson, a World War II Army Air Corps pilot. Of the 110 Federal Aviation Administration approved air engine schools in the nation, this was the only one located in a prison. And the school at the Tracy institution was ranked among the top 10 in America. Airline representatives kept close tab on inmates enrolled in the two classes. "They come in and ask to have this man or that man when he is released," noted James Brower, head of the Vocational Education Program at DVI. Inmates enrolled in the class run the gauntlet of the crime scene, serving time for such offenses as armed robbery and murder. After spending 7 hours a day, 5 days a week for 18 months and passing rigid FAA-supervised tests, they earn coveted A and P—air frame and power plant—licenses.

"We have a very high rate of success with men enrolled in the A and P courses," noted Associate Prison Supt. John Hacker who added: "Some men have asked that their parole be delayed a few months to enable them to complete the course. It's that important to them."

Kerr said surveys showed fewer than 10% of the inmates who have been graduated during the 20 years the air frame-air engine program had been in existence at DVI had been arrested after being released. At the time about 40% of all prisoners released in California eventually returned to prisons. One inmate summed it up: "If we can't make it on the outside after being licensed airplane mechanics, we'll never be able to make it."

COUNTRY CLUB OF PRISONS

EIGHTY-TWO-YEAR-OLD JOHN D. (FRENCHY) FLORENCE had just harvested his carrots. "Best crop I've had in years," said the old felon. Nearby, Jesse Houston, 70, tended his peach and nectarine orchard, worked happily in his garden of snapdragons, lilies of the Nile and hollyhocks. "Spring is the prettiest time of the year,"

CHARLES HILLINGER

observed the bank robber. "The fruit trees are in blossom, all the different colors of the flowers. The Santa Lucia Mountains are like green carpets of velvet."

Florence and Houston were inmates of the "country club" of penitentiaries, California Men's Colony, West Facility, San Luis Obispo. "As far as we know," explained Supt. Harold V. Field, "this is the only prison for old men in the nation." If it were not for the 12-foot fence surrounding West Facility's 43 acres, a visitor might imagine he were in a Palm Springs resort rather than on the grounds of one of California's state prisons. Men in their 50s, 60s, 70s and 80s, dressed in T-shirts and white shorts played tennis, gray-haired felons were on putting greens and handball courts, others played paddle tennis, shuffleboard and roque. On a shaded patio a bridge tournament was in progress. The prison Toastmasters Club was in session in the auditorium. Lawns were blanketed with tanned men in shorts sunbathing. "Here we have no cells," said the prison superintendent. "Our residents live in 60 open dorms. We feel treatment is more humane than at any other prison in America. These men are perhaps the best adjusted prisoners in the nation. At their age they do not have the overt hostilities of younger men. Arguments and fist fights common among prisoners seldom occur here."

This is a prison where guards preface all inmates' names with "Mr." The ratio of guards to prisoners is less than at any other prison in the country. It is perhaps the only prison where an announcement such as this is broadcast over the PA system: "Will all gardeners please report to the yard crew office for your garden seeds." Vegetable plots and flower gardens are among unique features. Many of the 1,430 old felons—a large percentage, lifers—are assigned individual crop beds where they grow vegetables of their choice. Vegetables produced go to the prison kitchen. Many paroled from the colony become landscape gardeners.

"Frenchy" Florence, one of scores of prisoners over 80, grew watermelons, casabas, carrots, cantaloupes, onions, tomatoes, corn and celery. Houston, the bank robber with a flowerbed, was the prison's shuffleboard champion for three years. Aim of the prison was to motivate the men to be physically and mentally active. Some, however, like Simon Birdow, 78, a thief, are permitted to "retire" with the colony doctor's permission. Known as the "philosopher," Birdow said he would spend the remainder of his days in prison "sitting on the porch soaking up the sun." Many enroll in high school and college courses or learn a trade.

California Men's Colony West Facility is adjacent to the medium-security East Facility, just west of San Luis Obispo. West Facility was established because prison authorities, desperate for bed space, decided it was feasible to house older men in inexpensive quarters. Lodged at the facility are the entire spectrum of felons, except arsonists, because of wooden barracks.

It is one of few prisons in the world where inmates like lifer Ward "Sweetpea" Blackburn refused to appeal for parole because he preferred to stay locked up. "I'm going to stay here all my life," said the 68-year-old inmate. "I like it here. This is where my friends are. I don't think I could cope with the world on the other side of the fence." For most old-timers, however, hope springs eternal. As 82-year-old "Frenchy" Florence puts it: "Sure, this is a great prison. But I hope to God I don't die in this joint. I want a taste of freedom before I go. I know, if given the chance, this time I'll be able to make it on the outside."

"NOW WE'RE GOING TO THE GAS CHAMBER"

"NOW WE'RE GOING TO THE GAS CHAMBER. Follow me," the murderer said. Armed guards on rooftop catwalks overlooking the San Quentin yard kept their eyes glued on the small group. "You will be constantly under the gun during your three hours within these walls. Don't worry. Everything will be cool," advised their prisoner-guide. The weekly tour of California's oldest correctional institution was under way. In the gas chamber the guide tells the visitors. "From 1938 until now cyanide pellets took the lives of 190 men and four women in this room. Thirty seconds after the cyanide pellets were dropped the condemned convict was unconscious and 11 1/2 minutes later he was dead." Asked about the traditional last meal, the guide recalled an old prison story: "One con asked for fresh strawberries. When told strawberries were out of season the con said: 'I'll wait.'"

At the time of our visit to San Quentin, every Wednesday groups of no more than 40 men and women, primarily law students, police officers and attorneys, had been admitted to tour the prison. All on the tour were carefully screened. The tour was under the direction of Nicola Frye, 36, who had trained 11 convicts to serve as guides. She was an elementary school teacher for seven years before becoming San Quentin's historian. Frye was in the process of establishing a museum in the prison that dated back to 1852 and was writing a history of San Quentin. Married and mother of two teen-age daughters, she was spending two days a week inside the prison. Each prisoner-guide was responsible for six to eight visitors on each tour. Frye and a sergeant of the guards accompanied each group. The guides provided facts, figures and statistics and answered questions. "We think letting the public seeing what goes on inside San Quentin is an excellent idea," said Lt. Jim McCullough, assistant to the warden.

The inmate who served as head tour guide added: "It's good for the public to come in here. You're paying for this place. It gives you a clear idea what a prison is." Visitors are not permitted to wear blue trousers, blue slacks or blue skirts to avoid being mistaken for prisoners, all of whom wear blue pants. Before the tour, everyone removes his or her shoes, jewelry, belts, and empties all pockets before going through a metal detector. No purses, wallets or money are permitted inside the walls.

A sergeant warns that San Quentin is where the state's most violent criminals are housed, that incidents inside the prison are not uncommon. He cautions everyone to stick close together and adds: "As for a hostage policy, there is none."

San Quentin was vastly overcrowded at the time. Prisoners were housed two to each of the 44-square cells. The prison was designed for 2,700 inmates. The day of the tour there were 3,354 men incarcerated there. Of that number, 1,700 had been under "lockdown" since a riot six months earlier in which 60 prisoners and seven guards were injured. Those inmates involved in the riot were confined to their cells day and night, with their meals taken to them. "There are violent men in here. Irrational things happen. There are stabbings and murders. Inmate against inmate, black against white against Latinos, inmates killing each other. It doesn't make sense," one of the prisoner guides said. "Some inmates will kill you with a marshmallow. They'll use anything. Rip your neck with eyeglasses. There are drugs in here better than you can get on the outside. We have marijuana coming out of our ears." Asked how prisoners get the drugs, the guide replied: "Visitors. Relatives. Friends. Sometimes even the guards bring it in."

The tour weaves through the prison furniture factory, the exercise yard, gym, chapel, and the cafeteria. It goes through a cellblock where the prisoners hoot and whistle at the women. Other men are sleeping on the double bunks, watching TV, reading, typing. There is a wash basin and open toilet in each cell. Some cells have signs on outside bars that read: "Please Knock Before Entering," "Do Not Disturb," "Will Be Back Soon."

"We want you to see how we live jammed together like caged animals," a guide said. "Note the tiers of cells in a cellblock. In summer it's hotter than hell. In winter it's cold. No air conditioning or heaters here." In the gym prisoners are shooting baskets, punching bags. Others play baseball and football. Games played with outside teams are always played at home, home being, San Quentin, of course. In preparing her history of the prison, Nicola Frye has freedom of movement. She had talked to many of the 103 men on Death Row. One prisoner talks about guards: "Some are excellent and vastly underpaid. Some are bad and grossly overpaid. The guards are like people everywhere on the outside. Some good. Some bad."

CHAPTER THIRTY-EIGHT

*This "ripply" airplane is in fact a kite, a style popularized by David Jue,
Chinese-American kite-maker extraordinaire.*

KITES & PUMPERNICKEL

KITE FLYER

STREAMERS AND RING-SHAPED SECTIONS of the 15-foot centipede wriggled in the breeze as the giant insect lofted over downtown Los Angeles streets. "It's just like one I made when a boy in China," shouted the 70-year-old man as he let out more string. David F. Jue (rhymes with dew), the Chinese kite maker of Palo Alto, was visiting friends in Chinatown in Los Angeles when someone said, "Go fly a kite!" And one of the most famous kite fliers since Benjamin Franklin did just that.

He reached into the trunk of his car and pulled out his bamboo strut, rice-paper centipede from dozens of homemade kites he fashioned in his garage. Other kites in his car included a redtail hawk, flying lampshade, pine tree, schoolhouse, fish and butterfly.

Jue migrated to Fresno from Kwongtung Province when he was 14. "I couldn't speak one word of English," he recalled. In time he went into the noodle business, and by his own admission, did quite well. "I retired and moved to Palo Alto when my son came back from the Army and enrolled at Stanford," he related. "But I was too young to stay retired so I became a stockbroker in San Francisco," he continued.

Jue had as much success with the stocks as he had with the noodles. He retired again—this time from Sutro & Co. He grew restless. Watching neighbor children at play his thoughts drifted to his childhood in China. "Flying kites was the height of excitement. Kites were part of our culture," he said. "Kites date back before written history in China. We used kites for family protection. Our family secured reed flutes to kites. The musical kites fluttered over our home frightening away thieves.

"We fished with kites, flying them above lakes, tying a long string to the kite tail. At the end of the string we placed a hook with bait. When the fish bit, we pulled in the kite." Jue talked about the annual Chinese festival *Ascending on High.* "It was nine days of kite flying each September. The last day of the festival we let our kites go, string and all. All of the evil, bad luck and sickness, we believed, were carried away by the kites."

Jue put his thoughts to work. He began fashioning the kites he remembered from his boyhood and distributed them to boys and girls of Palo Alto. It became his full time hobby. He was making more than 400 of his ornate Oriental kites a year.

The Chinese kite flyer of San Jose wrote a book: *Chinese Kites, How to Make and Fly Them.* No wonder whenever David Jue showed up people were always telling him to "go fly a kite!"

THE KINGS OF PUMPERNICKEL

CLAUDE GRABSKI JR., known in baking circles as the "Pumpernickel Prince" said he owed his success to a 300-year-old culture he kept in an earthen pot. "Mr. Felix brought the culture to this country from his home in Lodz, Poland," said Grabski, Mr. Felix's grandson. "How Mr. Felix came into possession of the culture, I never knew. But as far back as I can remember, my grandfather and my father warned: 'Guard the culture with your life. It's the secret to your success in pumpernickel.'"

When we met Mr. Felix's grandson, the Grabskis had been producing pumpernickel for 83 years in Los Angeles using the ancient culture as a starter. The original Grabski, Claude's grandfather, was a white-mustached pumpernickel baker affectionately known by hundreds throughout Southern California simply as "Mr. Felix."

"Mr. Felix was king of pumpernickel bakers here as well as on the continent before he migrated to America," noted Henry Bederski, one of two bakers working with the third generation Grabski in the pink pumpernickel palace at 1620 East 3rd Street. "Mr. Felix," said Bederski, "died in Los Angeles in 1939. In his lifetime he was cited by the czar of Russia for his pumpernickel. And Albert Einstein wrote Mr. Felix a letter saying his pumpernickel was the best he ever tasted!"

The pumpernickel palace wasn't a pretentious place. It was an old brick building. No signs proclaimed that pumpernickel was produced there with Mr. Felix's famous old recipe. Pumpernickel was baked there in old brick ovens just as it was in the old country when Mr. Felix left home to make his fortune in America.

But the Grabskis had always had modest aspirations even though Mr. Felix's brother, Wladyslaw Grabski, was prime minister of Poland in 1920. Mr. Felix's brother, the prime minister, was best remembered as the creator of zloty, the Polish currency. Mr. Felix, his son Claude Sr., who died in 1968 at age 65, and Claude Jr., all made comfortable livings on pumpernickel. But none of the three ever attempted to become the tycoon of the pumpernickel trade.

For example, the Felix Baking Company did not even sell its pumpernickel at the bakery. The loaves were distributed mostly to German sausage outlets and German meat markets in the Los Angeles area. Claude Jr., and his two bakers delivered the delicious pumpernickel hot out of the oven.

These days Claude Grabski Jr., Bederski and Jim Ricketts, a Swede with a Welsh name, were baking only 1,100 loaves of pumpernickel a day. "Only I know what's in the bread," said the third generation Grabski. "Henry Bederski and Jim Ricketts have worked beside my father and me for years, yet, they don't know Mr. Felix's secret formula. When my two sons get old enough, they, too, will know pumpernickel as Mr. Felix knew it."

CHAPTER THIRTY-NINE

Richard Lenfestey (left) and Lonnie McCraney with one of their antique stoves.

POTBELLIES, GUM & GARLIC

POTBELLIES

THE OLD SCHOOLHOUSE IN PALOMA, a Calaveras County hamlet, had not had any students in 25 years, but it was home to a former mail carrier and nearly 100 of his potbellied friends. Richard Lenfestey, 53, had filled the two-room Paloma school with turn-of-the-20th century cast iron stoves. The school had been vacant nine years, a victim of the elements and vandals, when Lenfestey bought it in 1972 for $5,250 from the local school district. Then he and his stoves moved in.

"We had a roughhouse crowd around here then. Every door and every desk was removed from the school. The tin roof was dangling in the air from the structure's sad state of disrepair," said Lenfestey. He bought his first cast iron heating stove in 1956 from a local rancher for $30. Made in 1857, it was a prized possession.

The old cast iron stoves were a full-time pastime for Lenfestey. The Paloma schoolhouse had become the home and headquarters of his Paloma Stove Works. He bought and sold rare potbellied and cook stoves. "Every time I travel America looking for stoves, I find most of them in the Midwest. They are becoming harder and harder to locate. In the past I would drive 6,000 to 8,000 miles looking for stoves and come home with as many as 50 in a big truck and trailer," explained Lenfestey. "On my last trip I returned with only 15."

He had a boneyard with thousands of rusted, dirty and grime-encrusted grates, dampers, rings, ash pans, door handles, oven racks and other stove parts. He sold old stoves for as little as $150 and as much as $2,500. Most were ornate with nickel crowns and elaborate scrollwork.

Like his stoves, Lenfestey was a throwback. He drove a 1931 Model-A coupe. "I found the old Tin Lizzie rusting away on a Lodi farm. I saved it from melting into the ground," he related. He grew up in Stockton, where he delivered mail for 16 years. "I would have preferred to have been a fireman on steam engine trains but I came along too late. Steam engines were phased out and replaced by diesels," he continued. "I have always been fascinated by boilers. So, since I couldn't be a railroad fireman, I began collecting potbellied and cast iron cook stoves."

Lenfestey's sidekick, Lonnie McCraney, 37, lived in Paloma, population less than 100, with his wife and two children. McCraney went to the old elementary-school-now-home-for-potbellies from first to fourth grade. He repaired and restored the old stoves in a shop behind the schoolhouse.

McCraney wore a black T-shirt bearing the words ROUND OAK MEDICINE MAN. Lenfestey wore a similar T-shirt inscribed ROUND OAK CHIEF. Most of their stoves were Round Oak, made in Dowagiac, Michigan, the furnace capital of America at the turn of the 20th century. At that time, the Beckwith Round Oak Stove Co. was the largest potbellied stove manufacturer in the nation. In 1900, its popular four-hole cook stove sold for $27; the most expensive heating stove sold for $36.

Paloma is an old gold mining town 35 miles northeast of Stockton. Gold was first discovered here in 1849. Mining for the precious metal continued off and on until 1909. Upward of 5,000 people lived here in the gold boom. The town boasted three hotels, two churches, livery stables, stores, several saloons and even a horse race track. Now, among a handful of scattered homes, the only relic of the gold mining days is the schoolhouse, home of the Paloma Stove Works.

GUM

To civic leaders, the town historian and local politicians alike in San Luis Obispo, the narrow alley is an eyesore. "It's vulgar and tacky," lamented town historian Louisiana Clayton Dart. Most people over 35 usually react negatively the first time they see it. But the young people love it.

Gum Alley is probably unique. It is a narrow walkway from Higuera Street, San Luis Obispo's main street, to a large parking lot. Since 1969 both adults and children have been sticking wads of chewing gum on the red brick wall fronting the south side of the alley. No one is quite sure how the practice stated. But the result is there for all to see. Stuck to the wall are thousands of globs of chewing gum, some of it fashioned in a myriad of designs. The gum-plastered wall even has an owner— the Me and You Dress Shop.

"When I bought the building the gum came with it," explained Hiro Nasta, 30. "I love it. People are amazed by it. They've never seen anything like it anywhere before." Harry May, a disc jockey who went by the name Captain Buffoon on KSLY, the local radio station, led his listeners on bimonthly tours of the Gum Alley gallery. It's a tradition for visiting high school football teams to stop by the alley and stick gum on the wall before each game. "People go by every day and stick gum on the wall. There's a local saying that if you're chewing gum and walk by Gum Alley, it is bad luck if you don't put it on the wall," said Roberta Byrnes, 22, of Riverside, a senior at Cal Poly San Luis Obispo.

Elsie Cook who owned and operated Cook's Variety Store two doors from Gum Alley for 30 years said the previous owner of the dress shop cleaned the gum off the wall from time to time. "It wasn't easy to get rid of the gum. But she was ecology minded and wanted everything to look nice," said Mrs. Cook. Out-of-towners often drop into Mrs. Cook's store just to buy gum to chew and stick in Gum Alley. "They want to leave their mark, I guess," said Mrs. Cook, who says she had never stuck any gum on the wall. "I was brought up in the old school where we were always taught to roll your gum in paper before disposing of it," she said.

GARLIC

Noses twitch and taste buds tingle when travelers pass through Gilroy, a small Central California town. It's garlic. Gilroy, 72 miles south of San Francisco, is the garlic capital of America. For years Joseph Gubser Jr., was the garlic king of America. Garlic is almost exclusively a California industry. All but a few acres of the 7,500-acre commercial garlic crop is grown in California and 90% of that is raised in and around Gilroy. Garlic growers were finishing off harvest of a record 80-million-pound crop on our visit there. "America's a nation of garlic eaters," beamed cherubic "Garlic Joe" Gubser. "More and more housewives are seasoning favorite dishes with garlic to the delight of husbands across the land," Gubser said.

Gubser was the largest garlic grower in America and the world's leading garlic trader. When not overseeing the planting, growing and harvesting of his Gilroy garlic fields, he traveled the world buying and selling the pungent plant. His warehouses were stacked to the rafters with 5 million pounds of just harvested, bright white garlic bulbs. He was one of 60 to 100 garlic growers in California.

"The number varies because of the nature of the crop," explained Gubser. "Garlic prices fluctuate terribly. It's probably the most volatile crop on the market. Being a garlic grower is like mining gold. A few people hit it at the right time and make a fortune. Others lose their shirt." Gubser said one of the many strange things about the plant is that it grows best on a narrow band of land that spans the earth— between the 35th and 45th parallels. California, Italy, Spain, Southern Russia and China are the world's top garlic producers.

"Garlic needs a lot of rain during the early part of its growth and absolutely no rain the last few weeks before it's harvested," continued Gubser. "There's only one crop a year, and it takes nine months for the plant to mature. Consumption is funny too. Some of the biggest garlic eaters in the country are in New Orleans. Florida is booming as a big garlic-eating market. Garlic also is big in New York City.

"Then there are other places like sections of the Midwest—Iowa and Nebraska—where garlic consumption is practically zilch. It seems like the big garlic eaters on earth are people living near the equator— Cubans and Puerto Ricans, for example. I just shipped 2,000 50-pound sacks to the Fiji Islands. That's a fabulous amount of garlic for a tiny equatorial island."

According to most researchers the plant originated in the Kirgiz area of Siberia many centuries ago. In the Book of Numbers, Chapter 11, the children of Israel complained because they had to eat manna instead of the garlic to which they were accustomed in Egypt. "Garlic has very powerful properties," wrote the Roman historian, Pliny. "The very smell of it drives away serpents and scorpions. "Garlicke maketh a man winke, drinke and stinke," wrote Thomas Nash, 16th-Century English novelist.

Medicinal values have been attributed to garlic down through the ages. References to garlic were quite common in the herbals—books on medicinal properties of plants—widely distributed from the 16th to the 18th-Century. Missionaries introduced garlic to California. The first major commercial producer in the state, however, was Gubser's father, Joseph Gubser Sr. The Gubsers are Swiss by descent. The Swiss are not known to be big garlic consumers. There is, however, a well-known Swiss garlic pill used as an aid in digestion.

Some scalp specialists swear that massaging the head with a little garlic each day will keep baldness away. In Hong Kong pickled garlic is popular as an hors d'oeuvre. During the flu epidemic of World War I, thousands of Americans tied garlic bulbs around their necks thinking it would keep the germ away. The reason perhaps being in ancient times garlic was thought to be the antidote for all evils.

When travelers drive through Gilroy, it isn't the garlic in the fields that tingle the taste buds. It's the processing fumes from garlic dehydration plants. Garlic bulbs are odorless unless bruised.

CHARLES HILLINGER

Junior McLarnon (left) and Ed Smith relaxing at their rest stop in Red Mountain.

POTPOURRI

ED AND JUNIOR'S HALF ACRE

YOU COULDN'T MISS ED AND JUNIOR'S HALF ACRE in Red Mountain, the old mining town on a lonely stretch of U.S. 395. It was the fence of highway signs that caught your eye, like the Speed Limit 50 sign that was one of the gates. Icy, Dips, Yield, Watch Out For Cattle, Right Lane Closed Ahead, Thru Traffic Merge Left and School Bus Stop 400 Feet are but a few of the nearly 100 road warnings that line the fence.

"A Caltrans official stopped one day wanting to know where the signs came from. He thought we stole them. I explained we bought them from a salvage yard. I showed him the receipts," said Ed Smith. Motorists and tour buses stopped out of curiosity when they spotted the fence and the incredible clutter littering the half acre. A Welcome sign hung out front. There are Caltrans rest stops along the freeways outside cities. Then there was Ed and Junior's rest stop.

David (Junior) McLarnon and Smith were pack rats, both 67 at the time of our 1990 interview. They collected everything. Using a metal detector, McLarnon collects memorabilia from old mining camps in the area. Smith came from a long line of pack rats. He had cans and packages of food and medicine, toys, dolls, buttons, hats, tools, kitchen utensils, furniture and much much more that he, his father and grandfather before him collected. He picked up an old razor blade sharpener and said: "Things like this most people never saw before.

"We get folks from around the world dropping in on us. Just lately a man from France was here. People stop, stretch their legs, spend a couple of hours looking at our stuff and visiting, then go on their way." Hunting and fishing friends passing through overnighted at Ed and Junior's. So, did truck drivers. They slept in their campers and trucks in a parking lot on the half acre or under the stars on a row of beds on the roof of Smith and McLarnon's house. "We enjoy visitors. We don't charge anybody. A lot of them would like to buy some of the stuff. We don't sell anything," said McLarnon.

The two men were hunting and fishing buddies for 40 years. Smith paid $760 for the half acre and a 1902 mining shack in 1964. For the first few years they stayed overnight in the shack on their fishing trips to and from the High Sierra. Smith lived in Orange County, McLarnon in Chula Vista. They were both married with children and grandchildren. McLarnon retired 11 years earlier. Smith retired in 1985. McLarnon was spending 90% of his time at the half acre, Smith 60%. Neither of their wives ever came to their place in Red Mountain.

The two men added several rooms and patios to the mining shack, all constructed of scrap material. The patios, rooms and the rest of the property were filled with what they called "PPJ"—pre-plastic junk. In his collection McLarnon had three-dozen turn-of-the-century watches thrown away by miners when the watches stopped running. He had mining equipment, rusted silverware, coins, porcelain pots and pans and dozens of skillets.

Old iron bedposts served as borders for plants and trees. A mining camp outhouse had carpet on the floor, walls and ceiling. A highway sign on the outhouse door proclaimed: "No Parking 8 a.m. to 12 Noon."

Charles Hillinger

Smith had 10,000 seashells he collected in the South Pacific when he was in the Navy in World War II. Many who visit the two men were regulars who dropped in to say hello whenever driving by Ed and Junior's private rest stop. It's a stop no one ever forgot.

A 19TH-CENTURY MAN

ITINERANT TINTYPE PHOTOGRAPHER JOHN COFFER described his life as "living the 1800s, A to Z." As far as Coffer knew, he was the only tintype photographer in the country traveling town to town in a horse-drawn wagon. "I enjoy the old ways. I ain't goin' back to the modern way of life. I'd rather do it the hard way and get it done better and more interesting," insisted the 28-year-old throwback to simpler times.

Coffer began his travels on the back roads of America leaving his hometown, Intercourse, Pennsylvania, in an Amish-built spring wagon pulled by his horse, Brownie. When I met him he had traveled more than 6,500 miles in his wagon through 20 states in two years. He avoided cities, staying mainly on gravel, dirt and two-lane country roads.

Coffer was supporting himself by photographing people with his 80-year-old Century No. 4 camera and printing the pictures on tintypes. "Tintypes have been around since 1865 when Hamilton L. Smith of Gambier, Ohio patented the positive photographic process made directly on iron plates and varnished with a tin, sensitized film," explained Coffer. From the 1860s down through the 1920s, itinerant tintype photographers were a highly visible part of the American landscape. "They traveled town to town just as I am doing today."

Coffer slept in the wagon, which doubled as his darkroom. He shaved with straight razor, using a kerosene lantern for light. He kept a journal with a dip pen. He cooked over a wood fire and did his own laundry on a scrub board. He ordered his old-fashioned clothes from mail-order catalogues. He carried an assortment of old clothes of all sizes for people to wear when posing for the tintypes.

For background he had a replica of a typical 19th-Century photographic canvas with a large painting of billowy clouds hovering over a scenic lake surrounded by trees. He sold his tintypes for as little as $3.75 and as much as $21.75 depending on size. "I'm seeing the country coast to coast, learning a lot about living the old way and making a living while I'm at it," he explained. "I have discovered a way to relive the 1800s. I don't ever want to rejoin the 20th-Century."

GRANDMA PRISBREY

G RANDMA PRISBREY created a whole village out of her pick-ings from the city dump in Simi Valley. "Some's got a bottle house. But nobody's got a bottle village," the 80-year-old pack rat proudly proclaimed. For 20 years Grandma Prisbrey moved thousands of bottles—plus tons of other junk—in an old Studebaker pickup a mile from the dump to her big backyard on the edge of town.

Without help, Grandma Prisbrey erected 13 bottle houses on her 44-foot-wide, 300-foot-deep property surrounded by a bottle fence. Most of the time she lived in a small trailer parked on the property, sometimes she spent a night in one of her bottle houses. A wide walkway leading from one bottle house to another the length of the bottle village contained thousands of pieces of junk artistically inlaid in concrete. "Everything you can imagine is in the walkway and stuffed in my bottle houses and lots you can't imagine," says Grandma Prisbrey. "Everything under the sun shows up at a dump if you wait long enough."

Cemented in the walkway and in the floors of her bottle houses were shreds of tile, old jewelry, scissors, rings, guns, tools, false teeth, pan lids, combs, curlers, license plates, signs, nails, nuts and bolts and much, much more. Next to a wishing well of 600 violet milk of magnesia bottles were a dozen doll heads, skewered on broomsticks. "Lots of people throw away just the heads and not the bodies," explained Grandma Prisbrey. There was a fountain fashioned from headlights, whisky bottles and neon light tubes, a garden where stems of flowers grew through discarded car and bedsprings and a path flanked with TV picture tubes.

"Everybody's called me Grandma seems like at least 30 years or so. My first name's Tressa, but few know it," Grandma Prisbrey mused. "I was born in Easton, Minnesota. My father was a blacksmith. When I was 15 I married a man 52. We had seven children. He died when he was 72. He'd be 117 if he were alive today. This thing started because of my pencils," she explained. "I collected pencils for 40 years and needed a place to display them. So, I started going to the dump for bottles to use to put up a building where I could properly display my pencils."

That was her first bottle house. Then she erected a schoolhouse made of bottles and filled with old books from the dump and Eclipse

CHARLES HILLINGER

desks—the old-fashioned desks with the inkwells. A huge round house built with 13,000 amber beer bottles was 24 feet across and had a round bar, round fireplace, round bed and round dresser. Another bottle house was filled with old coffeepots, old washboards and other junk from the dump, and one house, dubbed "Cleopatra's Bedroom," had a fancy gold quilted bed mounted on a dais.

Her bottle dollhouse was made of 6,000 bottles. The inside was cluttered with 600 discarded dolls from the dump. In the meditation bottle house, Grandma Prisbrey enjoyed entertaining guests by playing the Missouri Waltz and other nostalgic numbers on an old Mason & Hamlin piano. There was a shrine made of bottles with a statue of St. Francis of Assisi, a Madonna, a Star of David and a candelabrum of seven Manischewitz bottles.

"I'm the original designer of flip-top doll dresses," laughed Grandma Prisbrey, showing off scores of dolls with dresses festooned with flip-tops from beer and soft drink cans. "I was ambitious after raisin' seven kids," she sighed. "Never could sit still. Have to keep busy. That's how all this came about."

ROOT BEER FOAM

NEXT TIME YOU HAVE A ROOT BEER, think of Milton Blair and his 14 kids. The Blairs were harvesting 14 tons of yucca trees each week when we caught up with them. The yucca trees were on land leased from the Southern Pacific Railroad on the Mojave Desert at Hackberry Mountain in eastern San Bernardino County. Root beer foam comes from the sap of the thorny desert tree. "Harvesting Spanish daggers (yucca trees) is dirty, hard, nasty work," said Milton Blair, 50, as he revved up a chain saw to cut a yucca. Blair was blind in his left eye, the result of an accident when his eye was punctured by a yucca spine.

He and his oldest son, Milton Jr., 26, were cutting yucca trees and stripping the trunks of the dangerous spikes. The rest of the family hoisted the heavy yucca sections into a truck. "This is the best time of the year to cut daggers," said Melissa Blair, 17, her mouth bulging with a plug of chewing tobacco. It was February. "In summer we're wringing wet with sweat from sunup to sundown. Ants crawl up our bodies and bite. We get stuck with daggers and cactus. We gulp gallons of ice water," she said.

The Blairs sold the yucca to Ritter International, a Los Angeles firm, where it was processed for scores of uses including foam for root beer, an additive to carbonated beverages, shampoos, cosmetics and industrial deodorants. Yucca foam has been used for snow scenes in television and motion pictures. It was used by the Navy during World War II to smother fires. Don Emery, botanist for the U.S. Bureau of Land Management, noted: "The yucca is a renewable resource just as a tree in the forest, providing it is properly harvested as the Blairs are doing." The government required yucca to be harvested in a prescribed manner. The family divided its time harvesting yucca and running 200 head of cattle on their Lazy Daisy Ranch—450,000 acres of dry desert terrain leased from the railroad, the federal and state governments. They lived 14 miles by miserable dirt road from their nearest neighbor in a home without electricity, phone or television. Kerosene lamps furnished their light.

"My wife is secretary and bookkeeper of the outfit. I ain't worth a damn at that," said Blair. The Blairs had 10 boys and 4 girls. Their names and ages at the time of the interview: Milton Jr., 26, Joe, 24, Mary, 22, Susie, 21, Eddie, 19, Melissa, 17, Luke, 16, Dan, 14, Annie, 12, Austin, 9, Mark, 8, Johnny, 6, Mike, 4 and Matt, 2. The family lived in a three-bedroom home and bunkhouse. They used a wood stove for cooking and warmth. "The real chore is keeping track of our cows. They're scattered all over hell and gone," said Joe Blair. "We lost 25 head last year to spotlighters. Members of 'varmint clubs' drive out to the desert in pickup trucks armed with high-powered rifles. They use spotlights on their pickups to look for coyotes, bobcat and fox. They see an eye and WHAM! They shoot. Twenty-five pairs of those eyes last year belonged to our cows," Joe Blair said.

Biggest excitement of the week for the Blairs occurred every Saturday, the 40-mile drive to Needles, the closest town. "My wife and two of the girls spend a couple hours at the Seventh-Day Adventist Church and a couple hours shopping," explained Blair. "The rest of us wait for them at the Hungry Bear Café. We sit and drink coffee waiting for the women. Then we hop back into the pickup and head for the ranch."

CHARLES HILLINGER

CHAPTER FORTY-ONE

Mell Lazarus draws "Momma" on board
the Laugh Boat cartoonist cruise.

MELL'S MOMMA

"MOMMA"

"**M**OMMA IS THE REAL THING." At least that's what Mell Lazarus said and he ought to know. Mell's a personal friend. I have done several features about him over the years. I knew his late mother and was at her 80th birthday party. Mell was 45 in 1973 when I did an interview with him and his mother. Momma is the lovable, lonely old pensioner in Mell's comic strip syndicated around the world. His real mother, Frances Lazarus, was a widow at the time with three children, just like Momma in the comics. "Of course Momma in the comic strip is my mother," said the raw-boned, 6-foot cartoonist. "But my mother doesn't identify with her. She insists it's her sister, Helen."

In the strip, Mrs. Hobbs (Momma) is an elderly woman who lives alone. She has a married son, Thomas. Momma's other son, Francis' only apparent talent is dating girls. He borrows money from Momma to finance his dates. Marylou is Momma's comic strip daughter. She lives with a bunch of girls in an apartment.

"Momma is trying to keep control of her children—trying to justify her existence," said Lazarus. "She would like nothing better than have her son, Francis, move in with her and set up housekeeping. Francis is not too bright, but he's enthusiastic. Momma is jealous of Francis' girlfriends. She is making it impossible for Francis to get married. Nobody is good enough for him. As for Marylou, Momma considers her a pushover with men. Marylou has a succession of jobs. Momma feels every boss makes a pass at his secretary eventually." Lazarus said he, himself, was the prototype of the older son, Thomas. "Thomas and I are strictly suburban.

"My mother tells me she's not that kind of mother represented by Momma in the strip. But, of course, she is. She still has that control over my brother, my sister and me—after all these years. My mother still worries about us crossing the street, about bumping into things. It never changes. She worries about my wife. About my sister's husband. About my brother's wife."

Frances Lazarus was 72 at the time of the interview. Lazarus said the strip was done with affection. "Oh, I make Momma a little tough one week and sweeten her up the next. She gets put down once in a while. But, basically, she's got to come out on top, like all mommas are inclined to do." Lazarus admitted his comic strip Momma expressed essentially his values. "I worry about my daughters when they're out on dates. Sometimes my wife thinks I'm Momma. She says I try to run the family the way Momma in the strip runs hers."

Lazarus is a high school dropout. He quit at 16 to devote full time to cartooning. "World War II was on full blast. Most of the cartoonists were in service. I submitted single page fillers to comic magazines. Hardly anybody was around that could draw," he explained. He had his own commercial art service for a time. Then, in 1957, Lazarus started the comic strip Miss Peach, like Momma, appearing on comic pages in newspapers all over the world, with both strips read by upwards of 100 million people 365 days a year. Momma popped out of Mell Lazarus' pen for the first time in November, 1970. She is one of America's best-known mothers.

He does the two strips—Miss Peach and Momma—simultaneously, both the drawings and the writing. He works out of his home in San Fernando Valley. At the time of this interview Mell's wife, Hortense (Horty), and his three daughters, Marjorie, then 21, Susan, 18, and Cathy, 11, were his best critics. His father, a glassblower, had died in 1948.

Momma in the comic strip, like the cartoonist's real mother, had a steady stream of suitors over the years. "My mother puts down her boyfriends something terrible, just like I have Momma doing in the strip," Lazarus said. "None of them, of course, had ever been able to approach my father in character. They would sit on the couch for hours, just like Momma's friend in the comic strip. Woe to the suitor who can't do the Sunday New York Times crossword puzzle. My mother works them all. That's a prerequisite for a suitor."

Lazarus thinks the strip has been successful because "I happen to be delighted with my mother. She has a great sense of humor." And, how does Frances Lazarus feel about it? "I probably have the only boy in America," she mused, "who visits his mother for commercial purposes."

CHAPTER FORTY-TWO

*The Galloping Ghormleys walking along California
coast into Oregon, completing an 18-year odyssey.*

GALLOPING GHORMLEYS

CARL GHORMLEY AND HIS FAMILY have seen California as few others. The "Galloping Ghormleys" have walked the California coast—along the beach wherever possible, otherwise on cliff tops and headlands—from Mexico to the Oregon border.

It took the Rolling Hills family 18 years in "bits and pieces" to finish the strange odyssey. Ghormley, 61, and his wife, Harriett, 59, were tearful as they, their family and friends sprinted across the last few yards of beach on their 1,016-mile hike to Oregon. "This has been an incredible thing for our family, just sticking it out all these years," said Carl Ghormley, as the hikers embraced, shouted "Yahoos!" and tossed their hats into the air.

For the last mile across the wide sandy beach, family members took turns carrying a large American flag. As they scrambled over rocks, climbed steep cliffs and walked wide stretches of beach on their final four miles, the Ghormleys sang to the tune of "Onward Christian Soldiers":

"Onward Ghormley walkers! Forward on the beach!
With the Oregon border almost in our reach..."

It was the 4th of July. They sang "A Grand Old Flag" and other patriotic songs saluting the nation's birthday and sang time and time again a ditty they've been singing for years as they walked the shores of the Golden State:

"Mmmm Mmmm—would you like to take a walk?
Mmmm Mmmm—do you like to climb?
Mmmm Mmmm—gee, I better warn you,
The coast of California is gonna take a long, long time."

It had taken a long, long time, 18 years from the day the Ghormleys—Carl, Harriett and their four children, Justus, 21, Maggie, 16, Miles, 12, and Tom, 10—drove to Tijuana, walked to the U.S. border, and started walking north along the beach. That first day they hiked 13 miles to Coronado. That first year they walked 36.6 miles on weekends and vacations.

The year Carl broke his ankle they walked only 4.7 miles. The years they walked the most were 119.4 miles, 107.5 miles and 97.8 miles. They spent 177 days—or nearly six months—walking the coast. "It kept getting more complicated each year, more difficult getting everybody together for the walks," Harriet said. "We went through a period when the children were away at college. In time, all but Tom married. Grandchildren started coming along."

"And, the logistics didn't get any easier, either. The farther we progressed, the farther we had to drive to reach the starting point for our next walk," Carl added. By their fourth Thanksgiving on the hike they reached San Clemente, almost five years after they started, San Pedro, and on Easter in their 8th year, Santa Barbara.

Twelve years after they began, Maggie and her husband Tom LePley pushed the first of the Ghormley's six grandchildren, Kathleen America, across the Golden Gate Bridge. "When we reached a bay, we walked across the bridge to the other side. If we had walked the shores of the bays it would have taken us another 18 years," Miles explained. When the family sprinted across the Oregon line Tom LePley was carrying his daughter, Molly, 1, Janie had Teddie, 4 months, in a Snugli (front pack) and Miles was carrying Emily, 10 months.

The Ghormleys filled four journals with notes and photos, including detailed descriptions of wildlife, wildflowers and fascinating and funny happenings.

ABOUT THE AUTHOR

FOR 46 YEARS CHARLES HILLINGER ROAMED CALIFORNIA, the rest of the U.S., *and* the world doing nearly 6,000 human-interest stories on whatever he wanted to write about for the *Los Angeles Times*. His features and column "Charles Hillinger's America" were syndicated by the *Los Angeles Times* as well as the *Washington Post News Services* to more than 600 newspapers. His usual routine was to go out on the road for a week or two, come home and write a dozen or more stories, then go back out to track down other people and places to write about. Like many reporters for major metropolitan newspapers, Hillinger's had one adventure after another, including surviving five airplane crashes.

This "reporter's life" has taken him around the world twice, to the North and South Poles, Mount Everest, all 50 states, all the Canadian provinces, all the Mexican states, Central and South America, Russia, China, most every country in Europe, much of Africa, the Middle East, jaunts through the Far East, and also Australia, New Zealand, and throughout the Pacific islands. He was the first American journalist to travel through Siberia. He's also had datelines from such exotic places as Niue, Nauru, Andorra, Magadan, Xian, Sharjah, Addis Ababa, Bombay, Anadyr, Tuleneut, S'gogogsig, and the Galápagos. He's interviewed everyone from kings, queens, prime ministers, and presidents to people from all walks of life, the eccentric and oddball to "just folks."

Hillinger was one of six pool reporters for NASA aboard the aircraft carrier *Hornet* in the Pacific for the recovery of the Apollo 11 astronauts Neil Armstrong, Buzz Aldrin and Michael Collins on their splash-down return to Earth after the first flight to the moon. When three towering undersea mountains were discovered on the same day Armstrong and Aldrin stepped on the moon, it was Hillinger who named them after the astronauts.

Chuck Hillinger has won numerous writing awards, is past president of the Greater Los Angeles Press Club and author of two other well-received and reviewed books from Capra Press: *Charles Hillinger's America; People and Places in All 50 States* and *Hillinger's California; Stories from All 58 Counties*. He's also written: *Charles Hillinger's Channel Islands*, *The California Islands*, and *Bel-Air Country Club, A Living Legend*. His *America* book was issued as an audiobook. He did special features for George Schlatter's NBC prime-time television show *Real People*, which featured nearly 100 segments based on his newspaper articles, including many found in this book. Since he retired from the *Los Angeles Times* in 1992, his stories have appeared in 33 nationally-published magazines, and he is a member of the Society of American Travel Writers.

Born in Evanston, Illinois, he grew up in Park Ridge, both suburbs of Chicago. In the 7th through 10th grades he was a columnist and the youngest circulation manager of an accredited newspaper in America, the weekly *Park Ridge Advocate*. He was a copyboy and feature writer for the *Chicago Tribune* as a high school junior and senior. A graduate of Maine Township High School in Des Plains, Illinois, and of the University of California at Los Angeles, he has an honorary degree from Marymount College, Palos Verdes. Hillinger served three years in the Navy during World War II aboard the aircraft carrier *Attu* and the attack transport *Garrard*. His ship took part in the battle of Okinawa, and was with the Third Fleet when it sailed into Tokyo Bay as the war ended.

Hillinger is profiled in *Who's Who in the West* and *Who's Who in America*. He and his wife Arliene, listed in the *Who's Who of American Women* for her philanthropic work, were married in 1948. They have a son, Brad, a daughter, Tori Lindman, and four young granddaughters, Kristina, Brittani, Carlie, and Nicole.

In his foreword to *Charles Hillinger's America*, Charles Kuralt wrote: "Charles Hillinger has been a hero of mine since I first started reading his stories in the *Los Angeles Times* back in the sixties. He was always on the go, like the wandering scribes of yore, and like other well-known traveling writers of our time, the likes of John Steinbeck, James Agee, Calvin Trillin, William Least Heat Moon, John McPhee. But it seemed to me that Chuck Hillinger was a direct spiritual descendent of the greatest of them all, Ernie Pyle...."

From Bob Hope's forward to *Hillinger's California*: "I had a bird-eye's view of California and thought I knew it from every angle. Then, after reading the galley of *Hillinger's California* I realized how little I did know about California and how much there was to enjoy. The book is filled with surprises that make California different from every other state...."

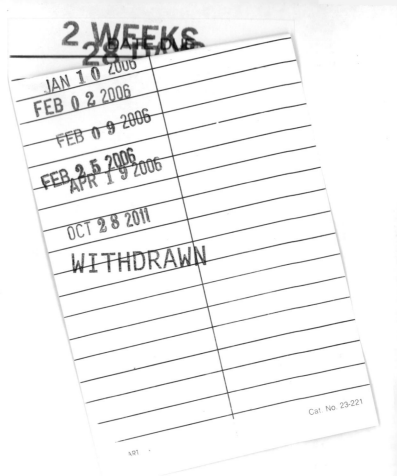

2 WEEKS

DATE DUE

JAN 1 0 2006
FEB 0 2 2006
FEB 0 9 2006
FEB 2 5 2006
APR 1 9 2006

OCT 2 8 2011

WITHDRAWN

Cat. No. 23-221

ART

979.4   Hillinger, Charles.
H65ca   California
         characters

Mechanics' Institute Library

3 1750 03327 0953